The Second Latchkey

by

A. M. Williamson And C. N. Williamson

The Second Latchkey
by A. M. Williamson And C. N. Williamson

Copyright © 2023

All Rights reserved.
No part of this publication may be reproduced, stored in a retrieval system, or transmitted in any form or by any means, electronic, mechanical, photocopying or Otherwise, without the written permission of the publisher.

The author/editor asserts the moral right to be identified as the author/editor of this work.

ISBN: 978-93-57483-33-9

Published by
DOUBLE 9 BOOKS
2/13-B, Ansari Road
Daryaganj, New Delhi – 110002
info@double9books.com
www.double9books.com
Tel. 011-40042856

This book is under public domain

ABOUT THE AUTHOR

C. N. Williamson

The Black & White magazine was started by British author and motorsport journalist Charles Norris Williamson (1859–1920). He is most well-known for his work on several books and travelogs alongside his wife, Alice Muriel Williamson. Williamson, who was raised at University College, London, and was born in Exeter, studied engineering there. Before becoming the founding editor of the Black and White in 1891, he worked as a writer for the Graphic for eight years. In 1881, he released a Life of Carlyle. Several of the Williamsons' novels and short tales went on to become movies.

A.M. Williamson

American-English novelist Alice Muriel Williamson (8 October 1858 – 24 September 1933), also known as the "C. N. and A. M. Williamson" and "Mrs. C. N. Williamson," wrote mostly under these aliases. Her father co-founded the Ohio State and Union Law Colleges, and she was born there in 1858. She took her maternal great grandfather's last name, "Livingston," as her own in 1890. Forget-Me-Not published her debut serial, "Confessions of a Stage-Struck Girl." Her sense of humor would eventually emerge as one of her most distinctive writing traits.

CONTENTS

CHAPTER I.
   A WHITE ROSE 7

CHAPTER II.
   SMITHS AND SMITHS 15

CHAPTER III.
   WHY SHE CAME 25

CHAPTER IV.
   THE GREAT MOMENT 31

CHAPTER V.
   THE SECOND LATCHKEY 40

CHAPTER VI.
   THE BEGINNING—OR THE END? 49

CHAPTER VII.
   THE COUNTESS DE SANTIAGO 56

CHAPTER VIII.
   THE BLUE DIAMOND RING 64

CHAPTER IX.
   THE THING KNIGHT WANTED 78

CHAPTER X.
   BEGINNING OF THE SERIES 86

CHAPTER XI.
   ANNESLEY REMEMBERS 95

CHAPTER XII.
   THE CRYSTAL 103

CHAPTER XIII.
　　THE SERIES GOES ON 112
CHAPTER XIV.
　　THE TEST 123
CHAPTER XV.
　　NELSON SMITH AT HOME 133
CHAPTER XVI.
　　WHY RUTHVEN SMITH WENT 142
CHAPTER XVII.
　　RUTHVEN SMITH'S EYEGLASSES 152
CHAPTER XVIII.
　　THE STAR SAPPHIRE 158
CHAPTER XIX.
　　THE SECRET 166
CHAPTER XX.
　　THE PLAN 180
CHAPTER XXI.
　　THE DEVIL'S ROSARY 188
CHAPTER XXII.
　　DESTINY AND THE WALDOS 197
CHAPTER XXIII.
　　THE THIN WALL 205
CHAPTER XXIV.
　　THE ANNIVERSARY 213
CHAPTER XXV.
　　THE ALLEGORY 222
CHAPTER XXVI.
　　THE THREE WORDS 230

CHAPTER I.
A WHITE ROSE

Even when Annesley Grayle turned out of the Strand toward the Savoy she was uncertain whether she would have courage to walk into the hotel. With each step the thing, the dreadful thing, that she had come to do, loomed blacker. It was monstrous, impossible, like opening the door of the lions' cage at the Zoo and stepping inside.

There was time still to change her mind. She had only to turn now ... jump into an omnibus ... jump out again at the familiar corner, and everything would be as it had been. Life for the next five, ten, maybe twenty years, would be what the last five had been.

At the thought of the Savoy and the adventure waiting there, the girl's skin had tingled and grown hot, as if a wind laden with grains of heated sand had blown over her. But at the thought of turning back, of going "home"—oh, misused word!—a leaden coldness shut her spirit into a tomb.

She had walked fast, after descending at Bedford Street from a fierce motor-bus with a party of comfortable people, bound for the Adelphi Theatre. Never before had she been in a motor-omnibus, and she was not sure whether the great hurtling thing would deign to stop, except at trysting-places of its own; so it had seemed wise to bundle out rather than risk a snub from the conductor, who looked like pictures of the Duke of Wellington.

But in the lighted Strand she had been stared at as well as jostled: a girl alone at eight o'clock on a winter evening, bare-headed, conspicuously tall if conspicuous in no other way; dressed for dinner or the theatre in a pale gray, sequined gown under a mauve chiffon cloak meant for warm nights of summer.

Of course, as Mrs. Ellsworth (giver of dress and wrap) often pointed out, "beggars mustn't be choosers"; and Annesley Grayle was worse off than a beggar, because beggars needn't keep up appearances. She should have thanked Heaven for good clothes, and so she did in chastened moods; but it was a costume to make a girl hurry through the Strand, and just for an instant she had been glad to turn from the white glare into comparative dimness.

That was because offensive eyes had made her forget the almost immediate future in the quite immediate present. But the hotel, with light-hearted taxis tearing up to it, brought remembrance with a shock. She envied everyone else who was bound for the Savoy, even old women, and fat gentlemen with large noses. They were going there because they wanted to go, for their pleasure. Nobody in the world could be in such an appalling situation as she was.

It was then that Annesley's feet began to drag, and she slowed her steps to gain more time to think. Could she—*could* she do the thing?

For days her soul had been rushing toward this moment with thousand-horsepower speed, like a lonely comet tearing through space. But then it had been distant, the terrible goal. She had not had to gasp among her heart-throbs: "Now! It is now!"

Creep as she might, three minutes' brought her from the turning out of the Strand close to the welcoming entrance where revolving doors of glass received radiant visions dazzling as moonlight on snow.

"No, I can't!" the girl told herself, desperately. She wheeled more quickly than the whirling door, hoping that no one would think her mad. "All the same, I *was* mad," she admitted, "to fancy I could do it. I ought to have known I couldn't, when the time came. I'm the last person to—well, I'm sane again now, anyway!"

A few long steps carried the girl in the sparkling dress and transparent cloak into the Strand again. But something queer was happening there. People were shouting and running. A man with a raucous, alcoholic voice, yelled words Annesley could not catch. A woman gave a squeaking scream that sounded both ridiculous and dreadful. Breaking glass crashed. A growl of human anger mingled with the roar of motor-omnibuses, and Miss Grayle fell back from it as from a slammed door in a high wall.

As she stood hesitating what to do and wondering if there were a fire or a murder, two women, laughing hysterically, rushed past into the hotel court.

"Hurry up," panted one of them. "They'll think we belong to the gang. Let's go into the hotel and stay until it's over."

"Oh, what is it?" Annesley entreated, running after the couple.

"Burglars at a jeweller's window close by—there are women—they're being arrested," one of the pair flung over her shoulder, as both hurried on.

"'Women ... being arrested ...'" That meant that if she plunged into the fray she might be mistaken for a woman burglar, and arrested with the guilty. Even if she lurked where she was, a prowling policeman might suppose she sought concealment, and bag her as a militant.

Imagine what Mrs. Ellsworth would say—and *do*—if she were taken off to jail!

Annesley's heart seemed to drop out of its place, to go "crossways," as her old Irish nurse used to say a million years ago.

Without stopping to think again, or even to breathe, she flew back to the hotel entrance, as a migrating bird follows its leader, and slipped through the revolving door behind the fugitives.

"It's fate," she thought. "This must be a *sign* coming just when I'd made up my mind."

Suddenly she was no longer afraid, though her heart was pounding under the thin cloak. Fragrance of hot-house flowers and expensive perfume from women's dresses intoxicated the girl as a glass of champagne forced upon one who has never tasted wine flies to the head. She felt herself on the tide of adventure, moving because she must; the soul which would have fled, to return to Mrs. Ellsworth, was a coward not worthy to live in her body.

She had room in her crowded mind to think how queer it was—and how queer it would seem all the rest of her life in looking back—that she should have the course of her existence changed because burglars had broken some panes of glass in the Strand.

"Just because of them—creatures I'll never meet—I'm going to see this through to the end," she said, flinging up her chin and looking entirely unlike the Annesley Grayle Mrs. Ellsworth knew. "To the *end*!"

She thrilled at the word, which had as much of the unknown in it as though it were the world's end she referred to, and she were jumping off.

"Will you please tell me where to leave my wrap?" she heard herself inquiring of a footman as magnificent as, and far better dressed than, the Apollo Belvedere. Her voice sounded natural. She was glad. This added to her courage. It was wonderful to feel brave. Life was so deadly, worse—so *stuffy*—at Mrs. Ellsworth's, that if she had ever been normally brave like other girls, she had had the young splendour of her courage crushed out.

The statue in gray plush and dark blue cloth came to life, and showed her the cloak-room.

Other women were there, taking last, affectionate peeps at themselves in the long mirrors. Annesley took a last peep at herself also, not an affectionate but an anxious one. Compared with these visions, was she (in Mrs. Ellsworth's cast-off clothes, made over in odd moments by the wearer) so dowdy and second-hand that— that—a stranger would be ashamed to——?

The question feared to finish itself.

"I *do* look like a lady, anyhow," the girl thought with defiance. "That's what he—that seems to be the test."

Now she was in a hurry to get the ordeal over. Instead of hanging back she walked briskly out of the cloak-room before those who had entered ahead of her finished patting their hair or putting powder on their noses.

It was worse in the large vestibule, where men sat or stood, waiting for their feminine belongings; and she was the only woman alone. But her boat was launched on the wild sea. There was no returning.

The rendezvous arranged was in what *he* had called in his letter "the foyer."

Annesley went slowly down the steps, trying not to look aimless. She decided to steer for one of the high-back brocaded chairs which had little satellite tables. Better settle on one in the middle of the hall.

This would give *him* a chance to see and recognize her from the description she had written of the dress she would wear (she had not mentioned that she'd be spared all trouble in choosing, as it was her only *real* evening frock), and to notice that she wore, according to arrangement, a white rose tucked into the neck of her bodice.

She felt conscious of her hands, and especially of her feet and ankles, for she had not been able to make Mrs. Ellsworth's dress quite long enough. Luckily it was the fashion of the moment to wear the skirt short, and she had painted her old white suede slippers silver.

She believed that she had pretty feet. But oh! what if the darn running up the heel of the pearl-gray silk stocking should show, or have burst again into a hole as she jumped out of the omnibus? She could have laughed hysterically, as the escaping women had laughed, when she realized that the fear of such a catastrophe was overcoming graver horrors.

Perhaps it was well to have a counter-irritant.

Though Annesley Grayle was the only manless woman in the foyer, the people who sat there—with one exception—did not stare. Though she had five feet eight inches of height, and was graceful despite self-consciousness, her appearance was distinguished rather than striking. Yes, "distinguished" was the word for it, decided the one exception who gazed with particular interest at that tall, slight figure in gray-sequined chiffon too old-looking for the young face.

He was sitting in a corner against the wall, and had in his hands a copy of the *Sphere*, which was so large when held high and wide open that the reader could hide behind it. He had been in his corner for fifteen or twenty minutes when Annesley Grayle arrived, glancing over the top of his paper with a sort of jaunty carelessness every few minutes at the crowd moving toward the restaurant, picking out some individual, then dropping his eyes to the *Sphere*.

For the girl in gray he had a long, appraising look, studying her every point; but he did the thing so well that, even had she turned her head his way, she need not have been embarrassed. All she would have seen was a man's forehead and a rim of smooth black hair showing over the top of an illustrated paper.

What he saw was a clear profile with a delicate nose slightly tilting upward in a proud rather than impertinent way; an arch of eyebrow daintily sketched; a large eye which might be gray or violet; a drooping mouth with a short upper lip; a really charming chin, and a long white throat; skin softly pale, like white velvet; thick, ash-blond hair parted in the middle and worn Madonna fashion—there seemed to be a lot of it in the coil at the nape of her neck.

The creature looked too simple, too—not dowdy, but too unsophisticated, to have anything false about her. Figure too thin, hardly to be called a "figure" at all, but agreeably girlish; and its owner might be anywhere from twenty to five or six years older. Not beautiful: just an average, lady-like English girl—or perhaps more of Irish type; but certainly with possibilities. If she were a princess or a millionairess, she might be glorified by newspapers as a beauty.

Annesley forced her nervous limbs to slow movement, because she hoped, or dreaded—anyhow, expected—that one of the dozen or so unattached men would spring up and say, constrainedly, "Miss Grayle, I believe?—er—how do you do?" If only he might not be fat or very bald-headed!

He had not described himself at all. Everything was to depend on her gray dress and the white rose. That seemed, now one came face to face with the fear, rather ominous.

But no one sprang up. No one wanted to know if she were Miss Grayle; and this, although she was ten minutes late.

Her instructions as to what to do at the Savoy were clear. If she were not met in the foyer, she was to go into the restaurant and ask for a table reserved for Mr. N. Smith. There she was to sit and wait to be joined by him. She had never contemplated having to carry out the latter clause, however; and when she had loitered for a few seconds, the thought rushed over her that here was a loop-hole through which to slip, if she wanted a loop-hole.

One side of her did want it: the side she knew best and longest as herself, Annesley Grayle, a timid girl brought up conventionally, and taught that to rely on others older and wiser than she was the right way for a well-born, sheltered woman to go through life. The other side, the new, desperate side that Mrs. Ellsworth's "stuffiness" had developed, was not looking for any means of escape; and this side had seized the upper hand since the alarm of the burglars in the Strand.

Annesley marched into the restaurant with the air of a soldier facing his first battle, and asked a waiter where was Mr. Smith's table.

The youth dashed off and produced a duke-like personage, his chief. A list was consulted with care; and Annesley was respectfully informed that no table had been engaged by a Mr. N. Smith for dinner that evening.

"Are you sure?" persisted Annesley, bewildered and disappointed.

"Yes, miss—madame, I am sure we have not the name on our list," said the head-waiter.

The blankness of the girl's disappointment looked out appealingly from wistful, wide-apart eyes. The man was sorry.

"There may be some misunderstanding," he consoled her. "Perhaps Mr. Smith has telephoned, and we have not received the message. I hope it is not the fault of the hotel. We do not often make mistakes; yet it is possible. We have had a few early dinners before the theatre and there is one small table disengaged. Would madame care to take it—it is here, close to the door—and watch for the gentleman when he comes?"

"When he comes!" The head-waiter comfortably took it for granted that Mr. Smith had been delayed, that he would come, and that it would be a pity to miss him. The polite person might be right, though with a sinking heart Annesley began to suspect herself played with, abandoned, as she deserved, for her dreadful boldness.

Perhaps Mr. Smith had been in communication with someone else more suitable than she, and had thrown over the appointment without troubling to let her know. Or perhaps he had been waiting in the foyer, had inspected her as she passed, and hadn't liked her looks.

This latter supposition seemed probable; but the head-waiter was so confident of what she ought to do that the girl could think of no excuse. After all, it would do little harm to wait and "see what happened." As Mr. Smith was apparently not living at the Savoy (he had merely asked her to meet him there), he might have had an accident in train or taxi. Annesley had made her plans to be away from home for two hours, so she could give him the benefit of the doubt.

A moment of hesitation, and she was seating herself in a chair offered by the head-waiter. It was one of a couple drawn up at a small table for two. Sitting thus, Annesley could see everybody who came in, and—what was more important—could be seen. By what struck her as an odd coincidence, the table was decorated with a vase of white roses whose hearts blushed faintly in the light of a pink-shaded electric lamp.

A quarter of an hour, twenty minutes, dragged along, and no Mr. Smith. Annesley could follow the passing moments on her wrist-watch in its silver bracelet, the only present Mrs. Ellsworth had ever given her, with the exception of cast-off clothes, and a pocket handkerchief each Christmas.

Every nerve in the girl's body seemed to prickle with embarrassment. She played with a dinner roll, changed the places of the flowers and the lamp, trying to appear at ease, and not daring to look up lest she should meet eyes curious or pitying.

"What if they make me pay for dinner after I've kept the table so long?" she thought in her ignorance of hotel customs. "And I've got only a shilling!"

Half an hour now, all but two minutes! There was nothing more to hope or fear. But there was the ordeal of getting away.

"I'll sit out the two minutes," she told herself. "Then I'll go. Ought I to tip the waiter?" Horrible doubt! And she must have been dreaming to touch that roll! Better sneak away while the waiter was busy at a distance.

Frightened, miserable, she was counting her chances when a man, whose coming into the room her dilemma had caused her to miss, marched unhesitatingly to her table.

CHAPTER II.
SMITHS AND SMITHS

Annesley glanced up, her face aflame, like a fanned coal. The man was tall, dark, lean, square-jawed, handsome in just that thrilling way which magazine illustrators and women love; the ideal story-hero to look at, even to the clothes which any female serial writer would certainly have described as "immaculate evening dress."

It was too good—oh, far too wonderfully good!—to be true that this man should be Mr. Smith. Yet if he were not Mr. Smith why should he——Annesley got no farther in the thought, though it flashed through her mind quick as light. Before she had time to seek an answer for her question the man—who was young, or youngish, not more than thirty-three or four—had bent over her as if greeting a friend, and had begun to speak in a low voice blurred by haste or some excitement.

"You will do me an immense service," he said, "if you'll pretend to know me and let me sit down here. You sha'n't regret it, and it may save my life."

"Sit down," answered something in Annesley that was newly awake. She found her hand being warmly shaken. Then the man took the chair reserved for Mr. Smith, just as she realized fully that he wasn't Mr. Smith. Her heart was beating fast, her eyes—fixed on the man's face, waiting for some explanation—were dilated.

"Thank you," he said, leaning toward her, in his hand a menu which the waiter had placed before the girl while she was still alone. She noticed that the hand was brown and nervous-looking, the hand of a man who might be a musician or an artist. He was pretending to read the menu, and to consult her about it. "You're a true woman, the right sort—brave. I swear I'm not here for any impertinence. Now, will you go on helping me? Can you keep your wits and not give me away, whatever happens?"

"I think so," answered the new Annesley. "What do you want me to do?" She took the pitch of her tone from his, speaking quietly, and wondering if she would not wake up in her ugly brown bedroom at Mrs. Ellsworth's, as she had done a dozen times when dreaming in advance of her rendezvous at the Savoy.

"It will be a shock when I tell you," he answered. "But for Heaven's sake, don't misunderstand. I shouldn't ask this if it weren't absolutely necessary. In case a man comes to this table and questions you, you must let him suppose that you are my wife."

"Oh!" gasped Annesley. Her eyes met the eyes that seemed to have been waiting for her look, and they answered with an appeal which she could not refuse.

She did not stop to think that if the dark eyes had not been so handsome they might have been easier to resist. She—the suppressed and timid girl, never allowed to make up her mind—let herself go with the wave of strong emotion carrying her along, and reached a resolve.

"It means trusting you a great deal," she answered. "But you say you're in danger, so I'll do what you ask. I think you can't be wicked enough to pay me back by trying to hurt me."

"You think right," the man said, and it struck her that his accent was not quite English. She wondered if he were Canadian or American. Not that she knew much about either. "A woman like you *would* think right!" he went on. "Only one woman out of ten thousand would have the nerve and presence of mind and the humanity to do what you're doing. When I came into this room and saw your face I counted on you."

Annesley blushed again in a rush of happiness. She had always longed to do something which would really matter to another soul. She had even prayed for it. Now the moment seemed to have come. God would not let her be the victim of an ignoble trick!

"I'm glad," she said, her face lit by a light from within. And at that moment, bending toward each other, they were a beautiful couple. A seeker of romance would have taken them for lovers.

"Tell me what you want me to do," Annesley said once more.

"The worst of it is, I can't tell you exactly. Two men may come into this restaurant looking for me. One or both will speak to me.

They'll call me a certain name, and I shall say they've made a mistake. You must say so, too. You must tell them I'm your husband, and stick to that no matter what the man, or men, may tell you about me. The principal thing now is to choose a name. But—by Jove—I forgot it in my hurry! Are you expecting any one to join you? If you are, it's awkward."

"I was expecting someone, but I've given him up."

"Was this table taken in his name or yours? Or, perhaps—but no, I'm sure you're *not*!"

"Sure I'm not what?"

"Married. You're a girl. Your eyes haven't got any experience of life in them."

Annesley looked down; and when she looked down her face was very sweet. She had long, curved brown lashes a shade or two darker than her hair.

"I'm not married," she said, rather stiffly. "I thought a table had been engaged in the name of Mr. Smith, but there was a misunderstanding. The head waiter put me at this table in case Mr. Smith should come. I've given him up now, and was going away when——"

"When you took pity on a nameless man. But it seems indicated that he should be Mr. Smith, unless you have any objection!"

"No, I have none. You'd better take the name, as I mentioned it to the waiter."

"And the first name?"

"I don't know. The initial I gave was N."

"Very well, I choose Nelson. Where do we live?"

Annesley stared, frightened.

"Forgive me," the man said. "I ought to have explained what I meant before asking you that, or put the question another way. Will you go on as you've begun, and trust me farther, by letting me drive with you to your home, if necessary, in case of being followed? At worst, I'll need to beg no more than to stand inside your front door for a few minutes if we're watched, and—but I see that this time I have passed the limit. I'm expecting too much! How do you know but I may be a thief or a murderer?"

"I hadn't thought of such a thing," Annesley stammered. "I was only thinking—it isn't *my* house. It doesn't even belong to my people. I live with an old lady, Mrs. Ellsworth. I hope she'll be in bed when I get back, and the servants, too. I have a key because—because I told a fib about the place where I was going, and consequently Mrs. Ellsworth approved. If she hadn't approved, I shouldn't have been allowed out. I could let you stand inside the door. But if any one followed us to the house, and saw the number, he could look in the directory, and find out that it belonged to Mrs. Ellsworth, not Mr. Smith."

"He couldn't have a directory in his pocket! By the time he got hold of one and could make any use of his knowledge, I'd be far away."

"Yes, I suppose you would," Annesley thought aloud, and a little voice seemed to add sharply in her ear: "Far away out of my life."

This brought to her memory what she had in her excitement forgotten: the adventure she had come out to meet had faded into thin air! The unexpected one which had so startlingly taken its place would end to-night, and she would be left to the dreary existence from which she had tried to break free.

She was like a pebble that had succeeded in riding out to sea on a wave, only to be washed back into its old place on the shore. The thought that, after all, she had no change to look forward to, gave the girl a passionate desire to make the most of this one living hour among many that were born dead.

"Mrs. Ellsworth's house," she said, "is 22-A, Torrington Square."

"Thank you." Only these two words he spoke, but the eager dark eyes seemed to add praise and blessings for her confidence.

"My name is Annesley Grayle," she volunteered, as if to prove to the man and to herself how far she trusted him; also perhaps as a bid for his name in payment of that trust. So at least he must have understood, for he said: "If I don't tell you mine, it's for your own protection. I'm not ashamed of it; but it's better that you shouldn't know—that if you heard it suddenly, it should be strange to you, just like any other name. Don't you see I'm right?"

"I dare say you are."

"Then we'll leave it at that. But we can't go on pretending to study this menu for ever! You came to dine with Mr. Smith. You'll dine with his understudy instead. You'll let me order dinner? It's part of the programme."

"Very well," Annesley agreed.

The man nodded to the head-waiter, who had been interested in the little drama indirectly stage-managed by him. Instead of sending a subordinate, he came himself to take the order. With wonderful promptness, considering that Mr. Smith's thoughts had not been near the menu under his eyes, several dishes were chosen and a wine selected.

"Madame is glad now that I persuaded her not to go?" the waiter could not resist, and Annesley replied that she was glad. As the man turned away, "Mr. Smith" raised his eyebrows with rather a wistful smile.

"I'm afraid you're sorry, really," he said. "If I'd come a minute later than I did, you'd have been safe and happy at home by this time."

"Not happy," amended the girl. "Because it isn't home. If it were, I shouldn't have told fibs to Mrs. Ellsworth to-night."

"That sounds interesting," remarked her companion.

"It's *not* interesting!" she assured him. "Nothing in my life is. I don't want to bore you by talking about my affairs, but if you think we may be—interrupted, perhaps, I'd better explain one or two things while there's time. I wanted to come here this evening to keep an engagement I'd made, but it's difficult for me to get out alone. Mrs. Ellsworth doesn't like to be left, and she never lets me go anywhere without her except to the house of some friends of mine, the only real friends I have. It's odd, but *their* name is Smith, and that saved my telling a direct lie. Not that a half-lie isn't worse, it's so cowardly!

"Mrs. Ellsworth likes me to go to Archdeacon and Mrs. Smith's because—I'm afraid because she thinks they're 'swells.' Mrs. Smith has a duke for an uncle! Mrs. Ellsworth said 'yes' at once, when I asked, and gave me her key and permission to stop out till half-past ten, though everyone in the house is supposed to be in bed by ten. She's almost sure to be in bed herself, but if she gets interested in one of the books I brought from the library to-day, it's possible she may be sitting up to read, and to ask about my evening.

"Our bedrooms are on the ground floor at the back of an addition to the house. What if she should hear the latchkey (it's old fashioned and hard to work), and what if she should come to the swing door at the end of the corridor where she'd see you with me? What would you say or do?"

"H'm! It would be awkward. But—isn't there a *young* Smith in your Archdeacon's family?"

"There is one, but I haven't seen him since I was a little girl. He's a sailor. He's away now on an Arctic expedition."

"Then it wasn't *that* Mr. Smith you came to meet at the Savoy?"

"No. They're not related." As Annesley returned in thought to the Mr. Smith who had thrown her over, she took from her bodice the white rose which was to have identified her for him, and found it a place in the vase with the other white roses. She had a special reason for doing this. The real Mr. Smith, if by any chance he appeared now, would be a complication. Without the rose he could not claim her acquaintance.

"Why do you do that?" her companion broke the thread of his questioning to ask.

The girl was tempted to tell some easy fib that the rose was faded, or too fragrant; but somehow she could not. They both seemed so close to the deep-down things of life at this moment that to speak the truth was the one possible thing.

"I arranged to wear a white rose for Mr. Smith to recognize me. We—have never seen each other," she confessed.

"Yet you say there's nothing interesting in your life!"

"It's true! *This* thing was—was dreadful. It could happen only to a girl whose life was not interesting."

"Now I understand why you put away the rose—for my sake, in case Mr. Smith should turn up, after all. Will you give it to me? I won't flaunt it in my buttonhole. I'll hide it sacredly, in memory of this evening—and of you. Not that I shall need to be reminded of anything which concerns this night—you especially, and your generosity, your courage. But it may be that the men I spoke of won't find me here. If they don't, the worst of your ordeal is over. It will only be to finish dinner, and let me put you into a taxi. To-morrow you can think that you dreamed the wretch who appealed to you, and be glad that you will never see him again."

Annesley selected her white rose from its fellows, dried its stem daintily with her napkin, and gave the flower to "Mr. Smith." Already it looked refreshed, as she herself felt refreshed, after five years of "stuffiness," by these few throbbing moments.

Their hands touched, and through Annesley's darted a little tingle of electricity that flashed up her arm to her heart, where it caught like a hooked wire. She was surprised, almost frightened by the sensation, and ashamed because she didn't find it disagreeable.

"It must be that people who're really *alive*, as he is, give out magnetism," she thought. And the thrill lingered as the man thanked her with eyes and voice.

When he had looked at the rose curiously, as if expecting to learn from it the secret of its wearer, he put the flower away in a letter-case in an inner breast pocket of his coat.

For once Annesley was face to face with romance, and even though she would presently go back to the old round (since the adventure she came out to meet had failed), she was stirred to a wild gladness in this other adventure. The *hors d'oeuvres* appeared; then soup, and wine, which Mr. Smith begged her to taste.

"Drink luck for me," he insisted. "You and you alone can bring it."

Annesley drank. And the champagne filliped colour to her cheeks.

"Now we'll go on and think out the problem of what may happen at your door — if Fate takes me there," the man said. "Your old friend's sailor son is no use to me. He can't be whisked back from the North Pole to London for my benefit. Perhaps I may be an acquaintance of Archdeacon Smith's, mayn't I, if worst comes to worst? I've been dining there, and brought you back in a taxi. Will that do? If there are fibs to tell, I'll tell them myself and spare you if possible."

"After all I've told to-night, one or two more can't matter," said Annesley. "They won't hurt Mrs. Ellsworth. It's the other danger that's more worrying — the danger from those men. I've thought of something that may help if they follow us to Torrington Square. They may ask a policeman whose house we've gone into, and find out it's Mrs. Ellsworth's, before you can get away. So it will be better not to tell them it's *yours*. You can be visiting. There is a Mr. Smith who comes sometimes from America, where he lives, though he's not American.

Even the policemen who have that beat may have heard of him from Mrs. Ellsworth's servants. There's a room kept always ready for him, and called 'Mr. Smith's room.'"

"That does help," said the man. "It's clever and kind of you to rack your brains for me. A Mr. Smith from America! It's easy for me to play that part, I'm from America. Perhaps you've guessed that?"

"But you're very different from Mrs. Ellsworth's Mr. Smith," Annesley warned him, hastily. "He's middle-aged, eccentric, and not good-looking. He comes to England for his 'nerves' when he has worked too hard and tired himself out. I think he's rich; and once he was robbed in some big hotel, so he likes to stay at a plain sort of house where there's no danger. He has a horror of burglars, and won't even stop at the Archdeacon's since they had a burglary a few years ago. He pays Mrs. Ellsworth for his room, I believe. A funny arrangement!—it came about through me. But that's not of importance to you."

"It may be. We can't tell. Better let me know as much as possible about these Smiths. There's Mrs. Ellsworth's Smith, and the Smith you came to meet— —"

"We needn't talk of *him*, anyway!"

There was a hint of anger in the girl's protest; but her resentment was for the man who had humiliated her by breaking his appointment— *such* an appointment!

She hurried on, trying to hide all signs of agitation. "You see, Mrs. Ellsworth once hoped to have Archdeacon Smith and his wife for friends. They didn't care for her, but they loved my father—oh, long ago in the country, where we lived. When he died and I hadn't any money or training for work, they were nice to Mrs. Ellsworth for my sake—or, rather, for my father's sake—and persuaded her to take me as her companion. She was glad to do it to please them; but soon she realized that they didn't mean to reward her by being intimate.

"Poor woman, I was almost sorry for her disappointment! You see, she's a snob at heart, and though 'Smith' sounds a common name, both the Archdeacon and his wife have titled relations. So have I— and that was another reason for taking me. She adores a title. Doesn't that sound pitiful? But she has few interests and no real friends, so she's never given up hope of 'collecting' the Smiths.

"That's why she lets me visit them. And when I happened to mention, for something to say, that the Archdeacon had an eccentric cousin in America who was afraid of hotels and even of visiting at their house because of a fad about burglars, she offered to give him the better of her two spare rooms whenever he came to England. I never thought he'd accept, but he did, only he would insist on paying.

"That's the story, if you can call it a story, for Mr. Ruthven Smith isn't a bit exciting nor interesting. When he appears—generally quite suddenly—he finds his room ready. He has his breakfast sent up, and lunches out at his club or somewhere. He mostly dines out, too, but he has a standing invitation to dine with Mrs. Ellsworth, and we always have good dinners when he is staying, to be ready in case of the worst."

The man smiled, rather a charming smile, Annesley could not help noticing.

"In case of the worst!" he repeated. "He must be deadly if his society bores you more than that of an old lady on whom, I suppose, you dance attendance morning, noon, and night. Now, my situation is so—er—peculiar that I ought to be thankful to exchange identities with any man. But I wouldn't with Mr. Ruthven Smith for all his money and jewels."

Annesley opened her eyes. "Did I say anything about jewels?" she asked.

"No, you didn't," the man assured her, "except in mentioning the name of Ruthven Smith. Anybody who has lived in America as long as I have, associates jewels with the name of Ruthven Smith. His 'Ruthven' lifts him far above the ruck of a *mere* Smith—like myself, for instance"; and he smiled again.

Annesley began curiously to feel as if she knew him well. This made her more anxious to give him help—for it would not be helping a stranger: it would be helping a friend.

"I've heard, of course, that he's something—I'm not sure what— in a firm of jewellers," she said. "But I'd no idea of his being so important."

"He's third partner with Van Vreck & Co.," her companion explained. "I've heard he joined at first because of his great knowledge of jewels and because he's been able to revive the lost art of making certain transparent enamels. The Van Vrecks sent for him from England years ago. He buys jewels for the firm now, I believe. No doubt that's why he's in such a funk about burglars."

"Fancy your knowing more about Mr. Smith than I know! Perhaps more than Mrs. Ellsworth knows!" exclaimed Annesley, forgetting the strain of expectation—the dread that a pair of mysterious, nightmare men might break up the dreamlike dinner-party for two.

"I don't know more about him than half America and Europe knows," laughed the man. "It's lucky I *do* know something, though, as I may have to be mistaken for Ruthven Smith, and add an 'N' to his initials. I suppose he's not in England now by any chance?"

"No. It must be six or seven months since he was here last," said Annesley. "I don't think Mrs. Ellsworth has heard from him. She hardly ever does until a day or two before he's due to arrive; neither do his cousins."

"A peculiar fellow, it would seem," remarked her companion. And then, out of a plunge into thought, "You say you've never seen the Mr. Smith you came to meet at the Savoy? How can you be sure it isn't old 'R. S.' as they call him at Van Vreck's, wanting to play you a trick—give you a surprise?"

Annesley shook her head. "If you knew Mr. Ruthven Smith, you'd know that would be impossible. Why, I don't believe he remembers when I'm out of sight that I exist."

"Still more peculiar! Miss Grayle, I haven't any right to ask you questions. But I shouldn't be a man if I weren't forgetting my own affairs—in—in curiosity, if you want to call it that (I don't!), about yours. No! I won't let it pass for ordinary curiosity. Can't you understand you're doing for me more than any woman ever has done, or any man would do? That does make a bond between us. You can't deny it. Tell me about this Mr. Smith whom you don't know and never saw, yet came to the Savoy Hotel to meet."

CHAPTER III.
WHY SHE CAME

Surprised by the abruptness of his question, Annesley's eyes dropped from the eyes of her host, which tried to hold them. She felt that she ought to be angry with him for taking advantage of her generosity—for it amounted to that! Yet anger would not come, only shame and the desire to hide a thing which would change his gratitude to contempt.

"Don't let's waste time talking about me," she said. "We haven't arranged——"

"We've arranged everything as well as we can. For the rest, I must trust to luck—and you. Do tell me why you came here, why you *thought* you came here, I mean; for I'm convinced you were sent for my sake by any higher powers there may be. I felt that, the minute I saw you. I feel it ten times more strongly now. I know that whatever your reason was, it's nothing to be ashamed of."

"I *am* ashamed," Annesley was led on to confess. "You'd despise me if I told you, for you can't realize what my life's been for five years. And that's my one excuse."

"Only a fool would want a woman like you to excuse herself for anything. I swear I wouldn't despise you. I couldn't. If you should tell me—knowing you as little, or as well, as I do, that you'd been plotting a murder, I'd be certain you were justified, and my first thought would be to save you, as you're saving me now."

Annesley felt again the man's intense magnetism. Suddenly she wanted to tell him everything. It would be a relief. She would watch his face and see how it changed. It would be like having the verdict of the world on what she had done—or meant to do.

"I saw an advertisement in the *Morning Post*," she said with a kind of breathless violence, "from a man who—who wanted to meet a girl with—a 'view to marriage.'"

The words brought a blush so painful that the mounting blood forced tears to her eyes. But she looked her *vis-à-vis* unwaveringly in the face.

That did not change at all, unless the interest in his eyes grew warmer. The sympathy she saw there gave Annesley a new and passionate desire to defend herself. If he had shown disgust, she would not have cared to try, she thought.

"I told you it was horrid, and not interesting or romantic," she dashed on. "But I was desperate. Mrs. Ellsworth is awful! I don't suppose you ever met such a woman. She's not cruel about starving my body. It's only my soul she starves. What business have *I* with a soul, except in church, where it's proper to think about such things? But she nags—*nags*! She makes my hair feel as if it were turning gray at the roots, and my face drying up—like an apple.

"I wasn't nineteen when I came to her. I'm twenty-three now, and I feel *old*—desiccated, thanks to those piling-up hundreds of days with her. They've killed my spirit. I used to be different. I can feel it. I can see it in the mirror. It isn't only the passing days, but having nothing better to look forward to. I'm too cowardly—or too religious or something, to kill myself, even if I knew how to, decently. But the deadliness of it all, the airlessness of her house and her heart!

"A man couldn't imagine it. She's made me forget not only my own youth, but that there's youth in the world. Why, at first I was so wild I should have loved to say dreadful things, or strike her. But now I haven't the spirit left to feel like that. My blood's turning white. The other day when I was reading aloud to Mrs. Ellsworth (I read a lot: the stupidest parts of the papers and the silliest books, that turn my brain to fluff) I caught sight of an advertisement in the Personal Column.

"I stopped just in time and didn't read it out. Only a glimpse I had, for I was in the midst of something else when my eyes wandered. But when Mrs. Ellsworth was taking her nap after luncheon I got the *Post* again and read the advertisement through carefully. The reason I was interested was because even the glance I took showed that the girl who was 'wanted' seemed in some ways rather like me. The advertisement said she must be from twenty-one to twenty-six; needn't be a beauty, but of pleasant appearance; money no object; the essentials were that she must have a fair education and be of good birth and manners, so as to command a certain position in society.

"I believe those were the very words. And it didn't seem too conceited to think that I answered the description. I'm not bad-looking, and my mother's father was an earl—an Irish one. I couldn't get the advertisement out of my head. It fascinated me."

"No wonder!" exclaimed Mr. Smith. He had been listening intently, and though she had paused, panting a little, more than once, he had not broken in with a word.

"Do you *honestly* think it no wonder?" Annesley flashed at him.

"It was like a prisoner seeing a key sticking in a door that has always been locked," he said.

"How strange you should think of that!" she cried. "It was the thought which came into my mind, and seemed to excuse me if anything could." Annesley felt grateful to the man. She was sure she could never have explained herself in this way or pleaded her own cause with the real Mr. Smith. A man cold-blooded enough to advertise for a wife "well-born and able to command a certain position in society" would have frozen her into an ice-block of reserve.

She might possibly have accepted his "proposition" (one couldn't speak of it in the ordinary way as a "proposal"), provided that, on seeing her, he had judged her suitable for the place; but she could never have talked her heart out to him as she was led on to do by this other man, equally a stranger, yet sympathetic because of his own trouble and the mystery which made of him a figure of romance.

"It isn't strange I should think of the prison door and the key," her companion said. "That was the situation. 'N. Smith' was rather clever in his way. There must be many girls of good family and good looks who are in prison, pining to escape. He must have had a lot of answers, that fellow; but none of the girls could have come within a mile of you. I'm selfish! I bless my lucky stars he didn't turn up here."

"I dare say it's the best thing that could happen," Annesley agreed with a sigh. "Probably he's horrible. But there was one thing: I thought, though he must be a snob and vulgar, advertising as he did for a wife of good birth, that very thing looked as if he were no *worse* than a snob. Not a villain, I mean. Otherwise, I shouldn't have dared answer. But I did answer the same day, while I had the courage. I posted a letter with some of Mrs. Ellsworth's, which she sent me out to drop into the box. His address was 'N. S., the *Morning Post*'; and I told him to send a reply, if he wrote, to the stationery shop and library where Mrs. Ellsworth makes me go every day to change her books."

"And the answer? What was it like? What impression did it give you?" questioned the man who sat in Mr. Smith's place.

"Oh, it was written in a good hand. But it was a stiff, commonplace sort of letter, except that it asked me to wear a white rose. White roses happen to be the ones I like best."

"So do I," said Mr. Smith. "Did he tell you to come to a table here and wait for him?"

"Not exactly. He was to meet me in the foyer. But if he did not, I was to understand he'd been delayed; and in that case I must come to the restaurant and inquire for a table engaged by Mr. N. Smith. Lots of times I decided not to do anything. But you see I came, and this is my reward."

"A poor one," her companion finished.

"I don't mean that! I mean he hasn't come at all. Maybe he never meant to. Maybe he got some letter he liked better than mine, and arranged to meet the girl somewhere else. A man of that sort wouldn't write to tell the straight truth in time, and save the unwanted one from humiliation."

"Are you very sorry he didn't?"

"No," Annesley said, frankly. "I'm not sorry. It's good to be able to help someone. I'm glad I came."

"So am I," Mr. Smith answered with a sudden change in his voice from calm to excitement. "And now the moment isn't far off, I think, for the help to be given. The men I spoke of are here. They're in the restaurant. You can't see them without turning your head, which would not be wise. They're speaking to a waiter. They haven't seen me yet, but they're sure to look soon. They're pointing to a table near us. It's free. The waiter's leading them to it. In an instant you'll have a better view of them than I shall. Now ... but don't look up yet."

From under her lashes Annesley saw—in the way women do see without seeming to use their eyes—two men conducted to a table directly in front of her. As she sat on her host's right, at the end of the table, not opposite to him, this gave her the advantage—or disadvantage—of facing the newcomers fully, while Mr. Smith, who had faced them as they entered, would have his profile turned toward their table.

The pair seated themselves in the same way that Annesley and her companion were placed, one at the right hand of the other. This caused the first man to face the girl fully and gave her the second in profile. One table only intervened between Mr. Smith's and that selected by the late arrivals, and the latter had hardly sat down when the party of four at the intermediate table rose to go.

Under cover of their departure, bowing of waiters and readjustment of ladies' sable or ermine stoles, Annesley ventured a lightning glance at the men. She saw that both were black-haired and black-bearded, with dark skins and long noses. There was a slight suggestion of resemblance between them. They might be brothers. They were in evening dress, but did not look, Annesley thought, like gentlemen.

Mr. Smith was eating *blennes au caviar* apparently with enjoyment. He called a waiter and told him to put more whipped cream on the caviare as yet untouched in the middle of Annesley's pancake.

"That's better, I think," he said, genially. And as the waiter went away, "What are they doing now?"

Annesley lifted her champagne glass as an excuse to raise her eyes. "I'm afraid they've seen us and are talking about you. Can't we—hadn't we better go?"

"Certainly not," replied Mr. Smith. "At least, *I* can't. But if you repent——"

"I don't," Annesley broke in. "I was thinking of you, of course."

"Bless you!" said her host. His tone was suddenly gay. She glanced at him and saw that his face was gay also, his eyes bright and challenging, his look almost boyish. She had taken him for thirty-three or four; now she would have guessed him younger.

Annesley could not help admiring his pluck, for he had said that the arrival of these men meant danger. She ought to be sorry as well as frightened because they had come, but at that moment she was neither. Her companion's example was contagious. Her spirits rose. And the thought flashed through her head, "This adventure won't end here!" If she had had time she would have been ashamed of her gladness; but there was no time. Smith was talking again in a suppressed yet cheerful tone.

"You won't forget that we're Mr. and Mrs. Nelson Smith?"

"No—no. I sha'n't forget."

"You may have to call me Nelson, and I—to call you Annesley. It's a pretty name, odd for a woman to have. How did you get it?"

"Oh, you don't want to hear that now!"

"Why not?—unless you'd rather not tell me. We can't do anything more till the blow falls, except enjoy ourselves and go on with our dinner. How did you come to be Annesley?"

"It was part of my mother's maiden name. She was an Annesley-Seton."

"There's a Lord Annesley-Seton, isn't there?"

"Yes."

"Related to you?"

"A cousin. But Grayle isn't a name in their set. He and his wife have forgotten my existence. I'm not likely to remind them of it."

"His wife was an American girl, wasn't she?"

"How odd that you should know!"

"Not very. I remember there being a lot in the papers about the wedding six or seven years ago. The girl was very rich—a Miss Haverstall. Her father's lost his money since then."

"How *can* you keep such uninteresting things in your mind—just now?"

"They're not uninteresting. They concern you!"

"Lord Annesley-Seton's affairs don't concern me, and never will."

"I wonder?" said Smith, looking thoughtful; and the girl wondered, too: not about her future or her relatives, but what the next few minutes would do with this strange young man, and how at such a time he could bear to talk commonplaces.

"If you're trying to keep me from being nervous," she whispered, "it's not a bit of use! I can't think of anything or any one except those men. They've stopped whispering. But they're looking at you. Now—they're getting up. They're coming toward us!

CHAPTER IV.
THE GREAT MOMENT

The men were staring so keenly at "Mr. N. Smith" that it seemed to Annesley he must feel the stab of eyes, sharp as pin-pricks, in his back. He had the self-control, however, not to look round, not even to change expression. No man in the restaurant appeared more calmly at ease than he.

The couple had accompanied their stare with eager whisperings. Then, as if on some hasty decision, they pushed back their chairs and got up. Taking a few steps they separated, approaching Smith on right and left. One, therefore, stood between him and Annesley as if to prevent an exchange of words or glances. There was something Eastern and oddly alien about them in spite of their conventional clothes.

"Mr. Michael Varcoe!" said the bigger and older, he who stood on the left of Smith. The other kept in the background, not to crowd with conspicuous rudeness between Annesley and her host. The man who spoke had a thick voice and a curious accent which the girl, with her small experience, was unable to place.

"No," answered "Smith," in a puzzled tone. "You mistake me for someone else."

"I think not," insisted the bearded man, in a hostile drawl. "I *think* not!"

"I'm *sure* not," echoed the other. "You are Michael Varcoe. There's no getting away from that."

The emphasis seemed to add, "And no getting away from *us*."

Excitement stirred Annesley to courage. "Why, how horrid!" she exclaimed, bending past the human obstacle; "people taking you for some *foreigner*! I'm sure you can't be like a man with such a name as—Michael Varcoe! Tell them who we are."

"My name is Nelson Smith," said her official husband. "My wife is not— —"

"Your wife!" repeated the man standing opposite Annesley. He stared with insolent incredulity. "'Mr. and Mrs. Nelson Smith.' A good name to take."

"It happens to have been given me." Slight sharpness broke the tolerance of Smith's tone.

"I don't believe you!" exclaimed the other.

Smith's black brows drew together. "It doesn't matter whether you believe or not," he said. "What does matter is that you should annoy us. I tell you I'm not Michael Varcoe, and never heard the name. If you're not satisfied, and if you don't go back to your dinner and let us finish ours in peace, I'll appeal to the management."

"Well!" grumbled the taller of the pair. "If you're not the man I want, you're his image—minus moustache and beard. You *must* be Varcoe!"

"Of course he's Varcoe," insisted the other.

"Of course he's not!" said Annesley, with just the right amount of irritation. "Our name is Smith. Nelson, do tell this—person to ask the head-waiter who engaged the table, and not stay here making a fuss."

"Anybody can engage a table in the name of Smith!" sneered the first speaker. "That is nothing. We go by something more convincing than a name. There are countries where men have been arrested on less resemblance—or put out of the way."

"Oh, Nelson, he's frightening me," faltered Annesley. "He must have lost his senses."

"You think that, do you?" The fierce eyes fixed her with a stare. "You tell me—*you*, madame, that you are this man's wife?"

"I do tell you so," the girl replied, firmly, "though I don't see that it's your affair! Now go away."

"Very well, we take your word," returned the man, in a tone which said that he did nothing of the sort. "And we go—back to our table, to let you finish your meal, Mr. and Mrs. Smith."

His black glance sprang like a tarantula from her face to her companion's, then to his friend's. The latter accepted the ultimatum and followed in sulky silence; but when the pair were seated at their own table, though they ordered food and wine, their attention was still for the alleged Mr. and Mrs. Smith.

Annesley tried to ignore the fact that they stared without ceasing, but she could not help being aware of their eyes. She felt faint, and everything in the room whirled giddily.

"Drink some champagne," said Smith's quiet voice.

The girl obeyed, and the ice-cold wine cooled the fire in blood and nerves.

"You have been splendid," Smith encouraged her. "I know you won't fail me now."

"I promise you I will not!" returned Annesley. "The worst is over. I feel ready for anything."

"How can I thank you?" he murmured. "If I had all the rest of my life to do it in, instead of a few minutes, it wouldn't be too much. You were perfect in your manner, not anxious, only annoyed; just the right air for a self-respecting Mrs. Smith."

They both laughed, and Annesley was surprised that she could laugh naturally and gaily. Presently she laughed again, when Mr. Smith remarked that she had missed her vocation in not being an actress—she, the country mouse, who had hardly been inside a theatre.

The two lingered over their dinner, watched with impatience by the men at the other table, who had ordered only one dish and paid for it immediately, that they might be ready for anything at an instant's notice. They had also a small bottle of wine, which they sipped abstemiously as an excuse to remain after their food had been eaten.

When at last Mr. and Mrs. Smith had finished their *bombe surprise*, and trifled with some fruit, Annesley said: "Evidently they don't care how long they have to wait! I suppose there's nothing for us to do but to go?"

"Oh, yes, there's still something," said Smith. "We'll have coffee in the foyer, and see what the enemy's next move is. It would be a mistake to let the brutes believe they're frightening us."

Annesley agreed in silence; but in her heart she was glad to lengthen out the adventure. Soon she would have to creep back to her dull modern substitute for a moated grange, and after that—not "the deluge"; nothing so exciting: extinction.

As they walked out of the restaurant together the girl glanced up at the dark profile, mysterious as a stranger's, yet familiar as a friend's. The man had told her nothing about himself except that he was in danger, and had given no hint as to what that danger was; but the girl's heart was warm with belief in him. If there were a question of crime, the crime was not his. His superiority over those creatures must be moral as well as physical and social.

By an odd coincidence, Mr. Smith steered for the sofa in the corner whence a man had stared from behind an open newspaper at a tall, lonely girl in gray, earlier in the evening. Annesley knew nothing of this coincidence, because she had not noticed the man; but even if she had, she would have forgotten him. She had been thinking of herself when she first trailed her gray dress over the red carpet of the foyer; now, returning, she thought of the man who was with her and the two who were certain to follow.

Scarcely were she and Smith seated before the others appeared. The men sat down in chairs drawn up at a little table; and not only must those in the corner pass by them in escaping, but every word spoken above a whisper must be overheard.

This fact did not embarrass Smith. He ordered coffee and cigarettes, and talked to Annesley in an ordinary tone about a motor trip which it would be pleasant to take. The watchers also demanded coffee. But the waiter they summoned was slow in fulfilling their order. When it was obeyed, before the pair had time to lift cup to lip, Mr. Smith took impish pleasure in getting to his feet.

"Come, dear," he said, "we'd better be off."

He laid on the table money for the coffee and cigarettes, with a satisfactory tip. Then without looking at their neighbours he and Annesley passed, walking shoulder to shoulder with a leisurely step toward the entrance.

"I suppose there's no chance of shaking them off?" the girl whispered.

"None whatever," said Smith. "But we've had the fun of cheating them out of their coffee, because they won't chance our stopping to pick up our wraps. They'll be on our heels till the end of the journey, so there's nothing for it except to stick to the original plan of my going home with you. I hope you don't mind? I hope you're not afraid of me now?"

"I'm not at all afraid," said Annesley.

"Thank you for that. If our taxi outruns theirs, I sha'n't need to trespass on your kindness beyond the doorstep. But if they overtake us, and are on the spot before you can vanish into the house and I can disappear in some other direction, are you still game to keep your promise—the promise to let me go indoors with you?"

"Yes, I am 'game' to the end—whatever the end may be," the girl answered; and she wondered at herself, because her heart was as brave as her words.

Five minutes later Annesley, wrapped in her thin cloak, was stepping into a taxi. As Smith followed and told the chauffeur where to drive, the two watchers shot through the revolving door in time to overhear, and also to order a taxi.

Annesley wondered for one dismayed instant why her companion should have given the real address. He might have mentioned some other street, and thus have gained time; but a second thought told her that, with the pursuing taxi so close upon their heels, an attempt to deceive would have been useless. The policy of defiance was the only one.

For a few moments neither the girl nor the man spoke, although Annesley felt that there were a thousand things to say. Every second was taking them nearer to Torrington Square; and their parting must come soon. After that, all would be blankness for her, as before this wonderful night.

Such thoughts made the girl a prisoner of silence; and "Mr. Smith" was also tongue-tied. Was he concentrating his mind upon some plan of escape from these mysterious enemies? She told herself this must be so; yet his first words proved that he had been thinking of the risk she ran.

"If the dragon comes out of her den and catches us at the door, will that mean a catastrophe for you, or can I be explained away?" he inquired.

"I don't know," said Annesley. "And somehow I don't care!"

"I care," the man replied. "I can't have harm come to you through me. But tell me, before we go farther—does it matter to you, Miss Grayle, that in a little while you and I may see the last of each other? I feel I have a sort of right to ask that question, because it matters such a lot to me. I've got to know you better in this one evening than I could in a year in a commonplace way. I don't want you to go out of my life, because you're the best thing that ever came into it. And if I dared hope that I might mean to you some day half what you've begun to mean for me already, why, I wouldn't *let* you go!"

Annesley clasped her hands under her cloak. They were cold yet tingling. Her blood was leaping; but she could not speak. She was afraid of saying too much.

"Can't you give me a grain of hope?" he went on. His voice was wistful. "We have so little time."

"What—do you want me to say?" Annesley stammered.

"I want you to say—that you don't wish to see the last of me to-night."

"I shouldn't be human if I *could* wish that!" the words seemed to speak themselves; and she, who had been taught to repress and hide emotion as if it were a vice, was glad that the truth was out. After all they had gone through together she couldn't send this man away believing her indifferent. "I—it doesn't seem as if we were strangers," she faltered on.

"Strangers! I should think not," he echoed. "We mayn't know much about each other's tastes, but we do know about each other's souls, which is more than can be said of most men and women acquainted for half a lifetime. As for our pasts, you haven't had one, and I—well, if I swear to you that I've never murdered anybody, or been in prison, or committed an unforgivable crime, will you take my word?"

"If you told me you *were* a murderer, or had committed some unforgivable crime, I—I don't feel as if I could believe it," Annesley assured him. "It—would hurt me to think evil of you. I'm sure it isn't you who are evil, but these men."

"You're an angel to feel like that and speak like that!" exclaimed Smith. "I don't deserve your goodness, but I appreciate it. I'd like to take your hand and kiss it when I thank you, but I won't, because you're alone with me, under my protection. To save me from trouble you've risked danger and put yourself in my power. I may be bad in some ways—most men are, or would be in women's eyes if women saw them as they are; but I'm not a brute. The worst I've ever done is to try to pay back a great injury, an eye for an eye, a tooth for a tooth. Do you blame me for that?"

"I have no right—I don't know what the injury was," said the girl; and, hesitating a little, "still—I don't think *I* could find happiness in revenge."

"I could, or anyhow, satisfaction: I confess that. About 'happiness,' I don't know much. But you could teach me."

"I?"

"Yes. Do you believe there can be such a thing as love at first sight?"

"I can't tell. Books say so. Perhaps——"

"There's no 'perhaps.' I've found that out to-night. I believe love that comes at sight must be the only real love—a sort of electric call from soul to soul. The thing that's happened is just this: I've met the one woman—my help-mate. If I come out of this trouble, and can ask a girl like you to give herself to me, will you do it?"

"Oh, you say this because you think you ought to be grateful!" cried Annesley. "But I don't want gratitude. This is the first time I've ever *lived*. I owe that to you. And it's more than you can owe to me."

The man laughed, a happy laugh, as though danger were miles away instead of on his heels. "You know almost as much about men as a child knows, Miss Grayle," he said, "if you think I'm one of the sort—if there *is* such a sort—who would tie himself to a woman for gratitude. I've just one motive in wanting you to marry me. I love you and need you. I couldn't feel more if I'd known you months instead of hours."

The wonder of it swept over Annesley in a flood. Even in her dreams—and she had had wild dreams sometimes—she had never pictured a man such as this loving her and wanting her. To the girl's mind he was so attractive that it seemed impossible his choice of her could be from the heart. She would wake up to a stale, flat to-morrow and find that none of these things had really happened.

Still, she might as well live up to the dream while it lasted, and have the more to remember.

"It's a fairy story, surely!" she said, trying to laugh. "There are so many beautiful girls in the world for a man like you, that I——"

"A man like me! What *am* I like?"

"Oh, it's hard to put into words. But—well, you're brave; I'm sure of that."

"I hope I'm not a coward. All normal men are brave. That's nothing. What else am I—to you?"

"Interesting. More interesting than—than any one I ever saw."

"If you feel that, you don't want to send me out of your life, do you?—after you've stood by and sheltered me from danger?"

"No-o. I don't want to send you out of my life. But——"

"There's only one way in which you can keep me and I can keep you—circumstanced as we are. We must be husband and wife."

"Oh!" The girl covered her face with both hands. The world was on fire around her.

"I frighten you. Yet you might have consented to marry that other Smith. You went to meet him, to decide whether he was possible."

"I know. But I see now, if he'd kept his appointment, it would have ended in nothing, even if—if he had been pleased with me. I couldn't have brought myself to say 'yes'."

"How can you be certain?"

"Because"—Annesley spoke almost in a whisper—"because he wasn't *you*."

Smith snatched her clasped hands and kissed them. The warm touch of the man's lips gave the girl a new, mysterious sensation. No man had ever kissed even her hands. Suddenly she felt sure that what she felt must be love—love at first sight, which, according to him, was an electric call from soul to soul. His kiss told her that they belonged to each other for good or evil.

"Darling!" he said. "You are mine. I sha'n't let you go. For love of you I'll free myself from this temporary trouble I'm in, and come back to claim you soon. When I ask you to be my wife you'll say to me what you *wouldn't* have said to the other Smith?"

"If I can escape to hear you. But—you don't know Mrs. Ellsworth."

"St. George rescued the princess from the dragon: so will I, though I've warned you I'm no saint. When we meet again I'll tell you what I am, and perhaps my real name, which is better than Smith, though it mayn't be as safe. Now, there are other things to say——"

But there was no time to say them, for the taxi stopped. The time seemed so short since the Savoy that Annesley couldn't believe they were in Torrington Square. Perhaps the chauffeur had made a mistake? She looked out, hoping that it might be so; but before her were the darkened windows of the dull, familiar house, 22-A. The great moment was upon them.

CHAPTER V.
THE SECOND LATCHKEY

Without another word Smith opened the door and sprang out. As Annesley put her hand into his to descend she gave him the latchkey. It had been inside the neck of her dress, and the metal was warm from the warmth of her heart.

"Take this," she whispered. "If *they* are watching, it will be best for you to have the key."

Mr. Smith bestowed a generous tip on the driver, and was rewarded with a loud, cheerful "Thank you, sir!" which must have reached the ears of a chauffeur in the act of stopping before a house near by. Annesley, glancing sidewise at the other taxi, thought that it drew up with suspicious suddenness, as if it had awaited a "cue."

There was little doubt in her mind as to who the occupants were, and her heart beat fast, though she controlled herself to walk with calmness across the strip of pavement. On the doorstep she turned to wait for her companion, and, without seeming to look past him, saw that no one got out from the neighbouring taxi.

"They don't care whether we guess who they are or not," was her thought. "They mean to find out whether we have a latchkey and can let ourselves into a house in this square. When they see us go in, will they believe the story and drive away, or—will they stay on?"

What would happen if the watchers persisted Annesley dared not think; but she knew that she would sacrifice herself in any way rather than send the man she loved (yes, she *did* love him!) out to face peril.

Having paid the chauffeur, Mr. N. Smith joined the figure on the doorstep, and fitted into the lock Annesley's latchkey. Then he opened the door for the girl, and followed her in with a cool air of proprietorship which ought to have impressed the watchers. A minute later, if another proof had been needed that Mr. and Mrs. Smith were actually at home, it was given by a sudden glow of red curtains in the two front windows of the ground floor.

This touch of realism meant extra risk for Annesley in case Mrs. Ellsworth were awake; but she took it with scarcely a qualm of fear. The house was quiet, and there were ten chances to one against its mistress being on the alert at this hour, so long past her bedtime.

When the girl had switched on the lights of the two-branched chandelier over the dining table she beckoned to her companion, who noiselessly followed her from the dark corridor into the room. There, with one sweeping glance at the dull red walls, the oil-painted landscapes in sprawling gilt frames, the heavy plush curtains, the furniture with its "saddle-bag" upholstery, the common Turkish carpet, and the mantel mirror with tasteless, tasselled draperies, "Nelson Smith" seemed to comprehend the deadly "stuffiness" of Annesley Grayle's existence.

The look of Mrs. Ellsworth's middle-class dining room, and the atmosphere whence oxygen had been excluded, were enough to tell him, if he had not realized already, why the lady's companion had gone out to meet a strange man "with a view to marriage."

To Annesley, however, for the first time, this room was neither hideous nor depressing. It seemed years since she had seen it. She was a different girl from the spiritless slave who had crept out after luncheon, in the wake of her mistress: that short, shapeless form with a large head set on a short neck, and a trailing, old-fashioned dress of black.

Now, with a man holding her hands and calling her an angel—a "dear, brave angel!"—it looked to the girl a beautiful room. There was glamour upon it, and upon the rest of the world. Surely life could never seem commonplace again!

"Ssh!" Annesley whispered. "We mustn't wake Mrs. Ellsworth, or she'll run to the front door in her dressing gown and call 'Police!' She's old, but her ears are sharp as a cat's. She can almost hear one *thinking*. But I'm glad she can't quite. How frightful if she could!"

"Nothing about her need be frightful to you any more," said the man. "You have saved me. Soon it will be my turn to rescue you."

"I haven't saved you yet," the girl reminded him. "*They* are sure to be waiting to see whether you come out. But I've thought of one more thing to make them believe that you live here. I can steal softly upstairs to the front room on the second floor, above the drawing room—the one we call 'Mr. Smith's'—to turn on the lights, and then those hateful creatures will think— —". She hesitated, and the colour sprang to her cheeks.

"That Mr. and Mrs. Nelson Smith have gone to their room," the man finished her sentence. His eyes beamed love and gratitude, a glorious reward. "You're wonderful! You forget nothing that can help. Do you know, your trust, your faith in me, in spite of appearances, are the best things that have come into my life? You call those fellows 'hateful creatures,' because they're my enemies. Yet, for all you know, *they* may be injured innocents and I the 'hateful' one. This may be my way of getting into a rich old woman's house to steal her jewels and money—making you a cat's paw."

"Don't!" Annesley cut him short. "I can't bear to hear you say such things. I trust you because—surely a woman can tell by instinct which men to trust. I don't need proof."

"By Jove!" he exclaimed, his eyes fixed upon her face. "You are the kind of girl whose faith could turn Lucifer back from devil into archangel. I—you're a million times too good for me. I didn't even *want* to meet a white saint like you. But now I have met you, nothing on earth is going to make me give you up, if you'll stand by me. I'm unworthy, and I don't expect to be much better. But there's one thing: I can give you a gayer life than here. Perhaps I can even make you happy, if you don't ask for a saint to match yourself. You shall have my love and worship, and I'll be true as steel— —"

"Oh, listen!" Annesley broke in. "Don't you hear a sound?"

"Yes," he said. "A door creaked somewhere."

"Mrs. Ellsworth's bedroom door. What shall we do? There's just the short passage at the back, and then she'll be at the baize door that opens into the front corridor. Quick! You, not I, must go upstairs—to that second-floor front room I spoke of. Hurry! Before she gets to the swing door— —"

Without a word he obeyed, remembering his hat, which he had laid on the table. One step took him out of the lighted dining room into the dimness beyond. Another step and he was on the stairs. There, for the moment at least, he was safe from detection; for the staircase faced the front door, and Mrs. Ellsworth must approach from the back. She would come to the door of the dining room, and, expecting only the girl, would not think of spying at the foot of the stairs.

Besides, there was no light in the corridor except that which streamed through the reddish globes of the chandelier above the dining table. If only the man did not stumble on his way up, the situation might be saved.

He was alert, deft, quick-witted, and light of foot as a panther. Who but he would have remembered at such a moment to snatch up a compromising hat and take it with him?

Annesley stood still, rigid in every muscle, fighting to control her heart-throbs, that she might be ready to answer a flood of questions. She dared not even let her thoughts rush ahead. It was all she could do to face the present. The rest must take care of itself.

He had said that she would "make a good actress." Now was the moment to prove that he had judged her truly! She began to unfasten one of her long gray gloves. A button was loose. She must give it a few stitches to-morrow. Strange that there should be room for such a thought in her mind. But she caught at it gladly.

It calmed her as she heard a shuffling tread of slippered feet along the corridor; and she forced herself not to look up until she was conscious that a shapeless figure in a dressing gown filled the doorway, like a badly painted portrait too large for its frame.

"A nice time of night for you to be back!" barked the bronchitic voice hoarsened by years of shut windows. "Give you an inch and you take an ell! I told you half-past ten. Here it is eleven!"

Annesley looked up as if surprised. "Oh, Mrs. Ellsworth, you frightened me!" she exclaimed. "I was delayed. But it won't be eleven for ten minutes. This dining-room clock keeps such good time, you know. And I've been in the house for a few moments. I thought I came so softly! I'm sorry I waked you up."

"Waked me up!" repeated Mrs. Ellsworth. "I have not been to sleep. I never can close my eyes when I know anybody is out and has got to come back, especially a careless creature as likely as not to leave the front door unlatched. That's why I said half-past ten at *latest*! If I don't fall asleep before eleven I get nervous and lose my night's rest. You've heard me say that twenty times, yet you have *no* consideration!"

"This is the first time I've been out late," Annesley defended herself. As she spoke she looked at Mrs. Ellsworth as she might have looked at a stranger.

This fat old woman, with hard eyes, low, unintelligent forehead, and sneering yet self-indulgent mouth, had been for five years the mistress of her fate. The slave had feared to speak lest she should say the wrong thing, had hesitated before taking the most insignificant step, knowing that Mrs. Ellsworth's sharp tongue would accuse her of foolishness or worse. But now Annesley wondered at her bondage. If only the man upstairs could escape, never again would she be afraid of this old tyrant.

"You don't need to tell me how long you have been in," said Mrs. Ellsworth, blissfully ignorant that the iron chain was broken, and enjoying her power to wound. "I've been sitting up watching the clock. My fire's nearly out, and no more coals in the scuttle, the servants all three snoring while I am kept up. If I'm in bed with a cold to-morrow I shall have you to thank, Miss Grayle."

"I'll get you some more coal if you want it," said Annesley. "Hadn't you better go to bed now I am back?"

"Not till I've made you understand that this must never occur again," insisted the old woman. (Annesley was shocked at herself for daring to think that the unwieldy bulk in the gray flannel dressing gown looked like a hippopotamus.) "You don't seem to realize that you've done anything out of the way. You're as calm as if it was eight o'clock. Not a word of regret! Not a question as to *my* evening, you're so taken up with yourself and your smart clothes—clothes I gave you."

"I haven't had much chance to ask questions, have I?" Annesley ventured to remind her mistress. "Won't you tell me about your evening when you are in bed and I have made up your fire? You say it is bad for you to stand."

"I say so because it is the truth, and doctor's orders," rapped out Mrs. Ellsworth. "I thought I had been upset enough for one evening, but this last straw had to be added to my burden."

"Why, what can have upset you?" Annesley inquired, more for the sake of appearing interested than because she was so. But the look on her mistress's face told her that something really had happened.

"I don't care to be kept out of my bed, to be catechized by you," returned Mrs. Ellsworth, pleased that she had aroused curiosity and determined not to gratify it. "Turn on the light in the corridor and give me your arm. My rheumatism is very bad, owing to the chill I have caught, and if I stumble I may be laid up for a week."

The girl proffered a slender arm, hoping that the pounding of her heart might not be detected by Mrs. Ellsworth's hand. She wished that she could have slipped it under her right arm instead of the left, but owing to Mrs. Ellsworth's position in the doorway it was impossible to do so, except by pushing her aside.

She rejoiced, however, in the order to put on the light in the corridor, for this meant that after settling her mistress in bed and transferring the dining-room coal scuttle to the bedroom she must return to switch the electricity off. Then, with Mrs. Ellsworth out of the way, she could help the man upstairs to escape, if the watchers had abandoned the game.

The tyrant, shuffling along in heelless woollen slippers, made the most of her infirmity, and hung on the arm of her tall companion. In silence they passed through the baize door at the end of the corridor, so into the addition at the back of the house, which contained Mrs. Ellsworth's room and bath, with another small room suitable for a maid, and occupied by Annesley. This addition had been built a year or two before Annesley's arrival, and saved Mrs. Ellsworth the necessity of mounting and descending the stairs, as she used the dining room to sit in and seldom went into the drawing room on the floor above. Annesley was not surprised to see that the fire in her mistress's room was still a bank of glowing coals, for one of Mrs. Ellsworth's pleasures was to represent herself in the light of a martyr. The girl made no remark, however: she was far too experienced for such mistakes in tact.

Still in silence, she peeled the stout figure of its dressing gown and helped it into a short, knitted bed-jacket.

"When you get the dining-room scuttle, put out the light there and in the corridor," Mrs. Ellsworth said. "If you leave this door open you can see your way with the coals. No use your creaking back and forth just as I've settled down to rest. Besides, there's somebody else to think of. I hope he hasn't been disturbed already!"

"Somebody else?" echoed the girl with a gasp. There was no longer any fear that her curiosity had not caught fire. Mrs. Ellsworth was satisfied.

"Yes, somebody else," she condescended to repeat. "A certain person has come since you went out. I suppose, *in the circumstances*, you do not need to be told *who*."

"I—I don't know what you mean by 'in the circumstances'," Annesley stammered.

"That's not intelligent of you, considering where you have spent the evening," sneered Mrs. Ellsworth.

Annesley's ears tingled as if they had been boxed. Could it be that Mrs. Ellsworth knew of the trick played on her—knew that her companion had not been to the Smiths'?

"I'm afraid I don't understand," she deprecated.

Mrs. Ellsworth sat in bed staring up at her. "Either you are a fool," she said, "or else I have caught you or *him* in a lie. I don't know which yet. But I soon shall. Perhaps you were not the only person in this house who went out to-night with a latchkey. Now do you guess?"

"No, I don't," the girl had to answer, though a dreadful idea was whirring an alarm in her brain.

"I dare say he is back before this, being more considerate of my feelings than you, and less noisy," went on the old woman, anxious to prove that Annesley Grayle and nobody else was responsible for keeping her from rest. "Anyhow, what a man does is not my business. What you do, is. Now, did or did *not* a certain person walk in and surprise you at the Archdeacon's? Don't stand there blinking like an owl. Speak out. Yes or no?"

"No," Annesley breathed.

"Then you haven't been to the Smiths'. I can more easily believe you are lying than *he*. Hark! There he comes. Isn't that a latchkey in the front door?"

"It—sounds like it. But—perhaps it's a mouse in the wall. Mice—make such strange noises."

"They're not making this one. He never could manage that key properly. Nobody with ears could mistake the sound, with both my door and the baize door open between, as they are now.

"No! You aren't to run and let him in. I don't want him to think we spy on him. He's free to come and go as he pleases, but I wish he wasn't so fond of surprises. It's not fair to me, at my time of life. As I was sitting down to dinner he walked in. Of course I had to ask him to dine, though there wasn't enough food for two. However, he refused, saying he would drop in at the Archdeacon's——"

"Mr. Smith has come!" Annesley cried out, wildly, interrupting her mistress for the first time in all their years together. "Oh, he will go upstairs! I must stop him—I mean, speak to him! I——"

"You will do nothing of the kind!" Mrs. Ellsworth leaned out of bed and seized the girl's dress. Careless of any consequence save one, Annesley struggled to free herself. But the old hand with its lumpy knuckles was strong in spite of fat and rheumatism. It clung leechlike to chiffon of cloak and gown, and though Annesley tore at the yellow fingers, she could not loosen them.

Desperate, she cried out in a choked voice, "Mr. Smith! Mr. Smith!" then checked herself lest the wrong Mr. Smith should answer.

But her voice was like the voice of one who tries to scream in a nightmare. It was muffled; and though the two intervening doors were ajar—the door of Mrs. Ellsworth's bedroom and the baize door dividing the corridors old and new—her call did not reach even the real Mr. Smith. To be sure, he was slightly deaf, and had to use an electric apparatus if he went to the theatre or opera; still, Annesley hoped that her choked cry might arrest him, that he might stop and listen for it to come again, thus giving time for the man upstairs to change his quarters after the grating of the latchkey in its lock.

"Wicked, wicked girl!" Mrs. Ellsworth was shrilling. "How dare you hurt my hand? Have you lost your *senses*? Out of my house you go to-morrow!"

But Annesley did not hear. Her mind, her whole self, had escaped from her body and rushed out into the hall to intercept Mr. Ruthven Smith. It seemed that he *must* feel the influence and stop. If he did not, some terrible thing would happen—unless, indeed, the other man had heard and heeded the warning sound at the front door. What if those two met on the stairs, or in the room on the second floor? Her lover would believe that she had betrayed him!

"Mrs. Ellsworth," she said in a fierce, low voice utterly unlike her own, "you must let me go, or you will regret it. I don't want to hurt you, but—there's only one thing that matters. If——"

The words seemed to be beaten back against her lips with a blow. From somewhere above a sharp, dry explosion struck the girl's brain and shattered her thoughts like breaking glass.

Mrs. Ellsworth let go the chiffon cloak and dress so suddenly that Annesley almost lost her balance. The noise had dazed the girl. The world seemed full and echoing with it. She did not know what it was until she heard Mrs. Ellsworth gasp, "A pistol shot! In my house! *Thieves! Murder!*"

CHAPTER VI.
THE BEGINNING—OR THE END?

For one confused instant the girl stood statue-still, then, realizing that she was free, without a thought for Mrs. Ellsworth she ran out of the room. In the front corridor and in the dining room the electric light was still on; and as she reached the stairs Annesley saw Ruthven Smith standing near the top with a small pistol in his hand.

She feared that he would fire a second shot, and there was no time to reach him. Somehow, he must be stopped with a word—but what word? Everything depended on that. Sheer desperation inspired her.

"Stop! He's my lover!" she cried. "Don't shoot!"

Ruthven Smith—a tall, lanky figure in a long over-coat—kept his weapon aimed at someone out of the girl's sight, but he jerked his head aside for a glance down at her. It was a brief glance, for the man who dreaded burglars would not be caught napping. He turned again instantly to face a possible antagonist, eyes as well as weapon ready.

But the light from below had lit up his features for a second; and Annesley realized that disgust and astonishment were the emotions her "confession" had inspired.

The fact that he was inclined to believe her statement showed how low was his opinion of women. Annesley knew that he did not think highly of her sex, but he had liked her and she had liked him despite his eccentricities. His look said: "So you are the same as the rest! But in case you're lying, I sha'n't be thrown off guard."

The girl felt physically sick as she understood the irrevocability of what she had just said, and the way in which her words were construed. If she could have waited, "Nelson Smith" might have saved himself without compromising her, for he was above all things resourceful. In announcing that he was her "lover," she had committed him as well as herself. He would have to make the best of a situation she had recklessly created.

This she realized, but had no time to wonder how he would do it before he spoke.

"Mr. Ruthven Smith, what Miss Grayle says is the truth. We're engaged to be married. All I want is a chance to explain why you find me where I am. I'm not armed, so you can safely give me that chance."

"You know my name?" exclaimed Ruthven Smith, suspiciously. He still covered the other with his pistol, as Annesley could see now, because "Nelson Smith" had coolly advanced within a yard of the Browning's small black muzzle, and, finding the electric switch, had flooded the upper corridor with light.

"I've heard your name from Miss Grayle," said the younger man. "I know it must be you, because no other person has a right to make himself at home in this house as you are doing. I certainly haven't. But bringing her home a few minutes ago, after dining out, we saw a light in what she said was your room. She was afraid some thief had got in, and I proposed to her that I should take a quiet look round while she went to see if Mrs. Ellsworth was safe. No doubt she was all right, because I heard them talking together while I examined your premises. The next thing I knew, as I was coming down with the news that everything was quiet, you blazed away. It was quite a surprise."

"I fired in the air, not at you," Ruthven Smith excused himself, more or less convinced. Annesley clutched the banisters in the sudden weakness of a great revulsion from panic to relief. She might have known that *he* would somehow rescue her, even from her own blundering.

The shamed red which had stained Annesley's cheeks at Ruthven Smith's contempt died away. Her "lover"—he was openly that now—had miraculously made his presence in the other Smith's room, after eleven o'clock at night in this early bed-going household, the most natural thing in the world. At least, Ruthven Smith's almost apologetic tone in answering proved that he had been persuaded to think it so.

With Mrs. Ellsworth, however, it would be different. There would lie the stumbling-block; but with all danger from the Browning ended, the girl was in no mood to borrow trouble for the future, even a future already rushing into the arms of the present.

"I should always fire the first shot in the air," Ruthven Smith went on, "unless directly threatened."

"Lucky for me," replied the other. "I don't want to die yet. And it would have been hard lines, as I was trying to do you a good turn: rid you of a thief if there were one. But I suppose you or some servant must have left the light on in your room."

"I'm pretty sure I didn't," said Ruthven Smith, still speaking with the nervousness of a suspicious man, yet at the same time slowly, half reluctantly, pocketing his pistol. "We must find out how this happened. Perhaps there *has* been a thief——"

"No sign of anything being disturbed in your room," the younger man assured him. "However, you'd best have a look round. If you like"—and he laughed a frank-sounding laugh—"I'm quite willing to be searched before I leave the house, so you can make sure I'm not going off with any booty."

"Certainly not! Nothing of the kind! I accept your explanation," protested Ruthven Smith. He laughed also, though stiffly and with an effort. "I have no valuables in my luggage—I have brought none with me. It's not worth my while to open the boxes in my room, as there's nothing there to tempt a thief. Still, one gets a start coming to a quiet house, at this time of night, finding a light in one's windows that ought to be dark, and then seeing a man walk out of one's room. My nerves aren't over-strong. I confess I have a horror of night alarms. I travel a good deal, and have got in the habit of carrying a pistol. However, all's well that ends well. I apologize to you, and to Miss Grayle. When I know you better, I hope you'll allow me to make up by congratulating you both on your engagement."

As he spoke, in his prim, old-fashioned way, he began to descend the stairs, taking off his hat, as if to join the girl whom in thought he had wronged for an instant. "Nelson Smith" followed, smiling at Annesley over the elder man's high, narrow head sparsely covered with lank hair of fading brown.

It was at this moment Mrs. Ellsworth chose to appear, habited once more in a hurriedly donned dressing gown, a white silk scarf substituted in haste for a discarded nightcap. Panting with anger, and fierce with curiosity, she had forgotten her rheumatism and abandoned her martyred hobble for a waddling run.

Thus she pounced out at the foot of the stairway, and was upon the girl before the three absorbed actors in the scene had heard the shuffling feet in woollen slippers.

"What does this mean?" she quavered, so close to Annesley's ear that the girl wheeled with a start of renewed alarm. "Who's this strange man in my house? What's this talk about 'engagements'?"

"A strange man!" echoed Ruthven Smith, prickling with suspicion again. "Haven't you met him, Miss Grayle's fiancé?"

"Miss Grayle's fiddlesticks!" shrilled the old woman. "The girl's a baggage, a worthless baggage! In my room just now she *struck* me—beat my poor rheumatic knuckles! For five years I've sheltered her, given her the best of everything, even to the clothes she has on her back. This is the way she repays me—with insults and cruelty, and smuggles strange men secretly into my house at night, and pretends to be engaged to them!"

The dark young man in evening dress passed the lean figure in travelling clothes without a word and, putting Annesley gently aside, stepped between her and Mrs. Ellsworth.

"There is no question of 'pretending'," he said, sternly. "Miss Grayle has promised to marry me. If our engagement has been kept a secret, it's only because the right moment hadn't come for announcing it. I entered your house for a few moments to-night, for the first time, on an errand which seemed important, as Mr. Ruthven Smith will explain. I don't feel called upon to apologize for my presence in the face of your attitude to Miss Grayle. It was our intention that you should have plenty of notice before she left you, time to find someone for her place; but after what has happened, it's your own fault, madame, if we marry with a special licence, and I take her out of this house to-morrow. I only wish it might be now——"

"It *shall* be now!" Mrs. Ellsworth screamed him down. "The girl doesn't darken my doors another hour. I don't know who you are, and I don't want to know. But with or without you, Annesley Grayle leaves my house to-night."

"Mrs. Ellsworth, surely you haven't stopped to think what you're saying!" protested Ruthven Smith. "You can't turn a girl into the street in the middle of the night with a young man you don't know, even if she is engaged to him."

"I won't have her here, after the way she's treated me—after the way she's acted altogether," Mrs. Ellsworth insisted. "Let her go to your cousins' if you think they'd approve of her conduct. As for me, I doubt it. And I'm sure she lied when she said they'd asked her to dine with them to-night. I don't believe she went near them."

Ruthven Smith, who had made a surprise visit at the Archdeacon's and dined there, had heard no mention of Annesley Grayle being expected. For an instant he was silenced, but the girl did not lack a defender.

"She will not need to beg for Archdeacon Smith's hospitality," said the young man. "And even if Mrs. Ellsworth implored her to stay, I couldn't allow it now. I will see that Miss Grayle is properly sheltered and cared for to-night by a lady whose kindness will make her forget what she has suffered. As soon as possible we shall be married by special licence. Go to your room, dearest, and put together a few things for to-night and to-morrow morning—just what will fit into a hand-bag. If there's anything else you value, it can be sent for later. Then I'll take you away."

The words were brave and comforting, and a wave of emotion swept Annesley's soul toward the mysterious, unknown soul of her knight. It was so strong, so compelling a wave that she had no fear in trusting, herself to him. He was her refuge, her protector.

For a moment of gratitude she even forgot he was mysterious, forgot that a few hours ago she had been ignorant of his existence. When remembrance flooded her brain, her only fear was for him. What if the watchers should still be there when they went out of the house together?

She had turned to go to her room as he suggested when suddenly this question seemed to be shouted in her ear. Hesitating, she looked back, her eyes imploring, to meet a smile so confident that it defied fate.

Annesley saw that he understood what was in her mind, and this smile was the answer. For some reason he thought himself sure that the watchers were out of the way. The girl could not guess why, unless he had spied on the taxi from Ruthven Smith's window and saw it go. But she would soon learn.

Her room was a mere bandbox at the back of the "addition," behind Mrs. Ellsworth's bedroom and bath; and dashing into it now, the new, vividly alive Annesley seemed to meet and pity the timid, hopeless girl whose one safe haven these mean quarters had been. She tried to gather the old self into her new self, that she might take it with her and comfort it, rescuing it from the tyrant.

The two trunks she had brought five years ago were stored in the basement box-room; but under the camp bed was her dressing-bag, the only "lock-up" receptacle she possessed. In it she kept a few letters and an abortive diary which in some moods had given her the comfort of a confidant.

The key of this bag was never absent from her purse, and opening it with quivering hands, the girl threw in a few toilet things for the night, a coat, skirt, and blouse for morning, and a small flat toque which would not crush. Afterward—in that wonderful, dim "afterward" which shone vaguely bright, like a sunlit landscape discerned through mist—she could send for more of her possessions. But she would have nothing which had been given her by Mrs. Ellsworth, and she would return the dress and cloak she was wearing to-night.

Three minutes were enough for the packing of the bag; then, luggage in hand, she turned at the door for a last look, such as a released convict might give to his cell.

"Good-bye!" she said, with a thought of compassion for her successor. And passing Mrs. Ellsworth's room she would have thrown a farewell glance at its familiar chairs and tables, each one of which she hated with a separate hatred; but with a shock of surprise, she found the door shut.

That must mean that the dragon had retreated from the combat and retired to her lair!

Not to be chased from the house by the sharp arrows of insult seemed almost too good to be true. But when Annesley arrived, bag in hand, in the front corridor, it was to see Ruthven Smith standing there alone, and the door open to the street.

"Mrs. Ellsworth has gone to her room," he explained, "and—er—your friend—your fiancé—is looking for a taxi, not to keep you waiting. He didn't leave till Mrs. Ellsworth went. I don't think he would have trusted me to protect you without him, though I—er—I did my best with her. Good heavens, what a fury! I never saw that side of her before! I must say, I don't blame you for making your own plans, Miss Grayle. I—I don't blame you for anything, and I hope you'll feel the same toward me. I'd be sorry to think that—er—after our pleasant acquaintance this was to be our last meeting. Won't you show that you forgive me for the mistake I made—I think it was natural—and tell me what your married name will be?"

Annesley looked anxiously at the half-open front door. If only the absent one would return and save her from this new dilemma! If she did not speak, Mr. Ruthven Smith would think her harsh and unforgiving, yet she could not answer unless she gave the name adopted temporarily for convenience. She hesitated, her eyes on the door; but the darkness and silence outside sent a doubt into her heart, cold and sickly as a bat flapping in from the night.

What if he never came back? What if the watchers had been hiding out there, lying in wait and, two against one—both bigger men physically than he, and perhaps armed—they had overpowered him? What if she were never to see him again, and this hour which had seemed the beginning of hope were to be its end?

CHAPTER VII.
THE COUNTESS DE SANTIAGO

"You don't wish to tell me the name?" Ruthven Smith was saying.

The repetition irritated the girl, whose nerves were strained to snapping point. She could not parry the man's questions. She could not bear his grieved or offended reproaches. If he persisted, through these moments of suspense, she would scream or burst out crying. Trembling, with tears in her voice, she heard herself answer. And yet it did not seem to be herself, but something within, stronger than she, that suddenly took control of her.

"Why should I not wish to tell you?" the Something was saying. "The name is the same as your own—Smith. Nelson Smith." And before the words had left her lips a taxi drew up at the door.

There was one instant of agony during which the previous suspense seemed nothing—an instant when the girl forgot what she had said, her soul pressing to the windows of her eyes. Was it he who had come, or——

It was he. Before she had time to finish the thought, he walked in, confident and smiling as when she had left him a few minutes— or a few years—ago; and in the wave of relief which overwhelmed her, Annesley forgot Ruthven Smith's question and her answer. She remembered again, only with the shock of hearing him address the newcomer by the name she had given.

"I hear from Miss Grayle that we are namesakes," Mr. Ruthven Smith said, as "Nelson Smith" sprang in and took the girl's bag from her ice-cold hand.

"I—he asked me ... I told him," Annesley stammered, her eyes appealing, seeking to explain, and begging pardon. "But if——"

"Quite right. Why *not* tell?" he answered instantly, his first glance of surprise turning to cheerful reassurance. "Now Mrs. Ellsworth is eliminated, I'm no longer a secret. And I expect you'll like to meet Mr. Ruthven Smith again when you have a house to entertain him in."

So speaking, he offered his hand with a smile to his "namesake"; and Annesley realized from the outsider's point of view the peculiar attraction of the man. Ruthven Smith felt it, as she had felt it, though differently and in a lesser degree. Not only did he shake hands, but actually came out to the taxi with them, asking Annesley if he should tell his cousins of her engagement, or if she preferred to give the news herself?

It flashed into the girl's mind that it would be perfect if she could be married to her knight by Archdeacon Smith; but she had been imprudent too often already. She dared not make such a suggestion without consulting the other person most concerned, so she answered that she would write Mrs. Smith or see her.

"To say that you, too, are going to be Mrs. Smith!" chuckled the Archdeacon's cousin in his dry way, which made him seem even older than he was. "Well, you can trust me with Mrs. Ellsworth. If she goes on as she began to-night, I'm afraid I shall have to follow your example: 'fold my tent like an Arab, and silently steal away.' Ha, ha! By the by, I dare say she's owing you salary. I'll remind her of it if you like—tell her you asked me. It may help with the trousseau."

"Thank you, but my wife won't need to remind Mrs. Ellsworth of her debt," the answer came before Annesley could speak. "And she *will* be my wife in a day or two at latest. Good-night! Glad to have met you, even if it was an unpromising introduction."

Then they were off, they two alone together; and Annesley guessed that the chauffeur must have had his instructions where to drive, as she heard none given. Perhaps it was best that their destination should not be published aloud, for there are walls which have ears. It occurred to the girl that precautions might still have to be taken. But in another moment she was undeceived.

"I thought old Ruthven Smith would be shocked if he knew the 'safe refuge' I have for you is no more convent-like than the Savoy Hotel," her companion laughed. "By Jove, neither you nor I dreamed when we got out of the last taxi that we should soon be in another, going back to the place we started from!"

"The Savoy!" exclaimed Annesley. "Oh, but we mustn't go there, of all places! Those men——"

"I assure you it's safer now than anywhere in London!" the man cut her short. "I can't explain why—that is, I *could* explain if I cared to rig up a story. But there's something about you makes me feel as if I'd like to tell you the truth whenever I can: and the truth is, that for reasons you may understand some day—though I hope to Heaven you'll never have to!—my association with those men is one of the things I long to turn the key upon. I know that that sounds like Bluebeard to Fatima, but it isn't as bad as *that*. To me, it doesn't seem bad at all. And I swear that whatever mystery—if you call it 'mystery'—there is about me, it sha'n't hurt you. Will you believe this—and trust me for the rest?"

"I've told you I would!" the girl reminded him.

"I know. But things were different then—not so serious. They hadn't gone so far. I didn't suppose that Fate would give you to me so soon. I didn't dare hope it. I——"

"Are you *sure* you want me?" Annesley faltered.

"Surer than I've ever been of anything in my life before. It's only of you I'm thinking. I wanted to arrange my—business matters so as to be fair to you. But you'll make the best of things."

"You are being noble to me," said the girl, "and I've been very foolish. I've complicated everything. First, by what I told Mr. Ruthven Smith about—about *us*. And then—saying your name was Nelson Smith."

"You weren't foolish!" he contradicted. "You were only—playing into Fate's hands. You couldn't help yourself. Destiny! And all's for the best. You were an angel to sacrifice yourself to save me, and your doing it the way you did has made me a happy man at one stroke. As for the name—what's in a name? We might as well be in reality what we played at being to-night—'Mr. and Mrs. Nelson Smith.' There are even reasons why I'm pleased that you've made me a present of the name. I thank you for it—and for all the rest."

"Oh, but if it isn't *really* your name, we sha'n't be legally married, shall we?" Annesley protested.

"By Jove!" he exclaimed. "I hadn't thought of that. It's a difficulty. But we'll obviate it—somehow. Don't worry! Only I'm afraid we can't ask your friend the Archdeacon to marry us, as I meant to suggest, because I was sure you'd like it."

"I should. But it doesn't matter," said the girl. "Besides, I feel that to-morrow I shall find I've dreamed—all this."

"Then I've dreamed you, at the same time, and I'm not going to let you slip out of my dream, now I've got you in it. I intend to go on dreaming you for the rest of my life. And I shall take care *you* don't wake up!"

Afterward there came a time when Annesley called back those words and wondered if they had held a deeper meaning than she guessed. But, having uttered them, he seemed to put the thought out of his mind, and turn to the next.

"About the Savoy," he went on. "I want to take you there, because I know a woman staying in the hotel—a woman old enough to be your mother—who'll look after you, to please me, till we're married. Afterward you'll be nice to her, and that will be doing her a good turn, because she's apt to be lonesome in London. She's the widow of a Spanish Count, and has lived in the Argentine, but I met her in New York. She knows all about me—or enough—and if she'd been in the restaurant at dinner this evening she could have done for me what you did. I had reason to think she would be there when I bolted in to get out of a fix. But she was missing. Are you sorry?"

"If she'd been there, you would have gone to her table and sat down, and we—should never have met!" Annesley thought aloud. "How strange! Just that *little* thing—your friend being out to dinner—and our whole lives are to be changed. Oh, *you* must be sorry?"

"I tell you, meeting you and winning you in this way is worth the best ten years of my life. But you haven't answered my question."

"I'll answer it now!" cried the girl. "Meeting you is worth *all* the years of my life! I'm not much of a princess, but you *are* St. George."

"St. George!" he echoed, a ring of bitterness under his laugh. "That's the first time I've been called a saint, and I'm afraid it will be the last. I can't live up to that, but—if I can give you a happy life, and a few of the beautiful things you deserve, why, it's *something*! Besides, I'm going to worship my princess. I'd give anything to show you how I—but no. I was good before, when I was tempted to kiss you. You're at my mercy now, in a way, all the more because I'm taking you from your old existence to one you don't know.

"I sha'n't ask to kiss you—except maybe your little hand if you don't mind—until the moment you're my wife. Meantime, I'll try to grow a bit more like what your lover ought to be; and later I shall kiss you enough to make up for lost time."

If, five hours ago, any one had told Annesley Grayle that she would wish to have a strange man take her in his arms and kiss her she would have felt insulted. Yet so it was. She was sorry that he was so scrupulous. She longed to have him hold her against his heart.

The thought thrilled her like an electric shock a thousand times more powerful than the tingling which had flashed up her arm at the first touch of his hand, though even that had seemed terrifying then. But she sat still in her corner of the taxi, and gave him no answer, lest she should betray herself.

Her silence, after the warmth of his words, seemed cold. Perhaps he felt it so, for he went on after an instant's pause, as if he had waited for something in vain, and his tone was changed. Annesley thought it, by contrast, almost businesslike.

"You mustn't be afraid," he said, "that I mean to stay at the Savoy myself. Even if I'd been stopping there, I should move if I were going to put you in the hotel. But I have my own lair in London. I've been over here a number of times. Indeed, I'm partly English, born in Canada, though I've spent most of my life in the United States. Nobody at the Savoy but the Countess de Santiago knows who I am, and she'll understand that it may be convenient for me to change my name. Nelson Smith is a respectable one, and she'll respect it!

"Now, my plan is to ask for her (she'll be in by this time), have a few words of explanation on the quiet, not to embarrass you; and the Countess will do the rest. She'll engage a room for you next to her own suite, or as near as possible; then you'll be provided with a chaperon."

"I'm not anxious about myself, but about you," Annesley said. "You haven't told me yet what happened after you went upstairs at Mrs. Ellsworth's, and how you knew those men were gone. I suppose you did know? Or—did you chance it?"

"I was as sure as I needed to be," Nelson Smith answered. "A moment after I switched on the electricity in the room up there I heard a taxi drive away. I turned off the light so I could look out. By flattening my nose against the glass I could see that the place where those chaps had waited was empty; but in case the taxi was only turning, and meant to pass the house again, I lit the room once more, for realism.

"That's what kept me rather long—that, and waiting for the dragon to go. Otherwise I should have been down before Ruthven Smith trapped me.

"For a second it looked as if the game of life was up. And then I found out how much you meant to me. It was *you* I thought of. It seemed beastly hard luck to leave you fast in that old woman's clutches!"

Annesley put out her hand with a warm impulse. He took it, raising it to his lips, and both were startled when the taxi stopped. They had arrived at the Savoy: and though Annesley seemed to have lived through a lifetime of emotion, just one hour and thirty minutes had passed since she and her companion drove away from these bright revolving doors.

The foyer was as brilliant and crowded as when they left at half-past ten. People were parting after supper; or they were lingering in the restaurant beyond. Nobody paid the slightest attention to the newcomers, and Annesley settled down unobtrusively in a corner, while her companion went to scribble a line to the Countess de Santiago.

When he had finished, and sent up the letter, he did not return, and again the girl had a few moments of suspense, thinking of the danger which might not, after all, be over. Just as she had begun to be anxious, however, she saw him coming with a wonderful woman.

Annesley could have laughed, remembering how he had said the Countess would "mother" her. Any one less motherly than this Juno-like beauty in flame-coloured chiffon over gold tissue it would be hard to imagine.

The Spanish South American Countess was of a camelia paleness, and had almond-shaped dark eyes with brooding lashes under slender brows that met. In contrast, her hair was of a flame colour vivid as her draperies, and her lips were red.

At first glance Annesley thought that the dazzling creature could not be more than thirty; but when the vision had come near enough to offer her hand, without waiting for an introduction, a hardness about the handsome face, a few lines about the eyes and mouth, and a fullness of the chin showed that she was older—forty, perhaps.

Still, Annesley hoped that her lover had not asked the lady to "mother" his fiancée. She had not the air of one who would be complimented by such a request.

As Annesley put her hand into that of the Countess, she noticed that this hand was as wonderful as the rest of the woman's personality. It was very long, very narrow, with curiously supple-looking fingers exquisitely manicured and wearing many rings. Even the thumb was abnormally long, which fact prevented the hand from being as beautiful as it was, somehow, unforgettable.

"This is a pleasure and a surprise," began the Countess, smiling, her eyes appearing to take in the full-length portrait of Annesley Grayle with their wide, unmoving gaze. When she smiled she was still extremely handsome, but not so perfect as with lips closed, for her white teeth were too short, somewhat irregular, and set too wide apart. She spoke English perfectly, with a slight foreign accent and a roll of the letter "r."

"My friend—Nelson Smith" (she turned, laughing, to him), "has told me ex-*citing* news. We have known each other a long time. I think this is the best thing that can happen. And you will be a lucky girl. He, too, will be lucky. I see that!" with another smile.

Annesley was disappointed because the beautiful woman's voice was not sweet.

"Now you must engage her room," Nelson Smith said, abruptly. "It's late. You can make friends afterward."

"Very well," the Countess agreed. "And you—will you come to the desk? Yet, no—it is better not. Miss Grayle and I will go together—

two women alone and independent. Lucky it's not the season, or we might find nothing free at short notice. But Don—I mean Nelson—always did have luck. I hope he always will!"

She flashed him a meaning look, though what the meaning was Annesley could not guess. She knew only that she did not like the Countess as she had wished to like her lover's friend. There was something secret in the dark eyes, something repellent about the long, slender thumb with its glittering nail.

CHAPTER VIII.
THE BLUE DIAMOND RING

Annesley had not expected to sleep. There were a million things to think of, and it was one o'clock before she was ready to slip into bed in the green-and-white room with its bathroom annex. But the crowding experiences of five hours had exhausted the girl. Sleep fell upon her as her head nestled into a downy pillow, and she lay motionless as a marble figure on a tomb until a sound of knocking forced itself into her dreams.

She waked with a start. The curtains were drawn across the window, but she could see that it was daylight. A streak of sunshine thrust a golden wedge between the draperies, and seemed a good omen: for the sun had hidden from London through many wintry weeks.

The knocking was real, not part of a dream. It was at her door, and jumping out of bed she could hardly believe a clock on the mantelpiece which said half-past ten.

"Who is it?" she asked, timidly, fearing that the Countess de Santiago's voice might answer; but a man replied: "A note from a gentleman downstairs, please, and he's waiting an answer."

Annesley opened the door a crack, and took in a letter. The new master of her destiny had written:

> Hurrah, my darling, our affairs march! I have been arranging about the licence, *et cetera*, and I believe that you and I can join forces for the rest of our lives tomorrow—blessed day!
>
> How soon can you come down and talk over plans? I've a hundred to propose. Will you breakfast with me, or have you finished?
>
> Yours since last night, till eternal night,
> N. S.

The girl scribbled an answer, confessing that she had overslept, but promising to be down in half an hour for breakfast. She did not stop to think of anything but the need for a quick reply; yet when the note was sent, and she was "doing" her hair after a splash in the porcelain bath (what luxury for the girl who had been practically a servant!), she re-read her love-letter, spread on the dressing-table.

She liked her lover's handwriting. It seemed to express character—just such character as she imagined her knight's to be. There were dash and determination, and an originality which would never let itself be bound by convention.

Perhaps if she had been critical—if the handwriting had been that of a stranger—she might have thought it too bold. Long ago, when she was a very young girl, she had superficially studied the "science" of chirography from articles in a magazine, and had fancied herself a judge. She remembered disliking Mrs. Ellsworth's writing the first time she saw it, foreseeing the selfishness which afterward enslaved her. Since then she had had little time to practise, until the day when she heard from "Mr. N. Smith" after her answer to his advertisement in the *Morning Post*.

One reason for feeling sure she could never care for the man was because his handwriting prejudiced her in advance, it was so stiff, so devoid of character. How different, she reflected now, from the writing of the man who had taken his place!

She made such haste in dressing that her fingers seemed to be "all thumbs"; and when at length she was ready she gazed gloomily into the mirror. Last night she had not been so bad in evening dress; but now in the cheap, ready-made brown velveteen coat and skirt and plain toque to match, which had been her "best" for two winters, she feared lest *he* should find her commonplace.

"The first thing I do, when he's had time to look me over, must be to tell him he's free if he wants his freedom," she decided. And she kept her word, when in the half-deserted foyer she had shaken hands with a young man who wore a white rose in his buttonhole. "Please tell me frankly if you don't like me as well by daylight," she gasped.

"I like you better," he said. "You're still my white rose. See, I've adopted it as your symbol. I shall never wear any other flower on my coat. This is yours. No, it's *you*! And I've kept the one I took last night.

I mean to keep it always. No danger of *my* changing my mind! But you? I've lain awake worrying for fear you might."

He held her hand, questioning her eyes with his.

She shook her head, smiling. But he would not let the hand go. At that hour there was no one to stare. "The Countess didn't warn you off me?"

Annesley opened her eyes. "Of course not! Why, you told me you were old friends!"

"So we are—as friends go in this world: 'pals,' anyhow. She's done me several good turns, and I've paid her. She'd always do what she could to help, for her own sake as well as mine. But her idea of a man may be different from yours."

"She wasn't with me long," explained Annesley. "She said I needed sleep. After she'd looked at my room to see if it were comfortable, she bade me 'good-night,' and we haven't met this morning. The few remarks she did make about you were complimentary."

"What did she say? I'm curious."

"Well, if you must know, she said that you were a man few women could resist; and—she didn't blame *me*."

"H'm! You call that complimentary? Let's suppose she meant it so. Now we'll have breakfast, and forget her—unless you'd like her called to go with us on a shopping expedition I've set my heart on."

"What kind of a shopping expedition?" Annesley wanted to know.

"To buy you all the pretty things you've ever wished for."

The girl laughed. "To do that would cost a fortune!"

"Then we'll spend a fortune. Shall you and I do it ourselves, or would you like to have the Countess de Santiago's taste?"

"Oh, let us go without her," Annesley exclaimed, "unless you——"

"Rather *not*. I want you to myself. You darling! We'll have a great day—spending that fortune. The next thing we do—it can wait till after we're married—is to look for a house in a good neighbourhood, to rent furnished. But we'll get your swell cousins, Lord and Lady Annesley-Seton, to help us choose. Perhaps there'll be something near them."

"Why, they hardly know I exist! I doubt if Lady Annesley-Seton *does* know," replied the girl. "They'll do nothing to help us, I'm sure."

"Then *don't* be sure, because if you made a bet you'd lose. Take my word, they'll be pleased to remember a cousin who is marrying a millionaire."

"Good gracious!" gasped Annesley. "*Are* you a millionaire?"

Her lover laughed. "Well, I don't want to boast to you, though I may to your cousins, but if I'm not one of your conventional, stodgy millionaires, I have a sort of Fortunatus purse which is never empty. I can always pull out whatever I want. We'll let your people understand without any bragging.

"I think Lady Annesley-Seton, *née* Miss Haverstall, whose father's purse has flattened out like a pancake, will jump for joy when she hears what you want her to do. But come along, let's have breakfast!"

Overwhelmed, Annesley walked beside him in silence to the almost deserted restaurant where the latest breakfasters had finished and the earliest lunchers had not begun.

So the mysterious Mr. Smith was rich. The news frightened rather than pleased her. It seemed to throw a burden upon her shoulders which she might not be able to carry with grace. The girl had little self-confidence; but the man appeared to be troubled with no doubts of her or of the future. Over their coffee and toast and hot-house fruit, he began to propose exciting plans, and had got as far as an automobile when the voice of the Countess surprised them.

She had come close to their table without being heard.

"Good morning!" she exclaimed. "I was going out, but from far off I saw you two, with your profiles cut like silhouettes against all this glass and sunshine. I couldn't resist asking how Miss Grayle slept, and if there's anything I can do for her in the shops?"

As she spoke her eyes dwelt on Annesley's plain toque and old-fashioned shabby coat, as if to emphasize the word "shops." The girl flushed, and Smith frowned at the Countess.

"No, thank you," he replied for Annesley. "There's nothing we need trouble you about till the wedding to-morrow afternoon. You can put on your gladdest rags then, and be one of our witnesses. I believe that's the legal term, isn't it?"

"I do not know," said the Countess with a suppressed quiver in her voice, and a flash in the eyes fixed studiously on the river. "I know nothing of marriages in England. Who will be your other witness, if it's not indiscreet to ask?"

"I haven't decided yet," returned Smith, laconically.

"Ah, of course, you have *plenty* of friends to choose from; and so the wedding will be to-morrow?"

"Yes. One fixes up these things in next to no time with a special license. Luckily I'm a British subject. I never thought much about it before, but it simplifies matters; and I'll have been living in this parish a fortnight to-morrow. That's providential, for it seems that legally it must be a fortnight. I've been up since it was light, learning the ropes and beginning to work them. Even the hour's fixed—two-thirty."

(This was news for Annesley also, as there had been no time to begin talking over the "hundred plans" Smith had mentioned in his letter.)

"You are prompt—and businesslike!" returned the Countess, and again the girl blushed. She did not like to think of her knight of romance being "businesslike" in his haste to make her his wife. But perhaps the Countess didn't mean to suggest anything uncomplimentary. "At what church will the 'ceremony take place' as the newspapers say?" she went on. "It is to be a fashionable one?"

"No," replied, Smith, shortly. "Weddings in fashionable churches are silly unless there's to be a crowd; and my wife and I are going to collect our circle after we're married. I'll let you know in time where we are going. As you'll be with the bride you can't lose yourself on the way, so you needn't worry."

"I don't!" laughed the Countess. "I'm at your service, and I shall try to be worthy of the occasion. But now I shall take myself off, or your coffee will be cold. You have a busy day and it's late—even later than our breakfasts on the *Monarchic* three weeks ago. Already it seems three months. *Au revoir*, Don. *Au revoir*, Miss Grayle."

She finished with a nod for Annesley, and turned away. Smith let her go in silence; and the girl watched the tall figure—as perfect in shape and as perfectly dressed as a French model—walk out of the restaurant into the foyer.

She seemed to have taken with her the golden glamour which had made up for lack of sunshine in the room before her arrival; or if she had not taken it, at least it was dimmed. Annesley gazed after the figure until it disappeared, because she felt vaguely that it would be best not to look at her companion just then. She knew that he was angry, and that he wanted to compose himself.

The Countess was as handsome by morning light, in her black velvet and chinchilla, as at night in flame colour and gold. But—the girl hoped she was not ill-natured—she looked *meretricious*. If she were "made up," the process defied Annesley Grayle's eyes; yet surely never was skin so flawlessly white; and such golden-red hair with dark eyes and eyebrows must be unique.

"Great Scott, I thought she meant to spend the morning with us!" Smith broke out, viciously. "I realize, now I've seen you together, that she's not—the ideal chaperon. But any port in a storm!"

"I thought you liked her," Annesley said.

"So I do—within limits. At least I appreciate qualities that she has. But there are times—when a little of her goes a long way."

"I'm afraid she realized that you weren't making her welcome," Annesley smiled. "You weren't very nice to her, were you?"

"I was as nice as she deserved," the man excused himself.

"But she was good to me last night!"

"She owes it to me to be good. It's a debt I expect her to pay, that's all, and I'm not sure she's paying it generously. You needn't be too grateful, dear."

"Perhaps, as she's known you some time, she feels you're sacrificing yourself," Annesley defended the Countess. "I don't blame her!"

"She's sharp enough to see that I'm in great luck," said Smith. "But I suppose there's always a dash of the cat in a woman of her race. I hope there's no need to tell you that she has no right to be jealous. If she had, I wouldn't have put you within reach of her claws. There are assorted sizes and kinds of jealousy, though. Some women want all the lime-light and grudge sparing any for a younger and prettier girl."

Annesley laughed. "*Prettier!* Why, she's a beauty, and I——"

"Wait till I introduce you to Mrs. Nelson Smith, who's going to be one of the best-dressed, best-looking young women in London, and you'll be *sorry* for the poor old Countess," returned Smith, warmly. "You can afford then to heap coals of fire on her head, which can't make it redder than it is. Meanwhile, it occurs to me, from the way the wind blows, you'd better go carefully with the lady! Don't let her pump you about yourself, or what happened at Mrs. Ellsworth's. It's not her business. Don't confide any more than you need, and if she pretends to confide in *you* understand that it will be for a purpose. The Countess is no *ingénue!*

"But enough about her," he went on, abruptly. "She sha'n't spoil our first breakfast together, even by reminding me of gloomy meals I used sometimes to eat with her when we happened to find ourselves in each other's society on board the *Monarchic*. I was feeling down on my luck then, and she wasn't the one to cheer me up. But things are different now. Have you noticed, by the way, that she has a nickname for me?"

"Yes," Annesley admitted. "She calls you 'Don.'"

"It's a name she made up because she used to say, when we first met, I was like a Spaniard; and I can jabber Spanish among other lingos. It's more her native tongue, you know, than English. I only refer to it because I want you to have a special name of your own for me, and I don't want it to be that one. It can't be Nelson, because—well, I can never be at home as Nelson with the girl I love best—the one who knows how I came to call myself that. Will you make up a name for me, and begin to get used to it to-day? I'd like it if you could."

"May I call you 'Knight'?" Annesley asked, shyly. "I've named you my knight already in my mind and—and heart."

He looked at her with rather a beautiful look: clear and wistful, even remorseful.

"It's too noble a name," he said. "Still—if you like it, I shall. Maybe it will make me good. Jove! it would take something strong to do that! But who knows? From now on I'm your 'Knight.' You needn't wrestle with 'Nelson' except when we're with strangers.

"And—look here!" he broke off. "I've another favour to ask. Better get them all over at once—the big ones that are hard to grant. You reminded me last night that we wouldn't be legally married if I didn't use my own name. That may be true. I can't very well make inquiries. But just in case, I'm giving my real name and shall sign it in a register. That's why our marriage must be quietly performed in a quiet place. It shall be in church, because I know you wouldn't feel married if it wasn't, but it must be in a church where nobody we're likely to meet ever goes; and the parson must be one we won't stand a chance of knocking up against later.

"Managed the way I shall manage it, there'll be no difficulty. Mr. and Mrs. Blank will walk out of the vestry after they've signed their names, and—*lose themselves*. No reason why they should ever be associated with Mr. and Mrs. Nelson Smith. Do you much mind all these complications?"

"Not if they're necessary to save you from danger," the girl answered.

"By Jove, you're a trump! But I haven't come to the *big* favour yet. Now for it! When I write my real name in the register, I don't want you to look. Is that the one thing too much?"

Annesley tried not to flinch under his eyes. Yet—he had put her to a severe test. Last night, when he said that it would be better for her not to know his name, she had quietly agreed.

But there was the widest difference between then and now. At that time they had been strangers flung together by a wave of fate which, it seemed, might tear them apart at any instant. In a few hours all was changed. They belonged to each other. This man's name would be her name, yet he wished her to be ignorant of it!

If the girl had not thought of him truly as her knight, if she had not been determined to trust him, the "big favour" would indeed have been too big.

Despite her trust, and the romantic, new-born love in her heart, she was unable to answer for a moment. Her breath was snatched away; but as she struggled to regain it and to speak, a bleak picture of the future without him rose before her eyes. She couldn't give him up, and go on living, after the glimpse he had shown her of what life might be!

"No, it's not too much," she said, slowly. "It's only part of the trust I've promised to—my knight."

He gave a sigh of relief. "Thank you—and my lucky star for the prize you are!" he exclaimed. Some men would have offered their thanks to God, or to "Heaven." Annesley noticed that he praised his "star."

This was one of many disquieting things, large and small; for she had been brought up to be a religious girl, and was mentally on her knees before God in gratitude for the happiness which illuminated her gray life. She could not bear to think that God was nothing to the man who had become everything to her. She wanted to shut her eyes to all that was strange in him; but it was as difficult as for Psyche to resist lighting the lantern for a peep at her mysterious husband in his sleep.

For instance, there was the Countess de Santiago's reference to their association on board the *Monarchic*, which Knight had refrained from mentioning. He had spoken of it after the Countess had gone, to be sure; but briefly, and because it would have seemed odd if he had not done so. It had struck Annesley that his annoyance with the lady was connected with that sharp little "dig" of hers, and she could not sweep her mind clean of curiosity.

The moment the *Monarchic's* name was brought up she remembered reading a newspaper paragraph about the last voyage of that great ship from New York to Liverpool. Fortunately or unfortunately, her recollection of the paragraph was nebulous, for when she read news aloud to her mistress she permitted her mind to wander, unless the subject happened to be interesting. She tried to keep up a vaguely intelligent knowledge of world politics, but small events and blatant sensations, such as murders, burglaries, and "society" divorces, she quickly erased from her brain.

Something dramatic had occurred on the *Monarchic*. Her subconscious self recalled that. But it was less than a month ago that she had read the paragraph, therefore the sensation, whatever it was, must have happened when Knight and the Countess de Santiago were on board, coming to England, and she could easily learn what it was by inquiring.

Not for the world, however, would she question her lover, to whom the subject of the trip was evidently distasteful. Still less would she ask the Countess behind his back.

There was another way in which she could find out a sly voice seemed to whisper in Annesley's ear. She could get old numbers of the *Morning Post*, the only newspaper that entered Mrs. Ellsworth's house, and search for the paragraph. But she was ashamed of herself for letting such a thought enter her head. Of course she would not be guilty of a trick so mean. She would not try to unearth one fact concerning her Knight—his name, his past, or any circumstances surrounding him, even though by stretching out her hand she could reach the key to his secret.

He talked of things which at another time would have palpitated with interest: their wedding, their honeymoon, their homecoming, and Annesley responded without betraying absent-mindedness. It was the best she could do, until the effect of the "biggest favour" and the doubts it raised were blurred by new sensations. She would not have been a normal woman if the shopping excursion planned by Knight had not swept her off her feet.

The man with Fortunatus' purse seemed bent on trying to empty it—temporarily—for her benefit: if she had been sent out alone to buy everything she had ever wanted, with no regard to expense, Annesley Grayle would not have spent a fifth of the sum he flung away on evening gowns, street gowns, boudoir gowns, hats, high-heeled paste-buckled slippers, a gold-fitted dressing-bag, an ermine wrap, a fur-lined motor-coat, and more suede gloves and silk stockings than could be used (it seemed to the girl) in the next ten years.

He begged for the privilege of "helping choose," not because he didn't trust her taste, but because he feared she might be economical; and during the whole day in Bond Street, Regent Street, Oxford Street, and Knightsbridge she was given only an hour to herself. That hour she was expected to pass, and did pass, in providing herself with all sorts of intimate daintiness of nainsook, lace, and ribbon, too sacred even for a lover's eyes.

And Knight spent the time of his absence from her upon an errand which he did not explain.

"I'll tell you what I did—and show you—to-morrow when I come to wish you good morning," he said. "Unless you're going to be conventional and refuse to see me till we 'meet at the altar,' as the sentimental writers say. I think I've heard that's the smart thing. But I hope it won't be your way. If I didn't see you from now till to-morrow afternoon I should be afraid I'd lost you for ever."

Annesley felt the same about him, and told him so. They dined together, but not at the Savoy. The Countess's name was not mentioned, yet Annesley guessed it was because of her that Knight proposed an Italian restaurant.

When he left her at last at the door of her own hotel everything was settled for the wedding-day and after. Knight was to produce two friends, both men, to one of whom must fall the fatherly duty of giving the bride away. He suggested their calling upon her in the morning, while he was with her at the Savoy, in order that they might not meet as strangers at the church, and the girl thought this a wise idea.

As for the honeymoon, Knight confessed to knowing little of England, outside London, and asked Annesley if she had a choice. Would she like to have a week or so in some warm county like Devonshire or Cornwall, or would she enjoy a trip to Paris or the Riviera? It was all one to him, he assured her; only he had set his heart on getting back to London soon, finding a house, and beginning life as they meant to live it.

Annesley chose Devonshire. She said she would like to show it to Knight.

"I think you'll love it," she told him. "We might stay at several places I used to adore when I was a child. And if we get to Sidmouth, maybe you'll have a glimpse of those cousins you were talking about, the Annesley-Setons. I believe they have a place near by called Valley House; but I don't know whether they live there or let it."

"We'll go to Sidmouth," he said.

The girl smiled. His desire that she should scrape acquaintance with Lord and Lady Annesley-Seton seemed boyish and amusing to her, but she did not see how it could be brought about.

Next morning at eleven o'clock, when Annesley had been up for two hours, packing her new things in her new trunks and the gorgeous new dressing-bag, she was informed that Mr. Nelson Smith had arrived. The girl had forgotten that Knight had hinted at something to tell and something to show her on the morning of their marriage day, and expected to find his two friends with him; but he had come alone.

"We've got a half-hour together," he said. "Then Dr. Torrance and the Marchese di Morello may turn up at any minute. Torrance is an elderly man, a decent sort of chap, and deadly respectable. He'll do the heavy father well enough. Paolo di Morello is an Italian. I don't care for him; but the troublesome business about my name is a handicap.

"I can trust these men. And at least they won't put you to shame. You can judge them when they come, so enough talk about them for the present! This is my excuse for being here," and he put into Annesley's hand a flat, oval-shaped parcel. "My wedding gift to my bride," he added, in a softer tone. "Open it, sweet."

The white paper wrapping was fastened with small red seals. If the girl had had knowledge of such things she would have known that it was a jeweller's parcel. But the white, gold-stamped silk case within surprised her. She pressed a tiny knob, and the cover flew up to show a string of pearls which made her gasp.

"For the Princess, from her Knight," he said. "And here"—he took from the inner pocket of his coat a band of gold set with a big white diamond—"is your engagement ring. Every girl must have one, you know, even if her engagement *is* the shortest on record. I've the wedding ring, too. But it isn't the time for that. A good-sized diamond's the obvious sort of thing: advertises itself for what it is, and that's what we want. You'll wear it, as much as to say, 'I was engaged like everybody else.' But if there wasn't a reason against it, *this* is what I should like to put on your finger."

As he spoke, he hid the spark of light in his other hand, and from the pocket whence it had come produced another ring.

If she had not seen this, Annesley would have exclaimed against the word "obvious" for the splendid brilliant as big as a small pea which Knight put aside so carelessly. But the contrast between the modern ring with its "solitaire" diamond and the wonderful rival he gave it silenced her. She was no judge of jewellery, and had never possessed any worth having; but she knew that this second ring was a rare as well as a beautiful antique. It looked worthy, she thought, of a real princess.

Even the gold was different from other gold, the little that was visible, for the square-cut stone, of pale, scintillating blue, was surrounded by a frame of tiny brilliants encrusting the rim as far as could be seen on the back of the hand when the ring was worn.

"A sapphire!" Annesley exclaimed. "My favourite stone. Yet I never saw a sapphire like it before. It's wonderful—brighter than a diamond."

"It is a diamond," said Knight. "A blue diamond, and considered remarkable. It's what your friend Ruthven Smith would call a 'museum piece,' if you showed it to him. But you mustn't. He'd move heaven and earth to get it! Nobody must see it but you and me. It wouldn't be safe. It's too valuable. And if you were known to have it, you'd be in danger from all the jewel thieves in Europe and America. You wouldn't like that."

"No, it would be horrible!" Annesley shuddered. "But what a pity it must be hidden. Is it yours?"

"It's yours at present," said Knight, "if you'll keep it to yourself, and look at it only when you and I are alone together. I can't give it to you, precisely, to have and to hold (as I shall give you myself in a few hours), because this ring is more a trust than a possession. Something may happen which will force me to ask you for it. But again, it may *not*. And, anyhow, I want you to have the ring until that time comes. I've bought a thin gold chain, and you can hang it round your neck, unless—I almost think you're inclined to refuse?"

Another mystery! But the blue diamond in its scintillating frame was so alluring that Annesley could not refuse. She knew that she would have more pleasure in peeping surreptitiously at the secret blue diamond than in seeing the "obvious" white one on her finger.

"I can't give it up!" she said, laughing. "But I hope it isn't one of those dreadful historic stones which have had murders committed for it, like famous jewels one reads of. I should hate anything that came from *you* to bring bad luck."

"So should I hate it. If there's any bad luck coming, I want it myself," Knight said, gravely.

"I wish I hadn't spoken of bad luck to-day!" the girl remorsefully exclaimed. "But I am not afraid. Give me the ring."

He gave it, and pulled from his pocket the slight gold chain on which he meant it to hang. He was leisurely threading the ring upon this when two men looked in at the door of the reading room.

One of the pair was of more than middle age. He was tall, thin, and slightly stooping. His respectable clothes seemed too loose for him. His hair and straggling beard were gray, contrasting with the sallow darkness of his skin. He wore gold-rimmed spectacles, and peered through them as if they were not strong enough for his failing sight.

The other man was younger. He, too, was dark and sallow, but his close-cut hair was black. He was clean shaven and well dressed. He wore a high, almost painfully high, collar, which caused him to keep his chin in air. He might be a Spaniard or an Italian.

Annesley had certainly not seen him before. She told herself this twice over. Yet—she was frightened. There was something familiar about him. It must be her foolish imagination which took alarm at everything!

But, with fingers grown cold, she covered up the blue diamond.

CHAPTER IX.
THE THING KNIGHT WANTED

When Dr. Torrance, who was to give her away, and the Marchese di Morello, who was to be Knight's "best man," had been introduced to Annesley, she laughed at the stupid "scare" which had chilled her heart for a moment.

If Knight had remained with her after his friends finished their call, she might have confessed to him how she had fancied in the tall, dark young man a likeness to one of the dreaded *watchers*. Until Knight spoke their names she had feared that the pair looking in at the door were there to spy; that one, at all events, was disguised—cleverly, yet not cleverly enough quite to hide his identity. But Knight said good-bye, and went away with his friends, giving the girl no chance for further talk with him.

They did not meet again until—with the Countess de Santiago—Annesley arrived at the obscure church chosen for the marriage ceremony. There Dr. Torrance awaited them outside the door, and took charge of the bride, while the Countess found her way in alone; and Annesley saw through the mist of confused emotion her Knight of love and mystery waiting at the altar.

During the ceremony that followed he made his responses firmly, his eyes calling so clearly to hers that she answered with an almost hypnotized gaze. His look seemed to seal the promise of his words. In spite of all that was strange and secret and unsatisfying about him, she had no regrets. Love was worth everything, and she could but believe that he loved her. This strong conviction went with the girl to the vestry, and made it easier to turn away when his name—his real name, which she, though his wife, was not to know—was recorded by him in the book.

They parted from Torrance, Morello, and the Countess at the church door, an arrangement which delighted Annesley. In the haste of making plans, she and Knight had forgotten to discuss what they were to do after the wedding and before their departure; but Knight had found time to decide the matter.

"These people were the best material I could get hold of at a moment's notice," he remarked, coolly, when he and Annesley were in the motor-car he had hired for the journey to Devonshire. "We've used them because we needed them. Now we don't need them any longer. It seems to me that a newly married couple ought to keep only dear friends around them or no one. Later we can repay these three for the favour they've done us, if you call it a favour. Meanwhile, we'll forget them."

Knight had neglected no detail which could make for Annesley's comfort, or save her from any embarrassment arising from the hurried wedding. Her luggage had been packed by a maid in the hotel, and—all but the dressing-bag and a small box made for an automobile—sent ahead by rail to Devonshire. She and Knight were to travel in the comfortable limousine which would protect them against weather. It did not matter, Knight said, how long they were on the way.

At Exeter they would visit some good agency in search of a lady's maid. Annesley said that she did not need a woman to wait on her, since she had been accustomed not only to taking care of herself but Mrs. Ellsworth.

Knight, however, insisted that his wife must be looked after by a competent woman. It was "the right thing"; but his idea was that, in the circumstances, it would be pleasanter to have a country girl than a sharp, London-bred woman or a Parisienne.

In Exeter an ideal person was obtainable: a Devonshire girl who had been trained to a maid's duties (as the agent boasted) by a "lady of title." She had accompanied "the Marchioness" to France, and had had lessons in Cannes from a hair dresser, masseuse, and manicurist. Now her mistress was dead, and Parker was in search of another place.

She was a gentle, sweet-looking girl, and though she asked for wages higher than Mrs. Ellsworth had paid her companion, Knight pronounced them reasonable. She was directed to go by train to the Knowle Hotel at Sidmouth (where a suite had been engaged by telegram for Mr. and Mrs. Nelson Smith and maid) and to have all the luggage unpacked before their arrival.

Flung thus into intimate association with a man, almost a stranger, Annesley had been afraid in the midst of her happiness. She felt as a young Christian maiden, a prisoner of Nero's day, might have felt if told she was to be flung to a lion miraculously subdued by the influence of Christianity. Such a maiden could not have been quite sure whether the story were true or a fable; whether the lion would destroy her with a blow or crouch at her feet.

But Annesley's lion neither struck nor crouched. He stood by her side as a protector. "Knight" seemed more and more appropriate as a name for him. Though there were roughnesses and crudenesses in his manner and choice of words, all he did and said made Annesley sure that she had been right in her first impression. Not a cultured gentleman like Archdeacon Smith, or Annesley's dead father, and the few men who had come near her in early childhood before her home fell to pieces, he was a gentleman at heart, she told herself, and in all essentials.

It struck her as beautiful and even pathetic, rather than contemptible, that he should humbly wish to learn of her the small refinements he had missed in the past—that mysterious past which mattered less and less to Annesley as the present became dear and vital.

"I've knocked about a lot, all over the world," he explained in a casual way during a talk they had had on the night of their marriage, at the first stopping-place to which their motor brought them. "My mother died when I was a small boy, died in a terrible way I don't want to talk about, and losing her broke up my father and me for a while. He never got over it as long as he lived, and I never will as long as I live.

"The way my father died was almost as tragic as my mother's death," he went on after a tense moment of remembering. "I was only a boy even then; and ever since the 'knocking-about' process has been going on. I haven't seen much of the best side of life, but I've wanted it. That was why, for one reason, you made such an appeal to me at first sight. You were as plucky and generous as any Bohemian, though I could see you were a delicate, inexperienced girl, brought up under glass like the orchid you look—and are. I'm used to making up my mind in a hurry—I've had to—so it didn't take me many minutes to realize that if I could get you to link up with me, I should have the thing I'd been looking for.

"Well, by the biggest stroke of luck I've got you, sooner than I could have dared to hope; and now I don't want to make you afraid of me. I know my faults and failings, but I don't know how to put them right and be the sort of man a girl like you can be proud of. It's up to you to show me the way. Whenever you see me going wrong, you're to tell me. That's what I want—turn me into a gentleman."

When Annesley tenderly reassured him with loving flatteries, he only laughed and caught her in his arms.

"Like a prince, am I?" he echoed. "Well, I've got princely blood in my veins through my mother; but there are pauper princes, and in the pauper business the gilding gets rubbed off. I trust you to gild my battered corners. No good trying to tell me I'm gold all through, because I know better; but when you've made me shine on the outside, I'll keep the surface bright."

Annesley did not like the persistent way in which he spoke of himself as a black sheep who, at best, could be whitened, and trained not to disgrace the fold; yet it piqued her interest. Books said that women had a weakness for men who were not good and she supposed that she was like the rest. He was so dear and chivalrous that certain defiant hints as to his lack of virtue vaguely added to the spice of mystery which decorated the background of the picture—the vivid picture of the "stranger knight."

When they had been for three days in the best suite at the Knowle Hotel, and had made several short excursions with the motor, he asked the girl if she "felt like getting acquainted with her cousins."

She did not protest as she had at first. Already she knew her Knight well enough to be assured that when he resolved to do a thing it was practically done. She had had chances to realize his force of character in little ways as well as big ones; and she understood that he was bent on scraping acquaintance with Lord and Lady Annesley-Seton. Had he not decided upon Sidmouth the instant she mentioned their ownership of a place in the neighbourhood? She had been certain that he would not neglect the opportunity created.

"How are we to set about it?" was all she said.

"Oh, Valley House is a show place, I suppose you know," replied Knight. "I've looked it up in the local guide-book. It's open to the public three days a week. Any one with a shilling to spare can see the ancestral portraits and treasures, and the equally ancestral rooms of your distinguished family. Does that interest you?"

"Ye-es. But I'm a distant relation—as well as a poor one," Annesley reminded him with her old humility.

"You're not poor now. And blood is thicker than water—when it's in a golden cup. It's Lord and Lady Annesley-Seton's turn to play the poor relations. It seems they're stony. Even the shillings the public pay to see the place are an object to them."

"Oh, I'm sorry!" exclaimed Annesley.

"That's generous, seeing they never bothered themselves about you when they had plenty of shillings and you had none."

"I don't suppose they knew there *was* a me."

"Lord Annesley-Seton must have known, if his wife didn't know. But we'll let that pass. I was thinking we might go to the house on one of the public days, with the man who wrote the local guide-book. I've made his acquaintance through writing him a note, complimenting him on his work and his knowledge of history. He answered like a shot, with thanks for the appreciation, and said if he could help me he'd be delighted. He's the editor of a newspaper in Torquay.

"If we invite him to lunch here at the Knowle, he'll fall over himself to accept. Then we'll be able to kill two birds with one stone. He'll tell us things about the heirlooms at Valley House we shouldn't be able to find out without his help—or a lot of dreary drudgery—and also he'll put a paragraph about us in his newspaper, which he'll send to your cousins. Now, isn't that a combination of brilliant ideas?"

"Yes," laughed Annesley. "But why should you take so much trouble—and how can you tell that the editor's paragraph would make the Annesley-Setons want to know us?"

"As for the paragraph, you may put your faith in me. And as for the trouble, nothing's too much to launch my wife on the top wave of society, where she has every right to be. I want Mrs. Nelson Smith to have her chance to shine. Money would do the trick sooner or later, but I want it to be done sooner. Besides, I have a feeling I should like us to get where we want to be, without the noisy splash money-bags make when new-rich candidates for society are launched. Your people will see excellent reasons why their late 'poor relation' is worth cultivating.

"But trust them to save their faces by keeping their real motive secret!" with a touch of sarcasm. "I seem to hear them going about among their friends, whom they'll invite to meet us, saying how charming and unspoilt you are though you've got more money than you know what to do with— —"

"I!" With the protesting pronoun Annesley disclaimed all ownership of her husband's fortune, whatever it might be.

"It's the same thing. You and I are one. Whatever is mine is yours. I don't swear to make you a regular, unfailing allowance worthy of the new position you're going to have, because you see I do business with several countries, and my income's erratic; I'm never sure to the day when it will come or how much it will be. But there's nothing you want which you can't buy; remember that. And when we begin life in London, you shall have a standing account at as many shops as you like."

Annesley made no objection to Knight's plan for luring the journalist into his "trap," which was a harmless one. According to his prophecy, Mr. Milton Savage of the Torquay *Weekly Messenger* accepted the invitation from his correspondent, and came to luncheon on the day when the public were free to view Valley House.

He was a small man with a big head and eyes which glinted large behind convex spectacles. Annesley was charming to him, not only in the wish to please Knight but because she was kind-hearted and had intense sympathy for suppressed people. Mr. Savage was grateful and admiring, and drank in every word Knight dropped, as if carelessly, about the relationship to Lord Annesley-Seton.

Knight allowed himself to be pumped concerning it, and also his wife's parentage, letting fall, with apparent inadvertence, bits of information regarding himself, his travels, his adventures, and the fortune he had picked up.

"I'm the exception," he said, "to the proverb that 'a rolling stone gathers no moss.' I've gathered all I want or know what to do with; and now I'm married I mean to take a rest. I haven't decided yet where or how, but it will be somewhere in England. We're looking for a house in London, and later we might rent one in the country, too."

Annesley admired his cleverness in touching the goal; but somehow these smart hits disturbed rather than amused her. Knight's complexity was a puzzle to her. She could not understand, despite his explanations, why these fireworks of dexterity were worth while. Knight was a brave figure of romance. She did not want her hero turned into an intriguer, no matter how innocent his motive.

After luncheon they drove five or six miles in the motor to Valley House, a place of Jacobean times. There was an Italian garden, and an English garden containing every flower, plant, and herb mentioned by Shakespeare. Each garden had a distant view of the sea, darkly framed by Lebanon cedars and immense beeches, while the house itself—not large as "show" houses go—was perfect of its kind, with carved stone mantels, elaborate oak panelling and staircases, leaded windows, and treasures of portraits, armour, ancient books, and bric-à-brac which would have remade the family fortune if all had not been heirlooms.

There was not a picture on the walls nor an old piece of jewellery in the many locked glass cabinets of which Mr. Milton Savage could not tell the history as he guided the Nelson Smiths through hall and corridors and rooms with marvellous moulded ceilings. The liveried servant told off to show the crowd over the house had but a superficial knowledge of its riches compared with the lore of the journalist; and the editor of the Torquay *Weekly Messenger* became inconveniently popular with the public.

He was not blind to the compliment, however; and, motoring into Torquay at the end of the afternoon with his host and hostess, expressed himself delighted with his visit.

That night was his night for going to press, but he found time to write the paragraph which Nelson Smith expected. Next morning a copy of the *Messenger*, with a page marked, arrived at the Knowle Hotel, and another, also marked, went to Valley House.

The bride and bridegroom were at breakfast when the paper came. There were also three letters, all for Knight, the first which either had received since their marriage.

Knight cut open the envelopes slowly, one after the other, and made no comment. Annesley could not help wondering if the Countess had written, for an involuntary glance had made her sure that one of Knight's letters was from a woman: a purple envelope with a purple monogram and a blob of purple wax sealed with a crown. He read all three, put them back into their envelopes, rose, dropped them into the fire, watched them burn to ashes, and quietly returned to his seat. Then, as if really interested, he tore the wrapping off the Torquay *Messenger*.

"Now we shall see ourselves in print!" he said, and a moment later was reading to Annesley an account of "the two most interesting guests the Knowle Hotel has entertained this season." Mr. and Mrs. Nelson Smith were described with enthusiasm. They were young and handsome. He was immensely rich, she was "highly connected" as well as beautiful, having been a Miss Annesley Grayle, related on her mother's side to the Earl of Annesley-Seton.

The modesty of the young couple was so great, however, that, though the bridegroom was a millionaire well known in his adopted country, America, and the bride quite closely linked with his lordship's family, they had refused to make their presence in the neighbourhood known to the Earl and Lady. Instead they had visited Valley House with a crowd of tourists on a public day, expressing the opinion to a representative of the *Messenger* that it would be "intrusive" to present themselves to Lord and Lady Annesley-Seton. They were spending their honeymoon in Devonshire, and might find, during their motor tours, a suitable country place to buy or rent.

In any case, they would look for a house in which to settle on their return to London.

"Good for Milton Savage," laughed Knight. "Now we'll lie low, and see what will happen."

Annesley thought that nothing would happen; but she was wrong. The next morning a note came by hand for Mrs. Nelson Smith, brought by a footman on a bicycle.

The note was from Lady Annesley-Seton.

CHAPTER X.
BEGINNING OF THE SERIES

No man who had not known the seamy side of life could have guessed the effect of Milton Savage's paragraph upon the minds of Lord and Lady Annesley-Seton.

"I told you if you bet against me you would bet wrong," Knight said, when the astonished girl handed the letter across the breakfast table. Even he had hardly reckoned on such extreme cordiality. He had expected a bid for acquaintanceship with the "millionaire" and his bride, but he had fancied there would be a certain stiffness in the effort.

Lady Annesley-Seton had begun, "My dear Cousin," and her frank American way was disarming. She wrote four pages of apology for herself and her husband, explaining why they had neglected "looking up Mrs. Nelson Smith when she was Miss Annesley Grayle." The letter went on:

> I hadn't been married long when my husband read out of some newspaper the notice of a clergyman's death, and mentioned that he was a cousin by marriage whom he hadn't met since boyhood, although the clergyman's living was in our county—somewhere off at the other end.
>
> My husband thought there was a daughter, and I remember his remarking that we ought to write and find out if she'd been left badly off. Of course, it was *my* duty to have kept his idea alive, and to have carried it out. But I was young and having such a good time that I'm afraid it was a case of "out of sight, out of mind."
>
> We forgot to inquire, and heard no more. It was *horrid* of us, and I'm sure it was *our* loss. Probably we should have remembered if things had gone well with us: but

perhaps you know that my father (whose money used to seem unlimited to me) lost it all, and we were mixed up in the smash. We've been poorer than any church mice since, and trying to make ends meet has occupied our attention from that day to this.

I have to confess that, if our attention hadn't been drawn to your name, we might never have thought of it again. But now I've eased my conscience, and as fate seems to have brought us within close touch, do let us see what she means to do with us. We should so like to meet you and Mr. Nelson Smith, who is, apparently, more or less a countryman of mine.

I'm not allowed out yet, in this cold weather, after an attack of "flu"; but my husband will call this afternoon on the chance of finding you in, carrying a warm invitation to you both to "waive ceremony" and dine with us at Valley House *en famille*.

Looking forward to meeting you,

Yours most cordially,

Constance Annesley-Seton.

"Sweet of her, isn't it?" Annesley exclaimed when she and Knight had read the letter through.

Knight glanced at his wife quizzically, opened his lips to speak, and closed them. Perhaps he thought it would be unwise as well as wrong to disturb the girl's faith in Lady Annesley-Seton's disinterestedness.

"Yes, it's *real* sweet!" he said, exaggerating his American accent, but keeping a grave face.

They were duly "at home" that afternoon, though they had intended to go out, and the caller found them in a private sitting room filled with flowers, suggesting much money and a love of spending it. Annesley had put on Knight's favourite frock, one of the "model dresses" he had chosen for her in their whirlwind rush through Bond Street, a white cloth trimmed with narrow bands of dark fur; and she had never looked prettier.

Lord Annesley-Seton, a tall thin man of the eagle-nosed soldier type, wearing pince-nez, but youthful-looking for the forty-four years Burke gave him, could not help thinking her a satisfactory cousin to pick up: and Nelson Smith was far from being in appearance the rough, self-made man he had dreaded.

He was delighted with them both—so young, so handsome, so happy, so fortunate, and luckily so well bred. He did not make the short conventional call he had intended, but stayed to tea, and at last went home to give his wife an enthusiastic account of the visit.

"The girl's a lady, and might be a beauty if she had more confidence in herself—you know what I mean: taking herself for granted as a charmer, the way you smart women do," he said. "She isn't that kind. But with you to show her the ropes, she'll be liked by the right people. There's a softness and sweetness and genuineness that you don't often see in girls now. As for the man, you'll think him a ripper, Connie—so will other women. Has the air of being a gentleman born, and then having roughed it all over the world. A strong man, I should say. A man's man as well as a woman's. Might 'take' if he's started right."

"*We'll* see to that," said Constance Annesley-Seton, who was not too ill to go out but had not wanted to seem too eager.

She was less than thirty, but looked more because she had worried and drawn faint lines between her delicate auburn brows and at the corners of her greenish-gray eyes. There were also a few fading threads in the red locks which were her one real beauty; but she had a marvellous hair-varnish which prevented them from showing.

"We'll see to that! If they'll *let* us. Are they going to let us?"

"Yes, I think so," Annesley-Seton reassured her. "They're a pair of children, willing to be guided. They can have anything they want in the world, but they don't seem to know what to want."

"Splendid!" laughed Constance. "Can't we will them to want our house in town, and invite us to visit them?"

"I shouldn't wonder," replied her husband. "You might make a start in that direction when they come to dinner to-morrow evening."

Lord Annesley-Seton had outgrown such enthusiasms as he might once have had, therefore his account of the cousins encouraged Constance to hope much, and she was not disappointed. On the contrary, she thought that he had not said enough, especially about the man.

If she had not had so many anxieties that her youthful love of "larks" had been crushed out, she would have "adored" a flirtation with Nelson Smith. It would have been "great fun" to steal him from the pretty beanpole of a girl who would not know how to use her claws in a fight for her man; but as it was, Connie thought only of conciliating "Cousin Anne," and winning her confidence. Other women would try to take Nelson Smith from his wife, but Connie would have her hands full in playing a less amusing game.

She thought, seeing that the handsome, dark young man she admired had a mind of his own, it would be a difficult game to play; and Nelson Smith saw that she thought so. His sense of humour caused him to smile at his own cleverness in producing the impression; and he would have given a good deal for someone to laugh with over her maneuvers to entice him along the road he wished to travel.

But he dared not point out to Annesley the fun of the situation. To do so would be to put her against him and it.

She, too, had a sense of humour, suppressed by five years of Mrs. Ellsworth, but coming delightfully to life, like a half-frozen bird, in the sunshine of safety and happiness. Knight appealed to and encouraged it often, for he could not have lived with a humourless woman, no matter how sweet.

Yet he did not dare wake it where her cousins were concerned. Her sense of honour was more valuable to him than her sense of humour. He was afraid to put the former on the defensive, and he was glad to let her believe the Annesley-Setons were genuinely "warming" to them in a way which proved that blood was thicker than water.

The girl had wondered from the first why he was determined to make friends with these cousins whom she had never known, and he was grateful because she believed in him too loyally to attribute his desire to "snobbishness." He wished her to suppose he had set his heart on providing her with influential guidance on the threshold of a new life; and it was important that she should not begin criticizing his motives.

By the time dinner was over Constance Annesley-Seton had decided that the Nelson Smiths had been sent to her by the Powers that Be, and that it would be tempting Providence not to annex them. Not that she put it in that way to herself, for she did not trouble her mind about Providence. All she knew was that she and Dick would be fools to let the chance slip.

It was as much as she could do not to suggest the idea in her mind: that the Nelson Smiths should take the house in Portman Square; that she and her husband should introduce them to society, and that the Devonshire place should either be let to them or that they should visit there when they wished to be in the country, as paying guests.

But she controlled her impatience, limiting herself to proposing plans for future meetings. She suggested giving a dinner in honour of the bride and bridegroom, and inviting people whom it would be "nice for them to know" in town.

Knight said that he and "Anita" (his new name for Annesley, a souvenir of Spanish South America) would accept with pleasure. And the girl agreed gladly, because she thought her cousin and his wife were very kind.

After dinner Annesley-Seton and Knight followed Constance and "Anita" almost directly, the former asking his guests if they would like to see some of the family treasures which they could only have glanced at in passing with the crowd the other day.

"Before sugar went to smash, we blazed into all sorts of extravagances here," he said, bitterly, with a glance at the deposed Sugar King's daughter. "Among others, putting electric light into this old barn. We'll have an illumination, and show you some trifles Connie and I wish to Heaven a kind-hearted burglar would relieve us of.

"Of course the beastly things are heirlooms, as I suppose you know. We can't sell or pawn them, or I should have done one or the other long ago. They're insured by the trustees, who are the bane of our lives, for the estate. But a sporting sort of company has blossomed out lately, which insures against 'loss of use'—I think that's the expression. I pay the premium myself—even when I can't pay anything else!—and if the valuable contents of this place are stolen or burned, we shall benefit personally.

"I don't mind you or all the world knowing we're stony broke," he went on, frankly. "And everyone *does* know, anyhow, that we'd be in the deuce of a hole without the tourists' shillings which pour in twice a week the year round. You see, each object in the collection helps bring in those shillings; and 'loss of use' of a single one would be a real deprivation. So it's fair and above board. But thus far, I've paid my premium and got no return, these last three years. Our tourists are so disgustingly honest, or our burglars so clumsy and unenterprising, that, as you say in the States, 'there's nothing doing.'"

As he talked Dick Annesley-Seton sauntered about the immense room into which they had come from the state banqueting hall, switching on more and more of the electric candle-lights set high on the green brocade walls. This was known as the "green drawing room" by the family, and the "Room of the Miniatures" by the public, who read about it in catalogues.

"Come and look at our white elephants," he went on, when the room, dimly and economically lit at first, was ablaze with light; and Mr. and Mrs. Nelson Smith joined him eagerly. Constance followed, too, bored but resigned; and her husband paused before a tall, narrow glass cabinet standing in a recess.

"See these miniatures!" he exclaimed, fretfully. "There are plenty more, but the best are in this cabinet; and there's a millionaire chap, in New York—perhaps you can guess his name, Smith?—who has offered a hundred thousand pounds for the thirty little bits of ivory in it."

"I think that must have been the great Paul Van Vreck," Knight hazarded.

"I thought you'd guess! There aren't many who'd make such an offer. Think what it would mean to me if it could be accepted, and I could have the handling of the money. There are three small pictures in the little octagon gallery next door, too, Van Vreck took a fancy to on a visit he paid us from Saturday to Monday last summer. We never thought much of them, and they're in a dark place, labelled in the catalogue 'Artist unknown: School of Fragonard'; but *he* swore they were authentic Fragonards, and would have backed his opinion to the tune of fifteen thousand pounds for the trio, or six thousand for the one he liked best. Isn't it aggravating? In the Chinese room he went mad over some bits of jade, especially a Buddha nobody else had ever admired."

"He's one of the few millionaire collectors who is really a judge of all sorts of things," Knight replied. "But, great Scott! I'm no expert, yet it strikes me these miniatures are something out of the ordinary!"

"Well, yes, they are," Annesley-Seton admitted, modestly. "That queer one at the top is a Nicholas Hilliard. I believe he was the first of the miniaturists. And the two just underneath are Samuel Coopers. They say he stood at the head of the Englishmen. There are three Richard Cosways and rather a nice Angelica Kauffmann."

"It was the Fragonard miniature Mr. Van Vreck liked best," put in Constance. "It seems he painted only a few. And next, the Goya——"

"Good heavens! where is the Fragonard?" cried Dick, his eyes bulging behind his pince-nez. "Surely it was here——"

"Oh, surely, yes!" panted his wife. "It was never anywhere else."

For an instant they were stricken into silence, both staring at a blank space on the black velvet background where twenty-nine miniatures hung. There was no doubt about it when they had reviewed the rows of little painted faces. The Fragonard was gone.

"Stolen!" gasped Lady Annesley-Seton.

"Unless one of you, or some servant you trust with the key, is a somnambulist," said Knight. "I don't see how it would pay a thief to steal such a thing. It must be too well known. He couldn't dispose of it—that is if he weren't a collector himself; and even then he could never show it. But—by Jove!"

"What is it? What have you seen?" Annesley-Seton asked, sharply.

Knight pointed, without touching the cabinet. He had never come near enough to do that. "It looks to me as if a square bit of glass had been cut out on the side where the lost miniature must have hung," he said. "I can't be sure, from where I stand, because the cabinet is too close to the wall of the recess."

Dick Annesley-Seton thrust his arm into the space between green brocade and glass, then slipped his hand through a neatly cut aperture just big enough to admit its passage. With his hand in the square hole he could reach the spot where the miniature had hung, and could have taken it off the hook had it been there. But hook, as well as miniature, was missing.

"That settles it!" he exclaimed. "It *is* a theft, and a clever one! Strange we should find it out when I was demonstrating to you how much I wished it would happen. Hurrah! That miniature alone is insured against burglary for seven or eight hundred pounds. Nothing to what it's worth, but a lot to pay a premium on, with the rest of the things besides. I wish now I hadn't been so cheese-paring. You'll be witnesses, you two, of our discovery. I'm glad Connie and I weren't alone when we found it out. Something nasty might have been said."

"We'll back you up with pleasure," Knight replied. "What was the miniature like? I wonder if we saw it when we were here the other day, Anita? I remember these, but can't recall any other."

"Neither can I," returned Annesley. "But I am stupid about such things. We saw so many—and passed so quickly."

"I wonder if Paul Van Vreck was here in disguise among the tourists?" said Dick, beginning to laugh. "It would have been the one he'd have chosen if he couldn't grab the lot."

"Oh, surely no one in the crowd could have cut a piece of glass out of a cabinet and stolen a miniature without being seen!" Annesley cried.

"Dick is half in joke," Constance explained. "It would have been a miracle, yet the servants are above suspicion. Those horrid trustees never let me choose a new one without their interference. And, of *course* Dick didn't mean what he said about Mr. Van Vreck."

"Of course not. I understood that," Annesley excused herself, blushing lest she had appeared obtuse.

"All the same, to carry on the joke, let's go into the octagon room and see if the alleged Fragonard pictures have gone, too," said Annesley-Seton. He led the way, turning on more light in the adjoining room as he went; and, outdistancing the others, they heard him stammer, "Good Lord!" before they were near enough to see what he saw.

"They aren't gone?" shrieked his wife, hurrying after him.

"One of them is."

In an instant the three had grouped behind him, where he stood staring at an empty frame, between two others of the same pattern and size, charming old frames twelve or fourteen inches square, within whose boundaries of carved and gilded wood, nymphs held hands and danced.

"Are we *dreaming* this?" gasped Constance.

"Thank Heaven we're not!" the husband answered. "The two paintings are on wood, you see. So was the missing one. Someone has simply unfastened it from the frame, and trusted to this being a dark, out-of-the-way corner, not to have the theft noticed for hours or maybe days. By all that's wonderful, here's *another* insurance haul for me! What about the jade Buddha in the Chinese room?"

They rushed back into the green drawing room, and so to the beautiful Chinese room beyond, with its priceless lacquer tables and cabinets. In one of these latter a collection of exquisite jade was gathered together.

And the Buddha which Paul Van Vreck had coveted was gone!

CHAPTER XI.
ANNESLEY REMEMBERS

There was great excitement for the next few days at Valley House and throughout the neighbourhood, for the Annesley-Setons made no secret of the robbery, and the affair got into the papers, not only the local ones, but the London dailies.

Two of the latter sent representatives, to whom Lord Annesley-Seton granted interviews. Something he said attracted the reporters' attention to Mr. and Mrs. Nelson Smith, who had been dining at Valley House on the evening when the theft was discovered, and Knight was begged for an interview.

He was asked if he had formed an opinion as to the disappearance of the three heirlooms, and whether he knew personally Mr. Paul Van Vreck, the American collector and retired head of the famous firm of jewellers, who had wished to buy the vanished treasures.

Having spent most of his life in America, Knight had the theory that unless you wished to be misrepresented, the only safe thing was to let yourself be interviewed. He was accordingly so good-natured and interesting that the reporters were delighted with him. If he had been wishing for a wide advertisement of his personality, his possessions, and his plans, he could not have chosen a surer way of getting it.

The two newspapers which had undertaken to boom the "Valley House Heirloom Theft" had almost limitless circulations. One of them possessed a Continental edition, and the other was immensely popular because of its topical illustrations.

Snapshots, not so unflattering as usual, were obtained of the young Anglo-American millionaire and his bride, as they started away from the Knowle Hotel in their motor, or as they walked in the garden. Though Knight had disclaimed any personal acquaintance with the great Paul Van Vreck, he was able to state that Mr. Van

Vreck had been convalescing at Palm Beach, in Florida, at the time of the robbery. He had had an attack of pneumonia in the autumn, and instead of travelling in his yacht to Egypt, as he generally did travel early in the winter, he had been ordered by his doctors to be satisfied with a "place in the sun" nearer home.

Everyone in America knew this, Knight explained, and everyone in England might know it also, unless it had been forgotten. If Mr. Van Vreck were well enough to take an interest in the papers, he was sure to be amused by the coincidence that the things stolen from Valley House were among those he had wanted to buy.

Knight thought, however, that even if the clever thief or thieves had heard of Van Vreck's whim, no attempt would be made to dispose of the spoil to him. The elderly millionaire, though one of the most eccentric men living, was known as the soul of honour.

The relationship between young Mrs. Nelson Smith and Lord Annesley-Seton was touched upon in the papers; and though it was irrelevant to the subject in hand, mention was made of the Nelson Smiths' plan to live in London.

This gave Constance her chance. At an impromptu luncheon at the Knowle Hotel, before the intended dinner party at Valley House, she referred to the interest Society would begin to take in this "romantic couple."

"Everybody will have fallen in love with you already," she said, "from those snapshots in the *Looking Glass*. They make you both look such darlings—though they don't flatter either of you. All the people we know will be clamouring to meet you, so you must hurry and find a nice house, in the right part of town, before some other sensation comes up and you're forgotten. How would it be if you took *our* house for a couple of months, while you're looking round? Naturally, if you *liked* it, you could keep it on. We'd be delighted, for we have to let it when we can, and it would be a pleasure to think of you in it."

"If we're in it, you must both come and stay, and not only 'think' of us, but be with us: mustn't they, Anita?" Knight proposed. Of course Annesley said yes, and meant yes. Not that she really wanted her duet with Knight to be broken up into a chorus, but she longed to succeed as a woman of the world, since that was what he wanted her to be; and she realized that Lady Annesley-Seton's help would be invaluable.

So, through the theft at Valley House and the developments therefrom, the hidden desires of Nelson Smith and the daughter of the deposed Sugar King accomplished themselves, Connie still believing that she had engineered the affair with diplomatic skill, and Knight laughing silently at the way she had played into his hands.

Detectives were set to work by the two insurance companies, who hoped to trace the thief and discover the stolen Fragonards and the jade Buddha; but their efforts failed; and at the dinner party given in honour of the new cousins, Lord and Lady Annesley-Seton rejoiced openly in their good luck.

"All the same," Constance said, "I *should* like to know how the things were spirited out of the house, and where they are. It is the first mystery that has ever come into our lives. I wish I were a clairvoyante. It would be fun!"

"Did you ever hear of the Countess de Santiago, when you lived in America?" asked Knight in his calm voice. He did not glance toward Annesley, who sat at the other end of the table, but he must have guessed that she would turn with a start of surprise on hearing the Countess's name in this connection.

"The Countess de Santiago?" Connie echoed. "No. What about her? She sounds interesting."

"She *is* interesting. And beautiful." Everybody had stopped talking by this time, to listen; and in the pause Knight appealed to his wife. "That's not an exaggeration, is it, Anita?"

Annesley, wondering and somewhat startled, answered that the Countess de Santiago was one of the most beautiful women she had seen.

This riveted the attention which Knight had caught. He had his audience, and went on in a leisurely way.

"Come to think of it, she can't have been heard of in your part of the world until you'd left for England," he told Constance. "She's the most extraordinary clairvoyante I ever heard of. That's what made me speak of her. Unfortunately she's not a professional, and won't do anything unless she happens to feel like it. But I wonder if I could persuade her to look in her crystal for you, Lady Annesley-Seton?

"She's an old acquaintance of mine," he went on, casually. "I met her in Buenos Aires before her rich elderly husband died, about seven or eight years ago. She was very young then. I came across her again in California, when she was seeing the world as a free woman, after the old fellow's death. Then I introduced her by letter to one or two people in New York, and I believe she has been admired there, and at Newport."

"But I've only *heard* all that," Knight hastened to explain. "I've been too busy till lately to know at first hand what goes on in the 'smart' or the artistic set. *My* world doesn't take much interest in crystal-gazers and palmists, amateur or professional, even when they happen to be handsome women, like the Countess. But I ran against her again on board the *Monarchic* about a month ago, crossing to this side, and we picked up threads of old acquaintance. She was staying at the Savoy when I left London."

He paused a moment, and added:

"As a favour to me, she might set her accomplishments to work on this business. Only she'd have to meet you both and see this house, for I've heard her say she couldn't do anything without knowing the people concerned, and 'getting the atmosphere.'"

"Oh, we *must* have her!" cried Constance, and all the other women except Annesley chimed in, begging their hostess to invite them if the Countess came.

No one thought it odd that Mrs. Nelson Smith should be silent, for her remark about the Countess de Santiago's beauty showed that she had met the lady; but to any one who had turned a critical stare upon her then, her expression must have seemed strange. She had an unseeing look, the look of one who has become deaf and blind to everything outside some scene conjured up by the brain.

What Annesley saw was a copy of the *Morning Post*. Knight's mention of the Countess de Santiago's power of clairvoyance at the same time with the liner *Monarchic* printed before her eyes a paragraph which her subconscious self had never forgotten.

For the moment only her body sat between a young hunting baronet and a distinguished elderly general at her cousins' dinner table. Her soul had gone back to London, to the ugly dining room at

22-A, Torrington Square, and was reading aloud from a newspaper to a stout old woman in a tea gown.

She was even able to recall what she had been thinking, as her lips mechanically conveyed the news to Mrs. Ellsworth. She had been wondering how much longer she could go on enduring the monotony, and what Mrs. Ellsworth would do if her slave should stop reading, shriek, and throw the *Morning Post* in her face.

As she pictured to herself the old woman's amazement, followed by rage, she had pronounced the words:

SENSATIONAL OCCURRENCE ON
BOARD THE S.S. MONARCHIC

Even that exciting preface had not recalled her interest from her own affairs. She could remember now the hollow, mechanical sound of her voice in her own ears as she had half-heartedly gone on, tempted to turn the picture of her wild revolt into reality.

The paragraph, seemingly forgotten but merely buried under other memories, had told of the disappearance on board the *Monarchic* of certain pearls and diamonds which were being secretly brought from New York to London by an agent of a great jewellery firm. He had been blamed by the chief officer for not handing the valuables over to the purser.

The unfortunate man (who had not advertised the fact that he was an agent for Van Vreck & Co. until he had had to complain of the theft) excused this seeming carelessness by the statement that he had hoped his identity might pass unsuspected. His theory was that safety lay in insignificance.

He had engaged a small, cheap cabin for himself alone, taking an assumed name; had pretended to be a schoolmaster on holiday, and had worn the pearls and other things always on his person in a money belt. Even at night he had kept the belt on his body, a revolver under his pillow, and the door of his cabin locked, with an extra patent adjustable lock of his own, invented by a member of the firm he served. It had not seemed probable that he would be recognized, or possible that he could be robbed.

Yet one morning he had waked late, with a dull headache and sensation of sickness, to find that his door, though closed, was unfastened, and that all his most valuable possessions were missing from the belt.

Some were left, as though the thief had fastidiously made his selection, scorning to trouble himself with anything but the best. The mystery of the affair was increased by the fact that, though the man (Annesley vaguely recalled some odd name, like Jekyll or Jedkill) felt certain he had fastened the door, there was no sign that it had been forced open. His patent detachable lock, however, had disappeared, like the jewels.

And despite the sensation of sickness, and pain in the head, there were no symptoms of drugging by chloroform, or any odour of chloroform or other anæsthetic in the room.

It struck Annesley as strange, almost terrifying, that these details of the *Monarchic* "sensation" should come back to her now; but she could not doubt that she had actually read them, and the rest of the story continued to reprint itself on her brain, as the unrolling of a film might bring back to one of the actors poses of his own which he had let slip into oblivion.

She remembered how some of the more important passengers had suggested that everybody on board should be searched, even to the ship's officers, sailors, and employés of all sorts; that the search had been made and nothing found, but that a lady supposed to possess clairvoyant powers had offered Mr. Jekyll or Jedkill to *consult her crystal* for his benefit.

She had done so, and had seen wireless messages passing between someone on the *Monarchic* and someone on another ship, with whom the former person appeared to be in collusion. She had seen a small, fair man, dressed as a woman, hypnotizing the jewellers' agent into the belief that he was locking his door when instead he was leaving it unlocked.

Then she had seen this man who, she asserted firmly, was dressed like a woman, walk into his victim's cabin, hypnotize him into still deeper unconsciousness, and take from his belt three long strings of pearls and several magnificent diamonds, set and unset. These things she saw made up into a bundle, wrapped in waterproof cloth, attached to a faintly illuminated life-preserver, and thrown overboard.

Almost immediately after, she said, the life preserver was picked up by a man in a small motor-launch let down from a steam yacht. The launch quickly returned to the yacht, was taken up, and the yacht made off in the darkness.

No life belt was missing from the *Monarchic* and even if suspicion could be entertained against any "small, fair man" (which was not the case, apparently), there was no justification for a search. Therefore, although a good many people believed in the seeress's vision, it proved nothing, and the sensational affair remained as deep a mystery as ever when the *Monarchic* docked.

"The Countess de Santiago was the woman who looked in the crystal!" Annesley said to herself. She wondered why, if Knight had been vexed with the Countess for speaking of their friendship and of the *Monarchic*, as he had once seemed to be, he should refer to it before these strangers.

She looked down the table, past the other faces to his face, and the thought that came to her mind was, how simple and almost meaningless the rest were compared to his. Among the fourteen guests—seven women and seven men—though some had charm or distinction, his face alone was complex, mysterious, and baffling.

Yet she loved it. Now, more than ever, she loved and admired it!

The dinner ended with a discussion between Knight and Constance as to how the Countess de Santiago could be induced to pay a visit to Valley House, despite the fact that she had never met Lord and Lady Annesley-Seton. Like most women who had lived in Spanish countries, the Countess was rather a "stickler for etiquette," her friend Nelson Smith announced. Besides, her experience as an "amateur clairvoyante" made her quick to resent anything which had the air of patronage. One must go delicately to work to think out a scheme, if Lady Annesley-Seton were really in "dead earnest" about wanting her to come.

At this point Knight reflected for a minute, while everyone hung upon his silence; and at last he had an inspiration:

"I'll tell you what we can do!" he exclaimed. "My wife and I—you're willing, aren't you, Anita?—can ask her to stay over this weekend with us. I think she'll come if she isn't engaged; and we can invite you to meet her at dinner."

"Oh, you must invite us *all!*" pleaded a pretty woman sitting next to Knight.

"All of you who care to come, certainly," he agreed. "Won't we, Anita?"

"Oh, of course. It will be splendid if everybody will dine with us!" Annesley backed him up with one of the girlish blushes that made her seem so young and ingenuously attractive. "We can—send a telegram to the Countess."

She did her best to speak enthusiastically, and succeeded. No one save Knight and Constance guessed it was an effort.

Knight saw, and was grateful. Constance saw also, and smiled to herself at what she fancied was the girl's jealousy of an old friend of the new husband—an old friend who was "one of the most beautiful women" the girl had seen. Annesley's hesitation inclined Constance to be more interested than ever in the Countess de Santiago.

CHAPTER XII.
THE CRYSTAL

Motoring back from Valley House to the Knowle Hotel, Annesley was asking herself whether she might dare refer to the *Monarchic*, and mention the story she had read In the *Morning Post*. She burned to do so, yet stopped each time a question pressed to her lips, remembering Knight's eyes as he had looked at the Countess in the Savoy restaurant the day before the wedding.

Perhaps the wish would have conquered if some imp had not whispered, "What about that purple envelope, addressed in a woman's handwriting? Maybe it was from *her*, hinting to see him again, and that is what has put this plan into his head. Perhaps he brought up the subject of the Countess on purpose to make them invite her here!"

This thought caused the Countess de Santiago to seem a powerful person, with an influence over Knight, though he had appeared not to care for her. Could it be that he wanted an excuse to have her near him? The suggestion closed Annesley's mouth by making her afraid that she was turning into a suspicious creature, like jealous brides she had read about. She determined to be silent as a self-punishment, and firmly steered the *Monarchic* into a backwater of her thoughts, while Knight talked of the Valley House party and their credulous superstition.

"Every man Jack and every woman Jill of the lot believe in that crystal and clairvoyant nonsense!" he laughed. "I mentioned it for fun, but I went on simply to 'pull their legs.' I hope you don't mind having the Countess down, do you, child? Of course, I made it out to be a favour that so wonderful a being should consent to come at call. But between us, Anita, the poor woman will fall over herself with joy. She's a restless, lonely creature, who has drifted about the world without stopping anywhere long enough to make friends, and I have a notion that her heart's desire is to 'get into society' in England. This will give her a chance, because these good ladies and gentlemen who are dying to see what she's like, and persuade her to tell their pasts and futures, are at the top of the tree. It's a cheap way for us to make her happy—and we can afford it."

"Don't you believe she really is clairvoyant, and sees things in her crystal?" Annesley ventured.

It was then that Knight made her heart beat by answering with a question. "Didn't you read in the newspapers about the queer thing that happened on board the *Monarchic*?"

"Ye-es, I *did* read it," the girl said, in so stifled a voice that the reply became a confession.

"Why didn't you tell me so?"

"Because—the day I heard you were on the *Monarchic*, I couldn't remember what I'd read. It was vague in my mind——"

"No other reason?"

"Only that—that—I fancied——"

"You fancied I didn't like to talk about the *Monarchic*?"

"Well, when the Countess spoke of it, you looked—cross."

"I was cross. But only with the *way* she spoke—as if she and I had come over together because we were pals. That's all. Though I've every cause to hate the memory of that trip! When did you remember what you had read in the newspapers?"

"Only this evening."

"I thought so! At dinner. I saw a look come over your face."

"I didn't know you noticed me."

"I'm always noticing you. And I was proud of you to-night. Well! You remembered——"

"About a man on board being robbed, and a lady—an 'amateur clairvoyante,' seeing things in a crystal. I thought it must have been the Countess de Santiago."

"It was, though her name was kept out of the papers by her request. She's sensitive about the clairvoyance stuff: afraid people may consider her a professional, and look down on her from patronizing social heights. Of course, I suppose it's nonsense about seeing things in a glass ball, but I believe she *does* contrive to take it seriously, for she seems in earnest. She did tell people on board ship things about themselves—true things, they said; and they ought to know!

"As for the jewel affair," he added, "nobody could be sure if there was anything in her 'visions', but people thought them extraordinary—even the captain, a hard-headed old chap. You see, a yacht had been sighted the evening before the robbery while the passengers were at dinner. It might have kept near, with lights out, for the *Monarchic* is one of the huge, slow-going giants, and the yacht might have been a regular little greyhound. It seems she didn't answer signals. The captain hadn't thought much of that, because there was a slight fog and she could have missed them. But it came back to him afterward, and seemed to bear out the Countess's rigmarole.

"Besides, there was the finding of the patent lock, where she told the man Jedfield he ought to look for it."

"I don't remember that in the paper."

"It was in several, if not all. She 'saw' the missing lock—a thing that goes over a bolt and prevents it sliding back—in one of the lifeboats upon the boat-deck, caught in the canvas covering. Well, it was there! And there could be no suspicion of her putting the thing where it was found, so as to make herself seem a true prophetess. She couldn't have got to the place.

"*That's* why people were so impressed with the rest of the visions. We're all inclined to be superstitious. Even I was interested. Though I don't pin my faith in such things, I asked her to look into the crystal, and see if she could tell what had become of my gold repeater, which disappeared the same night."

"Oh!" exclaimed Annesley. "So *you* had something stolen?"

"It looked like it. Anyhow, the watch went. And the Countess lost a ring during the trip—a valuable one, I believe. She couldn't 'see' anything for herself, but she got a glimpse of my repeater in the pocket of a red waistcoat. Nobody on board confessed to a red waistcoat. And in the searching of passengers' luggage—which I should have proposed myself if I hadn't been among the robbed—nothing of the sort materialized.

"However, that proved nothing. Jedfield's pearls and other trinkets must have been somewhere on board, in someone's possession, if the yacht vision wasn't true. Yet the strictest search gave no sign of them.

It was a miracle how they were disposed of, unless they *were* thrown overboard and picked up by someone in the plot, as the Countess said."

"Is that why you hate to think of the trip—because you lost your watch?" Annesley asked.

"Yes. Just that. It wasn't so much the loss of the watch—though it was a present and I valued it—as because it made me feel such a fool. I left the repeater under my pillow when I got up in the middle of the night to go on deck, thinking I heard a cry. I couldn't have heard one, for nobody was there. And next morning, when I wanted to look at the time, my watch was equally invisible. Then there was the business of the passengers being searched, and the everlasting talk about the whole business. One got sick and tired of it. I got tired of the Countess and her crystal, too: but the effect is passing away now. I expect I can stand her if you can."

Annesley said that she would be interested. She refrained from adding that she did not intend to make use of the seeress's gift for her own benefit.

The Countess de Santiago wired her acceptance of the invitation, and appeared at the Knowle Hotel on Saturday with a maid and a good deal of luggage. Annesley had secretly feared that the effect of the beautiful lady on the guests of the hotel would be overpowering, and had pictured her, brilliantly coloured and exquisitely dressed, breaking like a sunburst upon the dining room at luncheon time.

But she had underrated the Countess's cleverness and sense of propriety. The lady arrived in a neat, tailor-made travelling dress of russet-brown tweed which, with a plain toque of brown velvet and fur, cooled the ruddy flame of her hair. It seemed to Annesley also that her lips were less red than before; and though she was as remarkable as ever for her beauty, she was not to be remarked for meretriciousness.

She was pleasanter in manner, too, as well as in appearance; and Annesley's heart—which had difficulty in hardening itself for long—was touched by the Countess's thanks for the invitation.

"You are so happy and wrapped up in each other, I didn't expect you to give a thought to me," the beautiful woman said. "You don't know what it means to be asked down here, after so many lonely days in town, and to find that you and Don are going to give me some new friends."

This note, which Knight also had struck in explaining the Countess's "heart's desire," was the right note to enlist Annesley's sympathy. One might have thought that both had guessed this.

Annesley and Knight gave their dinner party in a private room adjoining their own sitting room, and connecting also with another smaller room which they had had fitted up for a special purpose. This purpose was to enshrine the seeress and her crystal.

As Knight had said, she seemed to take her clairvoyant power seriously, and insisted that she could do herself justice only in a room arranged in a certain way. In the afternoon she directed that the furniture should be removed with the exception of one small table and two chairs. Even the pictures had to be taken down, and under the Countess's supervision purple velvet draperies had to be put up, covering the walls and window. These draperies she had brought with her, and they had curtain rings sewn on at the upper edge, which could be attached to picture hooks or nails.

From the same trunk came also a white silk table-cover embroidered in gold with figures representing the signs of the zodiac. There were in addition three purple velvet cushions: two for the chairs and one—the Countess explained—for the table, to "make an arm rest." By her further desire a large number of hot-house lilies in pots were sent for, and ranged on the floor round the walls.

As for the Turkish carpet of banal reds, blues, and greens, it had to be concealed under rugs of black fur which, luckily, the hotel possessed in plenty. It was all very mysterious and exciting, and Annesley could imagine the effective background these contrivances would give the shining figure of the Countess.

When, later on, she saw her guest dressed for dinner, the girl realized even more vividly the genius of the artist who had planned the picture. For the Countess de Santiago wore a clinging gown made in Greek fashion, of a supple white material shot with interwoven silver threads. She wore her copper-red hair in a classic knot with a wreath of emerald laurel leaves.

She would gleam like a moonlit statue in her lily-perfumed, purple shrine, Annesley thought, and was not surprised that the lady should achieve an instant success with the county folk who had begged for an invitation to meet her.

The Countess de Santiago did not seem to mind answering questions about her powers, which everyone asked across the dinner-table. She said that since her seventh birthday she had been able, under certain circumstances, to see hidden things in people's lives, and future events.

Her first experience, as a child, was being shut up in a darkened room, and looking into a mirror, where figures and scenes appeared, like waking dreams. She had been frightened, and screamed to be let out. Her mother had taken pity and released her, saying that after all it was what "might be expected from the seventh child of a seventh child, born on All Saints' Eve."

The Nelson Smiths' guests listened breathlessly to every word, and were enchanted when she promised to give each man and woman a short "sitting" with her crystal after dinner.

Nothing was said about the purple room, so that the surprise could not help being impressive.

It was a delightful dinner, well thought out between the host and head-waiter, but no one wished to linger over it. Never had "bridge fiends" been so eager to "get to work" as these people were to take their turn with the Countess and her crystal. At Lady Annesley-Seton's suggestion they drew lots for these turns, and Constance herself drew the first chance. She and the gleaming figure of the Countess went out together, and ten or twelve minutes later she returned alone.

Everyone stared eagerly to see if she looked excited, and it took no stretch of imagination to find her face flushed and her eyes dilated.

"Well? Has she told you anything wonderful?" A clamour of voices joined in the question.

"Yes, she has," replied Constance. "She's simply *uncanny*! She could pick up a fortune in London in one season, if she were a professional. She has told me in what sort of place the heirlooms are now, but that we shall never see them again."

So saying, Lady Annesley-Seton plumped down on a sofa beside her hostess, as the next person hurried off to plunge into the mysteries. "I feel quite weak in the knees," Constance whispered to Annesley. "Has she told you anything?"

"No," said the girl "I don't—want to know things."

She might have added: "Things told by *her*." But she did not say this.

Constance shivered. "The woman frightened me with what she *knew*. I mean, not about our robbery—that's a trifle—but about the past. That crystal of hers seems to be—a sort of *Town Topics*. But I must say she didn't foretell any horrors for the future—not for me personally. If she goes on as she's begun she can do what she likes with us all. Dear little Anne, you must ask her often to your house when you're 'finding your feet'—and I'm helping you—in London. I prophesy that she'll prove an attraction. Why, it would pay to have a room fitted up for her in purple and black, with relays of fresh lilies."

Annesley smiled. But she made up her mind that, if a room *were* done in purple and black with relays of lilies anywhere for the Countess de Santiago, it would not be in her house. Unless, of course, Knight begged it of her as a favour.

And even then—but somehow she didn't believe, despite certain appearances, that Knight was anxious to have his old friend near him. He had the air of one who was paying a debt; and she remembered how he had said, on the day of their wedding: "We will find a time to pay back the favours they've done us."

This visit and dinner and introduction to society was perhaps his way of paying the Countess. Only—was it payment in full, or an instalment? Annesley wondered.

Vaguely she wondered also what had become of Dr. Torrance and the Marchese di Morello. Would the next payment be for them, and what form would it take?

She was far from guessing.

There was no anti-climax that night in the success of the Countess with her "clients." They were deeply impressed, and even startled. Not one woman said to herself that she had been tricked into giving the seeress a "lead." There was nothing in the past hidden from that crystal and the dark eyes which gazed into it! As for the future, her predictions were remarkable; and she must have given people flattering accounts of their characters, as everyone thought the analysis correct.

What a pity, the women whispered, that such an astonishing person was not a professional, who could be paid in cash! As it was, she would expect to be rewarded with invitations: and though she was presentable, "You *know*, my dear, she's frightfully pretty, the red-haired sort, that's the most dangerous—not a bit safe to have about one's *men*. Still—no price is too high. We shall all be fighting for her—or over her."

And before the evening had come to an end the Countess de Santiago had had several invitations for town and country houses. To be sure, they were rather informal. But the beautiful lady knew when to be lenient, and so she accepted them all.

"She told me that our stolen things are hidden away for ever, and that we'll be robbed again," Connie said to her husband on the way back to Valley House.

"She told me the same," said Dick. "And I hope to goodness we may be. We've done jolly well out of that last affair!"

"Yes," his wife agreed. "The only thing I don't like about it is the *mystery*. It makes me feel as if something might be hanging over one's head."

"Over the trustees' heads!" laughed Lord Annesley-Seton. "I wish the other night could be what the Countess called the 'first of a series.'"

"The first of a series!" Constance repeated. "What a queer expression! What was she talking about?"

"She was—looking in her crystal," answered Dick, slowly, as if something he had seen rose again before his eyes.

Constance was pricked with curiosity. "You might tell me what the woman said!" she exclaimed.

"You haven't told me what message she had for you."

"I've just said that she prophesied we should be robbed again."

"That's only one thing. What about the rest?"

"Oh! A lot of stuff which wouldn't interest *you*!"

"You can keep your secret. And I'll keep mine," remarked Dick Annesley-Seton, aggravatingly. "Anyhow, for the present. We'll see how it works out."

"See how *what* works out?" his wife echoed.

"The series."

CHAPTER XIII.
THE SERIES GOES ON

After all, Annesley had not written to her friends, Archdeacon Smith and his wife, on leaving Mrs. Ellsworth's, to tell the surprising news of her engagement. She had asked Mr. Ruthven Smith not to speak of it to his cousins, because she would prefer to write. But then—the putting of the news on paper in a way not to offend them, after their kindness in the past, had been difficult.

Besides, there had been little time to think out the difficulties, and find a way of surmounting them. There had been only one whole day before the wedding, and that day she had spent with Knight, buying her trousseau. It had been a wonderful day, never to be forgotten, but its end had found her tired; and when Knight had said "good-bye" and left her, she had not been equal to composing a letter.

Nevertheless, she had tried, for it had seemed dreadful to marry and go away from London without letting her only friends know what had happened, what she was doing, and why she had not invited them to her wedding.

Ah, *why*? In explaining that she confronted the great obstacle. She had not known how to exonerate herself without hurting their feelings, or—telling a lie.

The girl hated lying. She could not remember that in her life she had ever spoken or written a lie in so many words, though, like most people who are not saints, she had prevaricated a little occasionally to save herself or others from some unpleasantness.

In this case no innocent prevarication would serve. Even if she had been willing to lie, she could think of no excuse which would seem plausible. Tired as she had been that last night as Annesley Grayle, and throbbing as she was with excitement at the thought of the new life before her, she did begin a letter.

It was a feeble effort. She tore it up and essayed another. The second was worse than the first, and the third was scarcely an improvement.

Discouraged, and so nerve-racked that she was on the point of tears, the girl put off the attempt. But days passed, and when no inspiration came, and she was still haunted by the thought of a duty undone, she compromised by telegraphing from Devonshire. Her message ran:

> Dear Friends—
>
> I beg you to forgive me for seeming neglect, but it was not really that. I am married to a man I love. It had to be sudden. I could not let you know in time, though I wanted to. I shall not be quite happy till I've seen you and introduced my husband. Say to your cousin he may explain as far as he can. When we meet will tell you more. Coming back to London in fortnight to take house in Portman Square and settle down. Love and gratitude always. My new name is same as yours.
>
> Annesley Smith.

To this she added her address in Devonshire, feeling sure that, unless the Archdeacon and his wife were hopelessly offended by her neglect and horrified at Ruthven Smith's story, they would write.

She cared for them very much, and it would always be a grief, she thought, that she and Knight had not been married by her old friend. Every night she prayed for a letter, waking with the hope that the postman might bring one: and five days after the sending of her telegram her heart leaped at sight of a fat envelope addressed in Mrs. Smith's familiar handwriting.

They forgave her! That was the principal thing. And they rejoiced in her happiness. All explanations—if "dear Annesley wished to make any"—could wait until they met. The kind woman wrote:

> Cousin James Ruthven Smith was loyal to his promise, and gave us no hint of your news. We did not, of course, know of the promise till after your telegram came, and we showed it to him. Then he confessed that he was in your secret; that he had been witness of a scene in which poor Mrs. Ellsworth made herself more than usually unpleasant; and that you had asked him

to let you tell us the glad tidings of your engagement and hasty wedding.

I say "poor Mrs. Ellsworth" because it seems she has been ill since you left, and has had other misfortunes. The illness is not serious, and I imagine, now I have heard fuller details of her treatment of you, that it is merely a liver and nerve attack, the result of temper. If she had not been confined to bed, and very sorry for herself, I am sure nothing could have prevented her from writing to us a garbled account of the quarrel and your departure.

As it turned out, I hear she rang up the household after you went that night, had hysterics, and sent a servant flying for the doctor. He—a most inferior person, according to Cousin James—having a sister who is a trained nurse, put *her* in charge of the patient at once, where she has remained since. In consequence of the nurse's tyrannical ways, the servants gave a day's notice and left in a body.

Three temporary ones were got in as soon as possible from some agency; and last night (four days, I believe, after they were installed) a burglary was committed in the house.

Only fancy, *poor Ruthven*! He was afraid to stay even with us in our quiet house, when he came to London, because once, years ago, we were robbed! You know how reticent he is about his affairs, and how he never says anything concerning business. One might think that to *us* he would show some of the beautiful jewels he is supposed to buy for the Van Vrecks.

But no, he never mentions them. We should not have known why he came to England this time, after a shorter interval than usual, or that he had valuables in his possession, if it had not been for this burglary. As he was obliged to talk to the police, and describe to them what had been stolen from him (I forgot to mention that he as well as Mrs. Ellsworth was robbed, but you would have guessed that, from my beginning, even if you haven't read the morning papers before taking up my letter), there was no reason why, for once, he should not speak freely to us.

He has been lunching here and has just gone, as I write, but will transfer himself later to our house, as it has now become unbearable for him at Mrs. Ellsworth's. I fancy *that* arrangement has been brought to an end! Your presence in the *ménage* was the sole alleviation.

James, it appears, came to London on an unexpected mission, differing from his ordinary trips. You may remember seeing in the papers some weeks ago that an agent of the Van Vreck firm was robbed on shipboard of a lot of pearls and things he was bringing to show an important client in England—some Indian potentate. James tells us that *he* procured the finest of the collection for the Van Vrecks, and as he is a great expert, and can recognize jewels he has once seen, even when disguised or cut up, or in different settings, he was asked to go to London to help the police find and identify some of the lost valuables.

Also, he was instructed to buy more pearls, to be sold to the Indian customer, instead of those stolen from the agent on shipboard. James had not found any of the lost things; but he *had* bought some pearls the day before the burglary at Mrs. Ellsworth's.

Wasn't it *too* unlucky? I have tried to give the poor fellow a little consolation by reminding him how fortunate it is he hadn't bought *more,* and that the loss will be the Van Vrecks' or that of some insurance company, not *his* personally. But he cannot be comforted. He says that his not having ten thousand pounds' worth of pearls doesn't console him for being robbed of *eight* thousand pounds' worth.

James has little hope that the thieves will be found, for he feels that the Van Vrecks are in for a run of bad luck, after the good fortune of many years. They have lost the head of the firm—"the great Paul," as James calls him—who has definitely retired, and occupies himself so exclusively with his collection that he takes no interest in the business.

Then there was the robbery on the ship, which, in James's opinion, must have been the work of a masterly combination. And now another theft! The poor fellow has *quite* lost his nerve, which, as you know, has for years not been that of a young man. His deafness, no doubt, partly accounts for the timidity with which he has been afflicted since the first (and only other) time he was robbed. And now he blames it for what happened last night.

He's trained himself to be a light sleeper, and if he could hear as well as other people, he thinks the thief would have waked him coming into his room. Once in, the wretch must have drugged him, because the pearls were in a parcel under his pillow. But how the man—or men—got into the house is a mystery, unless one of the new servants was an accomplice.

Nothing was broken open. In the morning every door and window was as usual. Of course the servants are under suspicion; but they seem stupid, ordinary people, according to James.

As for Mrs. Ellsworth, he says she is making a fuss over the wretched bits of jewellery she lost, things of no importance. She, too, slept through the affair, and knew what had happened only when she waked to see a safe she has in the wall of her bedroom wide open.

It seems that in place of her jewel box and some money she kept there was an *insulting* note, announcing that for the first time something belonging to her would be used for a good purpose. To James this is the one bright spot in the darkness.

When Annesley had read this long letter with its many italics, she passed it to Knight who, in exchange, handed her a London newspaper with a page folded so as to give prominence to a certain column. It was an account of the burglary at Mrs. Ellsworth's house, which he had been reading.

Generous with money as "Nelson Smith" was, he was not a man who would allow himself to be "done," and in some ways the Annesley-Setons were disappointed in the bargain they arrived at with him. He appeared delighted with the chance of getting their London house, and of having them come to stay, in order to introduce his wife and himself to the brightest, most "particular" stars in the galaxy of their friends.

Yet, when it came to making definite terms he seemed to take it for granted that, as the Annesley-Setons would be living in the house as guests, they would not only be willing, but anxious, to accept a low price.

This had not been their intention. On the contrary, they had meant their visit and social offices to be a great, extra favour, which ought to raise rather than lower the rent. In some mysterious way, however, without appearing to bargain or haggle, Nelson Smith, the young millionaire from America, made his bride's relatives understand that he was prepared to pay so much, and no more. That they could take him on his own terms—or let him go.

Terrified, therefore, lest he and his money should slip out of their hands, they snapped at his carelessly made offer without venturing an objection. And they realized at the same time in a way equally mysterious, and to their own surprise, that not they but Mr. and Mrs. Nelson Smith would be master and mistress of the house in Portman Square. If there were ever a clash between wills, Nelson Smith's would prevail over theirs.

How this impression was conveyed to their intelligence they could hardly have explained even to each other. The man was so pleasant, so careless of finances or conventionalities, that not one word or look could be treasured up against him.

"The fellow's a genius!" Annesley-Seton said to Constance, when they were talking over the latest phase of the game. And they respected him.

Lady Annesley-Seton wished to bring to town the servants, including a wonderful butler, who had been transferred for economy's sake to Valley House. This proposal, however, Nelson Smith dismissed with a few good-natured words. He had his eye upon a butler whose brother was a chauffeur.

"Besides, it wouldn't be fair to Anita," he explained. "Your servants would scorn to take orders from her, and I want her to learn the dignity of a married woman with responsibilities of her own. That's the first step toward being the perfect hostess. She's the sweetest girl in the world, but she's timid and distrustful of herself. I want her to know her own worth, and then it won't be long before everyone around her knows it."

There was no answer to this except acquiescence, which Dick and Constance were obliged to give. They did give it: the more readily because they were inclined to suspect a hidden hint, a pill between layers of jam.

If the girl had been transferred from the earth to Mars, the new conditions of life could scarcely have been more different from the old than was life in Portman Square married to Nelson Smith, from the treadmill as Mrs. Ellsworth's slave-companion. What the Portman Square experiences of the bride would have been if Knight had allowed the Annesley-Setons to begin by ruling it would be dangerous to say. But he had taken his stand; and without guessing that she owed her freedom of action to her husband's strength of will, she revelled in it with a joy so intense that it came close to pain. Sometimes, if he were within reach, she ran to find Knight, and hugged him almost fiercely, with a passion that surprised herself.

"I'm so happy; that's all," she would explain, if he asked "What has happened?" "My soul was buried. You've brought it back to life."

When she said such things Knight smiled, and seemed glad. He would hold her to him for a minute, or kiss her hand, like an humble squire with a princess. But now and then he looked at her with a wistfulness that was like a question she could not hear because she was deaf. She never got any satisfaction, though, if she asked what the look meant.

"Oh, I don't know. I was only thinking of you," he would answer, or some other words of lover-language.

The Annesley-Setons' first move on the social chessboard was to make use of a pawn or two in the shape of "society reporters."

They knew a few men and women of good birth and no money who lived by writing anonymously for the newspapers. These people were delighted to get material for a paragraph, or photographs for their editors. Connie took her new cousin to the woman photographer who was the success of the moment; and, as she said to Knight, "the rest managed itself."

Meanwhile, an application was made to the Lord Chamberlain for Mrs. Nelson Smith's presentation by her cousin Lady Annesley-Seton at the first Court of the season. It was granted, and the bride in white and silver made her bow to their majesties. As for Knight, he laughingly refused Dick's good offices.

"No levees for me!" he said. "I've lived too long in America, and roughed it in too many queer places, to take myself seriously in knee-breeches. Besides, they have to know about your ancestors back to the Dark Ages, don't they, or else they 'cancel' you? My father was a good man, and a gentleman, but who *his* father was I couldn't tell to save my head. My mother was by way of being a swell; but she was a foreigner, so I can't make use of any of her 'quarterings,' even if I could count them."

Annesley was presented in February, and had by that time been settled in Portman Square long enough to have met many of her cousins' friends. After the Court, which launched her in society, she and Knight (with a list supplied by Connie) gave a dinner-dance. The Countess de Santiago was not asked; but soon afterward there was a luncheon entirely for women, in American fashion, at which the Countess was present.

When luncheon was over, she gave a short lecture on "the Science of Palmistry" and "the Cultivation of Clairvoyant Powers." Then there was tea; and the Countess allowed herself to be consulted by the guests—the dozen most important women of Connie's acquaintance.

Annesley, though she was not able to like the Countess, was pleased with the praise lavished upon her both for her looks and her accomplishments that afternoon. She had guessed, from the beautiful woman's constrained manner when they met at a shop the day after the dinner-dance, that she was hurt because she had not been invited: though why she should expect to be asked to every entertainment which the Nelson Smiths gave, Annesley could not see.

Vaguely distressed, however, by the flash in the handsome eyes, and the curt "How do you do?" the girl appealed to Knight.

"Ought we to have had the Countess de Santiago last evening?" she asked, perching on his knee in the room at the back of the house which he had annexed as a "den."

"Certainly not," he reassured her, promptly. "All the people were howling swells. The Annesley-Setons had skimmed the topmost layer of the cream for our benefit, and the Countess would have been 'out' of it in such a set, unless she'd been telling fortunes. You can ask her when you've a crowd of women. She'll amuse them, and gather glory for herself. But I'm not going to have her encouraged to think we belong to her. We've set the woman on her feet by what we've done. Now let her learn to stand alone."

The ladies' luncheon was a direct consequence of this speech; but complete as was the Countess's success, Annesley felt that she was not satisfied: that it would take more than a luncheon party of which she was the heroine to content the Countess, now that Nelson Smith and his bride had a house and a circle in London.

Occasionally, when she was giving an "At Home," or a dinner, Annesley consulted Knight. "Shall we ask the Countess?" was her query, and the first time she did this he answered with another question: "Do you want her for your own pleasure? Do you like her better than you did?"

Annesley had to say "no" to this catechizing, whereupon Knight briefly disposed of the subject. "That settles it. We won't have her."

And so, during the next few weeks, the Countess de Santiago (who had moved from the Savoy Hotel into a charming, furnished flat in Cadogan Gardens) came to Portman Square only for one luncheon and two or three receptions.

By this time, however, she had made friends of her own, and if she had cared to accept a professional status she might have raked in a small fortune from her séances. She would not take money, however, preferring social recognition; but gifts were pressed upon her by those who, though grateful and admiring, did not care for the obligation to admit the Countess into their intimacy.

She took the rings and bracelets and pendants, and flowers and fruit, and bon-bons and books, because they were given in such a way that it would have been ungracious to refuse. But the givers were the very women whose bosom friend she would have liked to seem, in the sight of the world: a duchess, a countess, or a woman distinguished above her sisters for some reason.

She worked to gain favour, and when she had any personal triumph without direct aid from Portman Square, she put on an air of superiority over Annesley when they met. If she suffered a gentle snub, she hid the smart, but secretly brooded, blaming Mrs. Nelson Smith because she was asked to their house only for big parties, or when she was wanted to amuse their friends.

She blamed Nelson, too; but, womanlike, blamed Annesley more. Sometimes she determined to put out a claw and draw blood from both, but changed her mind, remembering that to do them harm she must harm herself.

Once it occurred to her to form a separate, secret alliance with Constance Annesley-Seton. There were reasons why that might have suited her, and she began one day to feel her ground when Connie had telephoned, and had come to her flat for advice from the crystal. She had "seen things" which she thought Lady Annesley-Seton would like her to see, and when the séance was ended in a friendly talk, the Countess de Santiago begged Constance to call her Madalena. "You are my *first* real friend in England!" she said.

"Except my cousin Anne," Connie amended, with a sharp glance from the green-gray eyes to see whether "Madalena" were "working up to anything."

"Oh, I can't count *her*!" said the Countess. "She doesn't like me. She wouldn't have me come near her if it weren't for her husband. I am quick to feel things. You, I believe, really *do* like me a little, so I can speak freely to you. And you *know* you can to me."

But Constance, in the slang of her girlhood days, "wasn't taking any." She was afraid that Madalena was trying to draw her into finding fault with her host and hostess, in order to repeat what she said, with embroideries, to Nelson Smith or Annesley. She was not a woman to be caught by the subtleties of another; and in dread of compromising herself did the Countess de Santiago an injustice. If she had ventured any disparaging remarks of "Cousin Anne," they would not have been repeated.

The season began early and brilliantly that year, for the weather was springlike, even in February; and people were ready to enjoy everything. The one blot on the general brightness was a series of robberies. Something happened on an average of every ten or twelve days, and always in an unexpected quarter, where the police were not looking.

Among the first to suffer were Mr. and Mrs. Nelson Smith. The Portman Square house was broken into, the thief entering a window of the "den" on the ground floor, and making a clean sweep of all the jewellery Knight and Annesley owned except her engagement ring, the string of pearls which had been her lover's wedding gift, and the wonderful blue diamond on its thin gold chain. These things she wore by night as well as day; but a gold-chain bag, a magnificent double rope of pearls, a diamond dog-collar, several rings, brooches, and bangles which Knight had given her since their marriage, all went.

His pearl studs, his watch (a present out of Annesley's allowance, hoarded for the purpose), and a collection of jewelled scarf-pins shared the fate of his wife's treasures.

Unfortunately, a great deal of the Annesley-Seton family silver went at the same time, regretted by Knight far beyond his own losses. Dick was inclined to be solemn over such a haul, but Constance laughed.

"Who cares?" she said. "We've no children, and for my part I'm as pleased as Punch that your horrid old third cousins will come into less when we're swept off the board. Meanwhile, we get the insurance money for 'loss of use' again. It's simply splendid. And that dear Nelson Smith insists on buying the best Sheffield plate to replace what's gone. It's handsomer than the real!"

Neither she nor Dick lost any jewellery, though they possessed a little with which they had not had the courage to part. And this seemed mysterious to Constance. She wondered over it: and remembering how the Countess de Santiago had prophesied another robbery for them, telephoned to ask if she'd be "a darling, and look again in her crystal."

Madalena telephoned back: "I'll expect you this afternoon at four o'clock."

CHAPTER XIV.
THE TEST

Madalena had meant to go out that afternoon, but she changed her mind and stopped at home. "I know what you've come for," she said, as she kept Connie's hand in hers. It was an effective way she had, as if contact with a person helped her to read the condition of that person's mind.

"Do you really?" exclaimed Constance. "Why, I—but you mean you've guessed what has hap——"

"It's not guessing, it's *seeing*," answered the Countess. "I'm in one of my psychic moods to-day. A prophecy of mine has come true?"

"No-o—yes. Well, in a way you're right. In a way you're wrong. What is it you see?"

"I see that you've lost something—probably last night. This morning I waked with the impression. I wasn't surprised when you telephoned. Now, let me go on holding your hand, and *think*. I'll shut my eyes. I don't need my room and the crystal. Yes! The impression grows clearer. You *have* lost something. But it is not a thing to care about. You're glad it's gone."

"You *are* extraordinary!" Constance wondered aloud. "Can you see what I lost—and whether it was Dick's or mine, or both?"

"His," said Madalena, after shutting her eyes again. "*His*. And he does not care much, either. That seems strange. But I tell you what I *feel*."

"You are telling me the truth," Constance admitted. "Now, go on: tell what was the thing itself—and the way we lost it."

"I haven't seen that yet. I haven't tried. Perhaps I shall be able to, in the crystal; perhaps not. I don't always succeed. But—it comes to me suddenly that this thing isn't directly or entirely what brought you here?"

"Right again, O Witch!" laughed Connie. "I came to ask you to find out—you're so marvellous!-why I didn't lose *other* things, which I really *do* value."

The two women had been standing in the drawing room, Lady Annesley-Seton's hand still in the Countess's. But now, without speaking again, Madalena led her visitor into the room adjoining, which was fitted up much as the room at the Devonshire hotel had been for her first séance. The seeress gave herself, here at home, the same background of purple velvet; the floor was carpeted with black, and spread with black fur rugs; she was never without fragrant white lilies ranged in curious pots along the purple walls; but in her own house the appointments were more elaborate and impressive than the temporary fittings she carried about for use when visiting.

On her table was a cushion of cloth-of-gold, embroidered with amethysts and emeralds, the "lucky" jewels of her horoscope; and her gleaming ball of crystal lay like a bright bubble in a shallow cup of solid jet which, she told everyone, had been given her in India by the greatest astrologer in the world.

What was the name of this man, and when she had visited him in India, she did not reveal.

They sat down at the table, she and Constance Annesley-Seton, opposite each other. Madalena unveiled the crystal, which was hidden under a covering of black velvet when not in use. At first she gazed into the glittering ball in vain, and her companion watched her face anxiously. It looked marble white and expressionless as that of a statue in the light of seven wax candles grouped together in a silver candelabrum.

Suddenly, as it seemed to Constance's hypnotized stare, the statue-face "came alive." It was not the first time that Constance had seen this thrilling change. It invariably happened when the crystal began to show a picture; and so powerful was its effect on the nerves of the watcher in this silent, perfumed room, as to give an illusion that she, too, could see dimly what the seeress saw forming in those transparent depths.

"A man is there," Madalena said in a low, measured voice, as if she were talking in her sleep. "He is shutting a door. It is the front door of a house like yours. Yes, it *is* yours. There is the number over the door, and I recognize the street. It is Portman Square. He puts a latchkey in his pocket. How could he have got the key? I do not know. Perhaps I could find out, but there is no time. I must follow him.

"He is hurrying away. He carries a heavy travelling bag. A closed carriage is coming along—not a public one. It has been waiting for him I think. He gets in, and the coachman—who is in black—drives off very fast. They go through street after street! I can't be sure where. It seems to be north they are going. There's a park—Regent's Park, maybe. I don't know London well.

"The carriage is stopping—before a closed house in a quiet street. There is a little garden in front, and a high wall. The man opens the gate and walks in. The carriage drives off. The coachman must know where to go, for no word is said. Someone inside the house is waiting. He lets the man with the bag into a dark hallway. Now he shuts the door and goes into a room.

"There is a light. The first man puts the bag on a table; it is a dining table. The other man—much older—watches. The first one takes things out of the bag. Oh, a great deal of beautiful silver! I have seen it at your house. And there are other things—a string of pearls and a lot of jewellery. He pours it out of a brown handkerchief on to the table.

"But still the second man is not pleased. I think he is asking why there isn't more. The first man explains. He makes gestures. So does the other. They are quarrelling. The man who brought the bag is afraid of the older one. He apologizes. He seems to be talking about something that he will do. He goes to a mantelpiece in the room and points to a calendar. He touches a date with his forefinger."

"What date?" Lady Annesley-Seton cried out. It was forbidden to speak to the seeress in the midst of a vision, but Constance forgot in the strain of her excitement.

The Countess gave a gasp, fell back in her chair, and put her hands over her eyes. "Oh!" she stammered, as though she awoke from sleep. "How my head aches! It is all gone!"

"I'm so sorry!" Constance apologized. "It began to seem so real, I thought I was in that room with you. You are unaccountable! You couldn't know what happened. Yet you have been seeing the thief who stole our silver last night, and the Nelson Smiths' jewellery, but no jewellery of ours. That is the strange part of the affair, for I have a few things I adore—and they would have been easy to find. You didn't even know we *had* been robbed, did you?"

"No, of course not," said the Countess. "I am sorry! Was it in the papers?"

"It will be this evening and to-morrow morning! But the police must hear about this vision of yours, the vision of the man with the latchkey. It may help them."

"You must not tell the police!" Madalena said, "I have warned you all, that if you talked too much about me and my crystal, the police might hear and take notice. There are such stupid laws in England. I may be doing something against them. If you or Lord Annesley-Seton speak of me to the police I will go away, and you will never hear more of my visions—as you call them—in future. Unless you promise that you will let the police find the thieves in their own way, without dragging me in, I shall be so unnerved that my eyes will be darkened."

"Oh, I promise, if you feel so strongly about it," said Constance. "I didn't realize that it might do you harm to be mentioned to the police."

She wished very much to have Madalena go on looking in the crystal. She had been excited, carried out of herself for a few minutes, but she had not heard what she had come to hear—why she had been spared the loss of her personal treasures.

The desired promise hurriedly made, the Countess gave her attention once more to the crystal. For a time she could see nothing. The mysterious current had been severed by the diversion, and had slowly to be rewoven by the seeress's will.

"I can see only dimly," Madalena said. "It was clear before! I cannot tell you why the things you care for were left.... Something *new* is coming. It seems that this time I am looking ahead, into the future. The picture is blurred—like a badly developed photograph. The thing I see has still to materialize."

"Where?" whispered Constance, thrilled by the thought that some event on its way to her down the unknown path of futurity was casting a shadow into the crystal. "Where?"

"I see a beautiful room. There are a number of people there—men and women. You are with them, and Lord Annesley-Seton—and Nelson Smith and your cousin Anne. I know most of the faces—not all. Everyone is excited. Something has happened. They are talking it over.... Now I see the room more clearly. It is as if a light were turned on in the crystal. Oh, it is what you call the Chinese drawing room, at Valley House. I know why the room lights up, and why I see everything so much more clearly. It is because I myself am coming into the picture.

"The people want me to tell them the meaning of the thing that has happened. It seems that I know about it. I do not hesitate to answer. It must be that I have been consulting the crystal, for I seem sure of what I say to them! I point toward the door—or is it at something on the wall—or is it a person? Ah, the picture is gone from the crystal!"

"How irritating!" cried Lady Annesley-Seton, who felt that supernatural forces ought to be subject to her convenience. "Can't you make it come back if you concentrate?"

Madalena shook her head. "No, it will not come back. I am sure of that, because when the crystal clouds as if milk were pouring into it, I know that I shall never see the same picture again. Whether it is a cross current in myself or the crystal, I cannot tell; but it amounts to the same thing. I am sorry! It is useless to try any more. Shall we go to the other room and have tea?"

Constance did not persist, as she wished to do. She had to take the Countess's word that further effort would be useless, but she felt thwarted, as if the curtain had fallen by mistake in the middle of an act, and the characters on the stage had availed themselves of the chance to go home.

It was vexatious enough that Madalena had not been able to explain the mystery of last night. But this was ten times more annoying.

"Am I not to know the end of the act?" she asked as her hostess poured tea. The latter shrugged her shoulders, as if to shake off responsibility. "Ah, I cannot tell! Perhaps if— —"

She stopped, and handed her guest a cup.

"Perhaps if—*what*?"

"Oh, nothing!" Madalena tasted her own tea and put in more cream.

"Do tell me what you were going to say, *dear* Countess, unless you want me to die of curiosity."

"I should be sorry to have you do that!" smiled Madalena. "But if I said what I was going to say, you might misunderstand. You might think—I was asking for an invitation."

Instantly Constance's mind unveiled the other's meaning. There was to be an Easter party at Valley House—a very smart party. The Countess de Santiago wished to be a member of it. Lady Annesley-Seton, shrewd as she was, had a vein of superstition running through her nature, and, though one side of that nature said that the scene with the crystal had been arranged for this end, the other side held its belief in the vision.

"You mean," she said, "that if you should be at Valley House when the *thing* happens, and we are puzzled and upset about it, you might be able to help?"

"The fancy passed through my head. It was the picture in the crystal suggested it," Madalena explained. "Do have an éclair!" Face and voice expressed indifference; but Constance knew that the other had set her heart on being at Valley House for Easter; and there was really no visible reason why she shouldn't be there.

People liked her well enough: she was never a bore.

"Well, you must be 'in at the death,' with the rest of us," Lady Annesley-Seton assured her. "Of course, though it's my house, this Easter party is practically the Nelson Smiths' affair. You know what poverty-stricken wretches *we* are! They are paying all expenses, and taking the servants, so I suppose I am bound to go through the form of consulting Anne before I ask even *you*. Still——"

Madalena's eyes flamed. "Consult your cousin's husband!" she said. "It is only *he* who counts. As a favour to me, speak to him."

Constance smiled at the other over her teacup, with a narrowed gaze. "Why shouldn't I speak to them together?"

"Because I want to know what to think. If *he* says no, it will be a test."

"Very well, so be it!" said Constance, making light of what she knew was somehow serious. "I'll tackle Nelson alone without Anne."

"That is all I want. And if I am asked to be of your party, I think—I can't tell why, but I feel it strongly—that everybody may have some reason for being glad."

It seemed unlikely there would be a chance for a talk that evening, as Nelson Smith was dining at one of the clubs he had joined. The other three members of the household were to have a hasty dinner and go to the first performance of a new play—a play in which Knight was not interested. Afterward they expected to sup at the Savoy with the friend who had asked them to her box at the theatre; but the box was empty save for themselves.

While they wondered, a messenger brought a note of regret. Sudden illness had kept their would-be hostess in her room.

Without her, the supper was considered not worth while. The play had run late, and the trio voted for home and bed.

"If Nelson has come, I'll try and have a word with him to-night, after all," thought Constance, "provided I can keep my promise by getting Anne out of the way. Then I can phone to Madalena early in the morning, yes or no, and put her out of her suspense. No such luck, though, as that he will have got back from his club!"

He had got back, however. The entrance hall was in twilight when Dick Annesley-Seton let them into the house with his latchkey, for all the electric lights save one were turned off. That one was shaded with red silk, and in the ruddy glow it was easy to see the line of light under the door of the "den."

Annesley noticed it, but made no comment. Knight never asked her to join him in the den, but alluded to it as an untidy place, a mere work room which he kept littered with papers; and only the new butler, Charrington, was allowed to straighten its disorder.

This, of course, was not butler's business, but Knight said the footmen were stupid, and Charrington had been persuaded or bribed into performing the duty. Annesley's life of suppression had made her shy of putting herself forward; and though Knight had never told her that she would be a disturbing element in the den, his silence had bolted the door for her.

Constance, however, was not so fastidious.

"Oh, look!" she said, before Dick had time to switch on another light. "Nelson's got tired of his club, and come home!"

As she spoke, almost as if she had willed it, the door opened. But it was not Knight who came out. It was the younger Charrington, the chauffeur, called "Char," to distinguish him from his solemn elder brother, the butler.

The red-haired, red-faced, black-eyed young man stopped suddenly at sight of the newcomers. He had evidently expected to find the hall untenanted. Taking up his stand before the door, he barred the way with his tall, liveried figure, and it struck Constance that he looked aggressive, as if, had he dared, he would have shut the door again, almost in her face.

"I beg your pardon, madame!" he said in so loud a voice that it was like a warning to his master that an intruder might be expected. It occurred to her also, for the first time, that his accent sounded rather American, and he had forgotten to address her as "my lady."

This was odd, for his brother was the most typical British butler imaginable, as Nelson had remarked soon after the two servants had been engaged.

She stared, surprised; but Char still kept the door until his master showed himself in the lighted aperture. Then the chauffeur, saluting courteously, stepped aside.

"Funny that he should be here!" thought Constance. She might have been malicious enough to imagine that Nelson Smith had drunk too heavily at his club, and had been helped into the house by Char, who wished to protect him until the last; but he was unmistakably his usual self: cool, and more than ordinarily alert.

"Oh, how do you do?" he exclaimed. "I heard Char say 'Madame,' and thought it was Anita at the door."

"No, she has gone upstairs," explained Lady Annesley-Seton. "So has Dick. I alone had courage to linger! I feel like Fatima with the blood-stained key, in Bluebeard's house, you are such a bear about this den—you really *are*, you know!"

"I didn't expect you three so soon," said Knight, calmly. "If I'd known you had a curiosity to see Bluebeard's Chamber, I'd have had it smartened up. As it is, I shouldn't dare let you peep. You, the mistress of the house before we took it over, would be critical of the state I delight to keep it in. Untidiness is my *one* fault!"

"I'll put off the visit till a more propitious hour," Constance reassured him, "if you'll spare me a moment in the hall. It's only a word—about Madalena. She has asked me to call her that."

"The Countess de Santiago?" Knight questioned, smiling. He closed the door of the den, and came out into the hall, turning on still another of the lights.

"Yes. I've been to see her to-day. Will you believe it, she saw the *whole* affair of last night in her crystal—and the thief, and everything!"

"Oh, indeed, did she? How intelligent."

"But she says we mustn't mention her name to the police."

"She'd be lumped with common or garden palmists and fortune-tellers, I suppose."

"Yes, that's what she fears. But she wants to be in our Devonshire house party at Easter—to save us from something."

Knight looked interested. "Save us from what?"

"She couldn't see it distinctly in the crystal."

He laughed. "She could see distinctly that she wanted to be there. Well—we hadn't thought of having her. She seemed out of the picture with the lot who are coming—the Duchess of Peebles, for instance. But we'll think it over. Why don't you ask Anita? It occurs to me that she is the one to be consulted."

Now was the moment for Madalena's test.

"The Countess wished me to speak to you alone, and let you decide. Probably because you're such an old friend. I think she feels that Anita doesn't care for her."

Knight's face hardened. "She gave you *that* impression, did she? Yet, thinking Anita *doesn't* like her—and she's nearly right—she wants to come all the same. She wants to presume on my—er—friendship to force herself on my wife.... Jove! I guess that's a little too strong. It's time we showed the fair Madalena her place, don't you think so, Lady A?"

"What, precisely, is her place?" Connie laughed.

"Well, she seems determined to push herself into the foreground. My idea is that what artists call middle distance is better suited to her

The Second Latchkey

colouring. Seriously, I resent her putting you up to appeal to me—over Anita's head. I'm not taking any!

"Please tell her, or write—or phone—or whatever you've arranged to do—that we're both sorry—say '*both*,' please—that we don't feel justified in persuading you to add her to the list of guests this time, as Valley House will be full up."

"She will be hurt," objected Constance.

"I'm inclined to think she deserves to be hurt."

"Oh, well, if you've made up your mind! But—she's a charming woman, of course.... Still, I shouldn't wonder if there's something of the tigress in her, and she could give a nasty dig."

"Let her try!" said Knight.

In the morning Constance telephoned to the flat in Cadogan Gardens. She had not long to wait for an answer to her call.

The Countess was evidently expecting to hear from her early in the day.

"He wasn't in the right mood, I'm afraid, when I spoke to him," Connie temporized. "He seemed to resent your wish to—to—as he expressed it—'get at him over Anne's head.'"

"That is what I wanted to be sure of," Madalena answered. "Now—I *know*!"

CHAPTER XV.
NELSON SMITH AT HOME

The Countess de Santiago took her defeat like a soldier. But her line both of attack and defence was of the sapping-and-mining order.

Once she had cared as deeply as it was in her to care for the man known to London as "Nelson Smith." He was of the type which calls forth intense feeling in others. Men liked him immensely or disliked him extremely. Women admired him fervently or detested him cordially. It was not possible to regard him with indifference. His personality was too magnetic to leave his neighbours cold; and as a rule it was only those whom he wished to keep at a distance who disliked him.

As for Madalena de Santiago, for a time she had enjoyed thinking herself in love. There were reasons, she knew, why she could not hope to be the man's wife, and if he had chosen a plain woman to help him on in the world she would have made no objection to his marriage.

But at first sight she had realized that Annesley Grayle, shy and unconscious of power to charm as she was, might be dangerous.

Madalena had anxiously watched the two together, and at breakfast the day before the wedding she had distrusted the light in the man's eyes as he looked at the girl. It had seemed incredible that he should be in love with a creature so pale, so formless still in character (as Annesley appeared to Madalena); that a man like "Don" should be caught by a pair of gray eyes and a softness which was only the beauty of youth.

Still, the Countess had been made to suffer; and if she could have found a way to prevent the marriage without alienating her friend, she would have seized it. But she could think of no way, except to drop a sharp reminder of what Don owed to her. The hint had been unheeded. The marriage had taken place, and Madalena had been obliged to play the part of the bride's friend and chaperon.

Afterward, to be sure, she had been paid. Her reward had come in the shape of invitations and meetings with desirable people. Nelson Smith's marriage had given her a place in the world, and at first her success consoled her. Soon, however, the pain of jealousy overcame the anodyne. She could not rest; she was forever asking herself whether Don were glad of her success for her own sake, or because it distracted her attention from him.

Was he falling in love with his wife, or was his way of looking at the girl, of speaking to the girl, only an intelligent piece of acting in the drama?

Once or twice Madalena tried being cavalier in her manner to Annesley (she dared not be actually rude); and Nelson Smith appeared not to notice; but afterward the offender was punished—by missing some invitation. This might have been taken as the proof for which she searched, could she have been sure where lay the responsibility for the slight, whether on the shoulders of Annesley or of Annesley's husband.

Madalena strove to make herself believe that the fault was the girl's. But she could not decide. Sometimes she flattered her vanity that Annesley was trying to keep her away from Don. Again, she would wrap herself in black depression as in a pall, believing that the man was seeking an excuse to put her outside the intimacy of his life.

Then she burned for revenge upon them both; yet her hands were tied.

Her fate seemed to be bound up with the fate of Nelson Smith, and evil which might threaten his career would overwhelm hers also. She spent dark moments in striving to plan some brilliant yet safe *coup* which would ruin him and Annesley, in case she should find out that he had tired of her.

At last, by much concentration, her mind developed an idea which appeared feasible. She saw a thing she might do without compromising herself. But first she must be certain where the blame lay.

Constance Annesley-Seton's explanation over the telephone left her little doubt of the truth. She had the self-control to answer quietly; then, when she had hung up the receiver, she let herself go to pieces. She raged up and down the room, swearing in Spanish, tears tracing red stains on her magnolia complexion. She dashed a vase full of flowers on the floor, and felt a fierce thrill as it crashed to pieces.

"That is *you*, Michael Donaldson!" she cried. "Like this I will break you! That girl shall curse the hour of your meeting. She shall wish herself back in the house of the old woman where she was a servant! And you can do nothing—nothing to hurt me!"

Later that morning, when she had composed herself, Madalena wrote a letter to Lady Annesley-Seton:

> My Kind Friend,—
>
> I am sorry that I may not be with you for Easter, and sorry for the reason. I can read between the lines! But that does not interest you. Myself, I can do no more for your protection in the unknown danger which threatens; but again I am in one of those psychic moods, when I have glimpses of things beyond the veil.
>
> It comes to me that if the Archdeacon friend of your cousin could be asked to join your house party with his wife, and *especially* with his relative who is so rare a judge of jewels (is not his name Ruthven Smith?) trouble might be prevented.
>
> This is vague advice. But I cannot be more definite, because I am saying these things under *guidance*. I am not responsible, nor can I explain why the message is sent. I *feel* that it is important.
>
> But you must not mention that it comes from me. Nelson and his wife would resent that; and the scheme would fall to the ground. Write and tell me what you do. I shall not be easy in my mind until your house party is over. May all go well!
>
> Yours gratefully and affectionately,
>
> Madalena.
>
> P.S.—Better speak of having the Smiths, to Mrs. Nelson, not her husband. He might refuse.

Archdeacon Smith and his wife and their cousin, Ruthven Smith, were the last persons on earth in whom Constance would have expected the Countess de Santiago to interest herself. All the more, therefore, was Lady Annesley-Seton ready to believe in a supernatural influence. Madalena's request to be kept out of the affair would have meant nothing to her had she not agreed that the Nelson Smiths would object to the Countess's dictation.

Constance proposed the Smith family as guests in a casual way to Annesley when they were out shopping together, saying that it would be nice for Anne to have her friends at Valley House.

"The Archdeacon wouldn't be able to come," said Annesley. "Easter is a busy time for him, and Mrs. Smith wouldn't leave him to go into the country."

"What a dear, old-fashioned wife!" laughed Connie. "Well, what about their cousin, that Mr. Ruthven Smith who used to stay at your 'gorgon's' till our friends the burglar-band called on him? There are things in Valley House which would interest an expert in jewels. And you've never asked him to anything, have you?"

"Oh, yes," said Annesley, "he's been invited every time I've asked the Archdeacon and Mrs. Smith, but he always refused, saying he was too deaf and too dull for dinner parties. I'm sure he would hate a house party far worse!"

"Why not give the poor man a chance to decide?" Constance persisted. "He must be a nervous wreck since the burglary. A change ought to do him good. Besides, he would love Valley House. If you like to make a wager, I'll bet you something that he'd jump at the invitation."

Annesley refused the wager, but she agreed that it would be nice to have all three of the Smiths.

Constance was supposed to be hostess in her own house, though Knight was responsible for the financial side of the Easter plan, and it was for her to ask the guests, even those chosen by the Nelson Smiths. Remembering Madalena's hint that Nelson might refuse to add Ruthven Smith's name to the list, Connie gave Annesley no time to consult her husband. While her companion was being fitted for a frock at Harrod's, Lady Annesley-Seton availed herself of the chance to write two letters, one to Mrs. Smith, inviting her and the Archdeacon; another to Ruthven, saying that she wrote at "dear Anne's express wish" as well as her own.

She added cordially on her own account:

I have heard so much of you from Anne that it would be a pleasure to show you the Valley House treasures, which, I think, you would appreciate. Do come!

She stamped her letters and slipped them into the box at the Harrod post office before going to see if Anne were ready. Nothing more was said about the invitation for the Smiths until that evening at dinner, when it occurred to Annesley to mention it. Knight had come home late, just in time to dress, and she had not thought to speak of the house party.

"Oh, Knight," she said, "Cousin Constance proposed asking the Archdeacon and his wife and Mr. Ruthven Smith. I'm sure the Archdeacon can't come, but Mr. Ruthven might perhaps——"

"Oh, I don't think I'd have him with a lot of people he doesn't know and who don't want to know him," Knight vetoed the idea. "He's clever in his way, but it's not a social way. Among the lot we're going to have he'd be like an owl among peacocks."

"But he'd love their jewels," Annesley persevered. "They'll bring some of the most beautiful ones in England. You said so yourself."

"I'm thinking more of their pleasure than his," said Knight. "He's deaf as well as dull. The peacocks are invited already, and the owl isn't, so——"

"I'm afraid he is! When Anne agreed that she'd like to have the Smiths I wrote at once; and by this time they've got my letters," Constance broke in with a pretence at penitence. "Oh, dear, I have put my foot into it with the best intentions! What *shall* we do?"

"Nothing," said Knight. "If they've been asked, they must come if they want to. I doubt if they will."

That doubt was dispelled with the morning post. Mrs. Smith was full of regrets for herself and the Archdeacon, but Ruthven accepted in his precise manner with "much pleasure and gratitude for so kind an attention." The matter was settled, and Connie telephoned to Madalena.

"No Archdeacon; no Mrs. Archdeacon! But I've bagged the jewel-man. Will he be strong enough alone to spread over us that mantle of mysterious protection your crystal showed you?"

"I hope so," the Countess answered.

Yet the woman at the other end of the wire thought the voice sounded dull, and was disappointed, even vaguely anxious. Her anxiety would have increased if she could have seen the face of the seeress. Now that the match was close to the fuse, Madalena had a wild impulse to draw back. It was not too late. Nothing irrevocable had been done. Ruthven Smith's acceptance of the invitation to Valley House would mean only a few days of boredom for his fellow guests, unless—she herself made the next move in the game.

Before she decided to make it, she resolved to see the man of whom she thought as Michael Donaldson.

So far nothing had happened to raise any visible barrier between them. She was not supposed to know that he did not want her to join the Easter house party, and he and she and Annesley were on friendly terms. It would be easy for her to see Don, to see him alone, if she could only choose the right time, unless— —There was an "unless," but she thought the face of the butler would settle it.

There were certain times on certain days when Nelson Smith was "at home" for certain people. These days were not those when Annesley and Constance were "at home."

In fact, they had been chosen purposely in order not to clash.

The American millionaire had, from his first appearance in London, interested himself in more than one charitable society. Representatives of these associations called upon him during appointed hours, and were shown straight to his "den." Indeed, they were the only persons welcomed there, but the Countess de Santiago had some reason to expect that an exception might be made in her favour.

Luckily, the day when she heard the news from Lady Annesley-Seton was one of the two days in the week when Nelson Smith was certain not to be out of the house in the afternoon. Luckily also she knew that his wife was equally certain to be absent. "Anita" was going to play bridge at a house where Madalena was invited.

She got her maid to telephone an excuse—"the Countess had a bad headache." Had she said heartache it would have been nearer the truth. But one does not tell the truth in these matters.

Not for years—not since the strenuous times when Don had saved her from serious trouble and put her on the road to success had Madalena de Santiago been so unhappy. Whichever way she looked she saw darkness ahead, yet she hoped something from her talk with Don—just what, she did not specify to herself in words, but "*something*."

"I wish to see Mr. Nelson Smith on important business," she said, looking the butler straight in the eyes. It was he who opened the door of the Portman Square house on the "charity days." He gave her back look for look, losing the air of respectable servitude and suddenly becoming a human being.

"Mr. Smith is not alone," he answered, contriving to give some special meaning to the ordinary words which made them almost cryptic. "But I think he will be free before long, if you care to wait, madame, and I will mention that you are here."

"You must say it is important," she impressed upon him as she was ushered into a little reception room.

A few minutes later Charrington took her to the door of the "den," where Knight received her with casual cheerfulness.

"This is an unexpected pleasure!" he said.

"Don't let us bother with conventionalities, Don!" she exclaimed, her emotion showing itself in petulance. "I had to come and have an understanding with you."

"An understanding?" Knight was very calm, so calm that she—who knew him in many phases—was stung with the conviction that he needed to ask no questions. He was temporizing; and her anger—passionate, unavailing anger, beating itself like waves on the rock of his strong nature—broke out in tears.

"You know what I mean!" She choked on the words. "You're tired of me! There's nothing more I can do for you, and so—and so—oh, Don, say I'm wrong! Say it's a mistake. Say it's not you but *she* who doesn't want me. She's jealous. Only say that. It's all I want. Just to know it is not you who are so cruel—after the past!"

Knight remained unmoved. He looked straight at her, frowning. "What past?" he inquired, blankly.

"You ask me that—*you*?"

"We have never been anything to one another," Knight said. "Not even friends. You know that as well as I do. We've been valuable to each other after a fashion, I to you, you to me, and we can be the same in future if you don't choose to play the fool."

She was cowed, and hated herself for being cowed—hated Knight, too.

"What do you call playing the fool?" she asked.

"Behaving as you're behaving now; and as you've been behaving these last few weeks. I'm not blind, you know. You have been trying your power over me. I suppose that's what you'd call the trick. Well, my dear Madalena, it won't work. I hoped you might realize that without making a scene; but you wouldn't. You've brought this on yourself, and there's nothing for it now but a straight talk.

"My wife is not jealous. It's not in her to be jealous. If she doesn't like you, Madalena, it's instinctive mistrust. I don't think she's even seen the claws sticking out of the velvet. But *I* have. I've seen exactly what you are up to. You talk about our 'past'. You want to force my hand. You expect me, because I've been a decent pal, and paid what I thought was due, to pay higher, a fancy price. I won't. My wife had no hand in keeping you out of the Easter house party. It was I who said you weren't to be asked. You had to be taught that you couldn't dictate terms. You wouldn't take 'no' for an answer, so the lesson had to be more severe than I meant. Now we understand each other."

"I doubt it!" cried Madalena.

"You mean I don't understand *you*? I think I do, my friend. And I'm not afraid. If I'm not a white angel, certainly *you're* not. We're tarred with the same brush. Forget this afternoon, if you like, and I'll forget it. We can go back to where we were before. But only on the promise that you'll be sensible. No cat-scratchings. No mysteries."

It was all that the Countess de Santiago could do to bite back the threat which alone could have given her relief. Yet she did bite it back. Her triumph would be incomplete in ruining the man if he could not know that he owed his punishment to her. But she must be satisfied with the second best thing. She dared not put him on his guard, and she dared not let him guess that she meant to strike.

He would wonder perhaps, when the blow fell, and say to himself, "Can Madalena have done this?" She must so act that his answer would be, "No. It's an accident of fate." Knight was not the sort of man who for a mere wandering suspicion, without an atom of proof, would pull a woman down. And there would be no proof.

"You are not kind," was the only response she ventured. "And you are not just. I did not want to 'scratch.' I would not injure you for the world, even if I could. Yet it does hurt to think our friendship in the past has meant nothing to you, when it has meant so much to me. It hurts. But I must bear it. I shall not trouble you about my feelings again."

If she had hoped that her meekness might make him relent she was disappointed. He merely said, "Very good. We'll go back to where we were."

That same evening Madalena wrote to Ruthven Smith. She took pains to disguise her handwriting, and not satisfied with that precaution, went out in a taxi and posted the letter in Hampstead.

It was a short letter, and it had no signature; but it made an impression on Ruthven Smith.

CHAPTER XVI.
WHY RUTHVEN SMITH WENT

Never in his life had Ruthven Smith been blessed or cursed by an anonymous letter. He did not know what to make of it, or how to treat it. Instead of exciting him, as it might had he been a man of mercurial temperament, it irritated him intensely.

That was the way when things out of the ordinary happened to Ruthven Smith: he resented them. He was not—and recognized the fact that he was not—the type of man to whom things ought to happen. It was only one strange streak of the artistic in his nature which made him a marvellous judge of jewels, and attracted adventures to come near him.

He was constitutionally timid. He was conventional, and prim in his thoughts of life and all he desired it to give. He was a creature of a past generation; and whenever in time he had chanced to exist he would always have lagged a generation behind. But there was that one colourful streak which somehow, as if by a mistake in creation, had shot a narrow rainbow vein through his drab soul, like a glittering opal in gray-brown rock.

He loved jewels. He had known all about them by instinct even before he knew by painstaking research. He could judge jewels and recognize them under any disguise of cutting. He could do this better than almost any one in the world, and he could do nothing else well; therefore it was preordained that he should find his present position with some such firm as the Van Vrecks; and, being in it, adventures were bound to come.

Many attempts to rob him had doubtless been made. One had lately succeeded. His nerves were in a wretched state. He was "jumpy" by day as well as night; and sometimes, when at his worst, he even felt for five minutes at a time that he had better hand in his resignation to the firm who had employed him for nearly twenty years, and retire into private life, like a harried mouse into its hole.

But that was only when he was at his very worst. Deep down within him he was aware that, while the breath of life and his inscrutable genius were together in him, he could not, would not, resign.

It was part of Ruthven Smith, an intimate part of him, not to be able to decide for a long time what to do when he was confronted with one of those emergencies unsuited to his temperament. He was afraid of doing the wrong thing, yet was too reserved to consult any one. He generally counted on blundering through somehow; and so it was in the matter of the anonymous letter.

He had heard, and dimly believed, that it was morally wrong, and, still worse, quite bad form, to take notice of anonymous letters. But this one must be different, it seemed to him, from any other which anybody had ever received. Duty to his employers and duty to the one thing he really loved was above any other duty; and for fear of losing forever an immense, an unhoped-for advantage, which might possibly be gained, he dared not ignore the letter.

At all events, he had told himself, no matter what he might decide later, it was just as well that he had accepted the invitation to Valley House. Perhaps someone—he could not think who—was playing a stupid practical joke, with the object of getting him there. But he would risk that and go, and let his conduct shape itself according to developments.

For instance, if his eyes were able to detect the small detail mysteriously mentioned in the letter, he would feel bound to act as it suggested; yes, bound to act—but how unpleasant it would be!

And the worst of the whole unpalatable affair was that if he *did* act in that suggested way, and if he accomplished what he might, with dreadful deftness, be supposed to accomplish, it would be the moment when perhaps he might be fooled.

If the letter were written by a practical joker, he would be made to look ridiculous in the eyes of all who were in the secret. And that thought brought him back to the question which over and over he asked in his mind. Who could have written the anonymous letter?

It must be someone acquainted with him, or with his profession; someone who knew the Nelson Smiths and the Annesley-Setons well enough to be aware that there was to be an Easter party at Valley House. The writer hinted in vague terms that he was a private detective aware of certain things, yet so placed that he could have no handling of the affair, except from a distance, and through another person. He pretended a disinterested desire to serve Ruthven Smith, and signed himself, "A Well Wisher"; but the nervous recipient of the advice felt that his correspondent was quite likely to be of the class opposed to detectives.

What if there were some scheme for a robbery on a vast scale at Valley House, and this letter were part of the scheme? What if the band of thieves supposed to be "working" lately in London should try to make him a cat's paw in bringing off their big haul?

This was a terrifying idea, and more feasible than the one suggested by the anonymous writer, that Mrs. Nelson Smith should— oh, certainly it seemed the wildest nonsense!

Still, there was his duty to the Van Vrecks. They must be considered ahead of everything! So Ruthven Smith, nervous as a rabbit who has lost its warren, travelled down to Devonshire on Saturday afternoon, invited to stay at Valley House till Tuesday.

It was as Knight had said: the dull, deaf man was as completely out of the picture in that house party as an owl among peacocks; for he was an inarticulate person and could not talk interestingly even on his own subject, jewels. His idea of conversation with women was a discussion of the weather, contrasting that of England with that of America, or perhaps touching upon politics. He was afraid of questions about jewels lest he should allow himself to be pumped, and the information he might inadvertently give away be somehow "used."

But he was by birth and education a gentleman; and his relationship to Archdeacon Smith, whom everybody liked, was a passport to people's kindness.

Duchesses and countesses were of no particular interest to Ruthven Smith, but their adornments were fascinating. At Valley House one duchess and several countesses were assembled for the Easter party, and they were women whose jewels were famous. Most of these were family heirlooms, but their present owners had had the things reset, and no queen of fairyland or musical comedy could have owned more becoming or exquisitely designed tiaras, crowns, necklaces, earrings, dog-collars, brooches, bracelets, and rings than these great ladies.

For this reason the ladies themselves were interesting to Ruthven Smith, and he might have been equally so to them if he would have told them picturesquely all he knew about the history of their wonderful diamonds, pearls, emeralds, and rubies. It was too bad that he wouldn't, for there was not a famous jewel in England or Europe of which Ruthven Smith had not every ancient scandal in connection with it at his tongue's end.

But on his tongue's end it stayed, even when, for the sake of his own pleasure if nothing else, his hosts and hostesses tried to draw him out.

Nevertheless, he was not sorry that he had come. There was an element of joy in seeing, met together, and sparkling together, those exquisite, historic beauties of which he had read.

It had been a bother to Lady Annesley-Seton and her cousin Anne to decide how Ruthven Smith should be put at table. In a way, he was an outsider, the only one among the guests without a title or military rank which mechanically indicated his place in relation to others. Besides, no woman would want to have him to scream at.

Fortunately, however, there were two women asked on account of their husbands, and so—according to Connie's code—of no importance in themselves. Providence meant them to be pushed here and there like pawns on a chessboard; and they were pushed to either side of Ruthven Smith at the dinner-table on Saturday night.

Both had been placated by being told beforehand what a wonderful man he was, with frightfully exciting things to say, if he could tactfully be made to say them. But only one of the two had courage or spirit to rise to the occasion—the woman he was given to take in, a Lady Cartwright, married to Major Sir Elmer Cartwright, who was always asked to every house whenever the Duchess of Peebles was invited.

Lady Cartwright was Irish, wrote plays, had a sense of humour, and was not jealous of the Duchess. Because she wrote plays, she was continually in search of material, digging it up, even when it looked unpromising.

"I have heard such charming things about you," she began.

"I *beg* your pardon!" said Ruthven Smith, unable to believe his ears. And because he was somewhat deaf himself, he could not gauge the inflections of his own voice. Sometimes he spoke almost in a whisper, sometimes very loudly. This time he spoke loudly, and several people, surprised at the sound rising above other sounds like spray from a flowing river, paused for an instant to listen.

"What a wonderful expert in jewels you are," Lady Cartwright replied in a higher tone, realizing that she had a deaf man to deal with. "And that you have been one of the sufferers from that gang of thieves Scotland Yard can't lay its hands on."

Ruthven Smith was on the point of shrinking into himself, as was his wont if any personal topic of conversation came up, when it flashed into his mind that here was an opportunity. If he did not take it, so easy a one might not occur again. He braced himself for a supreme effort.

"Oh, yes, yes, I was robbed," he admitted. "A serious loss! Some fine pearls I had been buying—not for myself, but for the Van Vrecks. I seldom collect valuables for myself. I only wish these things had been mine. I should not have that sense of being an unfaithful servant—though I did my best——"

"Of course you did," Lady Cartwright soothed him. "But these thieves—if it's the same gang, as we all think—are too clever for the cleverest of us. As for the police, they seem to be nowhere. I haven't suffered yet, but each morning when I wake up, I'm astonished to find everything as usual. Not that it wouldn't *seem* as usual, even if the gang had paid us a visit and made a clean sweep of our poor possessions. They appear to be able to leak through keyholes, as nothing in the houses they go to is ever disturbed."

"Anyhow, they have latchkeys," retorted Ruthven Smith, with what for him might be considered gaiety of manner. "The thief or thieves who relieved me of my pearls—or rather, my employer's pearls—apparently walked in as a member of the household might have done."

Among those who had involuntarily suspended talk to hear what Ruthven Smith was saying about jewels and jewel thieves was Annesley. Though the party would never have been but for Knight and herself, Dick and Constance were playing host and hostess with all the outward responsibility of those parts. Lord Annesley-Seton had a duchess on his right, a countess on his left; Lady Annesley-Seton was fenced in by the duke and the count pertaining to these ladies; Mrs. Nelson Smith sat between two less important men, who liked the dinner provided by the American millionaire's miraculous new chef, and they could safely be neglected for a moment.

Annesley felt that Ruthven Smith was, in a way, her special guest, and she was anxious that he should not be the failure Knight had prophesied. She wanted him not to regret that he had flung himself on the tender mercies of this smart house party, and almost equally she wanted his two neighbours not to be bored by him. Knight would hate that. He attached so much importance to amusing the people whom he invited!

She listened and thought that Mr. Ruthven Smith and Lady Cartwright seemed to have begun well. Then, as she turned to Lady Cartwright's handsome husband (the Duchess of Peebles was talking to Dick Annesley-Seton just then), she caught the word "latchkey."

It seized her attention. She knew they were speaking of the burglary at Mrs. Ellsworth's house. She heard Ruthven Smith go on to explain in his high-pitched voice that the two woman servants had been suspected, but that their characters had "emerged stainless" from the examination.

"Besides," he continued, "neither of them had a latchkey to give to any outside person. The two women slept together in one room. At the time of the robbery there was no butler— —"

Annesley heard no more. Suddenly the door of her spirit seemed to close. She was shut up within herself, listening to some voice there.

"What became of your latchkey?" it asked.

The blood streamed to her face and made her ears tingle, as it used to do when she had been scolded by Mrs. Ellsworth. If any one had looked at her then, it must have been to wonder what Sir Elmer Cartwright or Lord John Dormer had said to make Mrs. Nelson Smith blush so furiously.

She was remembering what she had done with her latchkey. She had given it to Knight to open the front door, and so escape from the two watchers who had followed them in a taxi to Torrington Square. She had never thought of it from that moment to this. Could it be possible that some thief had stolen the latchkey from Knight, and used it when Mrs. Ellsworth's house was robbed?

Her thoughts concentrated violently upon the key. Had her neighbours spoken she would not have heard; but they did not speak. She was free to let her thoughts run where they chose. They ran back to the first night of her meeting with Nelson Smith, and her arrival with him at the house in Torrington Square. She recalled, as if it were a moment ago, putting the key into his hand, which had been warm and steady, despite the danger he was in, while hers had been trembling and cold. She said to herself that she must ask Knight, as soon as they were alone together, what he had done with the key, whether he had left it in the house or flung it away.

But of course he must have left it in the house, or close by, otherwise no thief would have known where it belonged. That made her feel guilty toward Ruthven Smith. She ought not to have been so utterly absorbed in her own affairs that night. She ought to have asked to have the key back, and then to have laid it where it could be found by Mrs. Ellsworth in the morning.

Perhaps, indirectly, *she* was responsible for the burglary at that house. And, now she thought of it, what a queer burglary it had been! The thieves must certainly have known something about Mrs. Ellsworth, or else, in helping themselves to her valuables, it would not have occurred to them to scrawl a sarcastic message.

That message had delighted Knight when he heard of it. He had laughed and said, "I like those chaps! They can have *my* money when they want it!"

Since then they *had* had his money, and other possessions. If the theory of the police were right, that a gang of foreign thieves was "working" London, Annesley was glad that she and Knight had been robbed. It made her feel less to blame for her carelessness in the matter of that latchkey.

At least, she had suffered, too, and so had Knight.

Could it be, she asked herself, that the *watchers* were somehow mixed up in the business? Were *they* members of the supposed gang? That did not seem likely, for how could a man like Knight have got involved with thieves? Yet it seemed, from what he had said that night at the Savoy—and never referred to again—as if he were somehow in their power.

How curiously like one of them Morello had been! She remembered thinking so, with a shock of fear. Then she had lost the feeling of resemblance, and told herself that she must have imagined it.

The two faces came back to her now, and again she saw them alike. She was glad that Knight had never invited Morello to call, and glad that when grudgingly she had asked one day after the two men who had witnessed their marriage, Knight had said, "Gone out of England. We just caught them in time."

As for the watchers, she had heard no more of them. Knight ignored the episode, or the part of it connected with those men. The memory of them was shut up in the locked box of his past, and he never left the key lying about, as apparently he had left the key of Mrs. Ellsworth's house.

Suddenly, while Annesley listened to Ruthven Smith, she became conscious that, as he talked to Lady Cartwright, his eyes had turned to her.

"This proves," the fancy ran through her head, "that if you look at or even think of people, you attract their attention."

She glanced away, and at her neighbours. They were both absorbed for the moment; she need not worry lest they should find her neglectful. She took some asparagus which was offered to her, and began to eat it; but she still had the impression that Ruthven Smith was looking at her. She wondered why.

"He can't be expecting me to scream at him across the table," she thought.

"Yes," he was saying to Lady Cartwright, "it was a misfortune to lose those pearls. Two I had selected to make a pair of earrings can scarcely be duplicated. But none of the things stolen from me compared in value to those our agent lost on board the *Monarchic*. I suppose you read of that affair?"

"Oh, yes," said Lady Cartwright, her voice raised in deference to her neighbour's deafness. "It was most interesting. Especially about the clairvoyant woman on board who saw a vision of the thief in her crystal, throwing things into the sea attached to a life-belt with a light on it, or something of the sort, to be picked up by a yacht. One would have supposed, with that information to go upon, the police might have recovered the jewels, but they didn't, and probably they never will now."

"I'm not sure the police pinned their faith to the clairvoyante's visions," replied Ruthven Smith, with his dry chuckle.

"Really? But I've understood—though the name wasn't mentioned then, I believe—that the woman was that wonderful Countess de Santiago we're so excited about. She is certainly extraordinary. Nobody seems to doubt *her* powers! I rather thought she might be here."

Ruthven Smith showed no interest in the Countess de Santiago. Once on the subject of jewels, it was difficult to shunt him off on another at short notice. Or possibly he had something to say which he particularly wished not to leave unsaid at that stage of the conversation.

"The newspapers did not publish a description of the jewels stolen on the *Monarchic*," he went on, brushing the Countess de Santiago aside. "It was thought best at the time not to give the reporters a list. To me, that seemed a mistake. Who knows, for instance, through how many hands the Malindore diamond may have passed? If some honest person, recognizing it from a description in the papers, for instance — —"

"The Malindore diamond!" exclaimed Lady Cartwright, forgetting politeness in her interest, and cutting short a sentence which began dully. "Isn't that the wonderful blue diamond that the British Museum refused to buy three years ago, because it hadn't enough money to spend, or something?"

"Quite so," replied Ruthven Smith, adding with pride: "But the Van Vrecks had enough money. They always have when a unique thing is for sale; and they are rich enough to wait for years, with their money locked up, till somebody comes along who wants the thing. That happened in the case of the Malindore diamond. The Van Vrecks hoped to sell it to Mr. Pierpont Morgan. But he died, and it was left on their hands till this last autumn."

"Ah, then that lovely blue diamond was sold with the other things the Van Vreck agent lost on the *Monarchic*?"

"*Was* to be sold if the prospective buyer liked it. He had married a white wife, you know, and— —"

"Oh, yes, of course. It was Lady Eve Cassenden. That marriage made a big sensation among us. *Horrid*, I call it! But she hadn't a penny, and they say he's the richest Maharajah in India."

"The Malindore diamond was once in his family, I understand, about five hundred years ago, when we first begin to get at its history," Ruthven Smith went on, ignoring the Maharajah as he had ignored the Countess de Santiago. "It was then the central jewel of a crown. But later, Louis XIV, on obtaining possession of it, had it set in a ring, and surrounded with small white brilliants. It still remains in that form, or did so remain until it was stolen from our agent on the *Monarchic*. What form it is in and where it is now, only those who know can say."

So strong was the call from Ruthven Smith's eyes to Annesley's eyes that she was forced to look up. She had been sure that she would meet his gaze fixed upon her, and so it was. He was staring across the table at her, with a curious expression on his long, hatchet face.

CHAPTER XVII.
RUTHVEN SMITH'S EYEGLASSES

Annesley could not read the look. Yet she felt that it might be read, if her soul and body had not been wrenched apart, and hastily flung together again, upside down, it seemed, with her brain where her heart had been, and vice versa.

Why had Ruthven Smith looked at her, as he spoke in his loud voice of the stolen Malindore diamond—a blue diamond set with small brilliants, in a ring? Had he found out that she—did he believe—but she could not finish the thought. It seemed as though the ring Knight had given her—*and told her to hide*—was burning her flesh!

Could *her* blue diamond be the famous diamond, about which the jewel expert was telling Lady Cartwright? A horrible sensation overcame the girl. She felt her blood growing cold, and oozing so sluggishly through her veins that she could count the drops—drip, drip, drip! She hoped that she had not turned ghastly pale. Above all things she hoped that she was not going to faint! If she did that, Ruthven Smith would think—what would he not think?

She found herself praying for strength and the power of self-control that she might reason with her own intelligence. Of course, if this were the diamond, Knight didn't dream that it had been stolen.

Just then a hand reached out at her left side and poured champagne into her glass. It was the hand of Charrington, the butler. Annesley saw that it was trembling. She had never seen Charrington's hand tremble before. Butlers' hands were not supposed to tremble. Charrington spilled a little champagne on the tablecloth, only a very little, no more than a drop or two, yet Annesley started and glanced up. The butler was moving away when she caught a glimpse of his face.

It was red, as usual, for his complexion and that of his younger brother were alike in colouring; but there was a look of *strain* on his features, as if he were keeping his muscles taut.

Sir Elmer Cartwright began to talk to her. His voice buzzed unmeaningly in her ears, as though she were coming out from under the influence of chloroform.

"What will become of me?" she said to herself, and then was afraid she had said it aloud. How awful that would be! Her eyes turned imploringly to Sir Elmer. He was smiling, unaware of anything unusual.

"Oh, yes!" she exclaimed at random. Fortunately it seemed to be the right answer; and the relief this assurance gave was like a helping hand to a beginner skating on thin ice. Sir Elmer went on to repeat some story which he said he had been telling the Duchess.

Annesley suddenly thought of a woman rider she had seen at a circus when she was a child. The woman stood on the bare back of one horse and drove six others, three abreast, all going very fast and noiselessly round a ring.

"I must drive my thoughts as she did the horses," came flashing into the girl's head. "I must think this out, and I must listen to Sir Elmer and go on giving him right answers, and I must look just as usual. *I must!*

"For Knight's sake!" She seemed to hear the words whispered. Why for Knight's sake? Oh, but of course she must try to think how it would involve him if the blue diamond was the famous one stolen from the Van Vrecks' agent on the *Monarchic*!

He would not be to blame, for if he had known, he would not have bought the diamond.

And yet, *might* he not have known? He had told her few details of his life before they met, but he had said that it had been hard sometimes, that he had travelled among rough people, and picked up some of their rough ways. He had confessed frankly that his ideas of right and wrong had got mixed and blunted. From the first he had never let her call him good.

Would it seem dreadful to him to buy a jewel which he might guess, from its low cost, had to be got rid of at almost any price?

Annesley was forced to admit, much as she loved Knight, that his daring, original nature (so she called it to herself) might enter into strange adventures and intrigues for sheer joy in taking risks. She imagined that some wild escapade regretted too late might have led him into association with the watchers. Maybe they had all three been members of a secret society, she often told herself, and Knight had left against the others' will, in spite of threats.

That would be like him; and brave and splendid as was his image in her heart, she could not say that he would never be guilty of an act which might be classed as unscrupulous.

This admission, instead of distressing, calmed her. Allowing that he had certain faults seemed to chase away a dreadful thought which had pressed near, out of sight, yet close as if it stood behind her chair, leaning over her shoulder.

For a moment she felt happy again. She would tell Knight what she had heard about the Malindore diamond, and how like its description was to hers. Then, no matter how much he might hate to let it go, he must show the blue diamond ring to Mr. Ruthven Smith and have its identity decided.

The girl drew a long breath, and determined to put the subject out of her mind until after dinner, so that Sir Elmer Cartwright need not think her a complete idiot.

But the deep sigh that stirred her bosom stirred also the fine gold chain on which hung the blue diamond. The chain lay loosely on her shoulders, lost, or almost lost among soft folds of lace. She wore it like that with a low dress, not only to prevent it from attracting attention and making people wonder what ornament she hid, but also because the thin band of gold, if seen, would break the symmetry of line. It was Knight who had given her this little piece of advice, the first time after their marriage that she had dined with him in evening dress, and since then she had never forgotten to follow it.

To-night, however, feeling suddenly conscious of the chain, she was on the point of looking down to make sure that it was shrouded in her laces. Something stopped her. With a quick warning thump of the heart she glanced across at Ruthven Smith.

A few minutes ago he had not been wearing his eyeglasses. Now they were on, pinching the high-bridged, thin nose. And he was peering through them at her—peering at her neck, her dress, as if he searched for something.

Ruthven Smith knew about the blue diamond. He knew that she wore it on a chain, hidden in her dress. The certainty of this shot through brain and body like forked lightning and seemed to sear her flesh. She was afraid. She could not tell yet of what she was afraid, but when she could disentangle her twisted thoughts one from another the reason would be clear.

Then it was as if her mind separated itself from the rest of her and began to run back along the path she had travelled with Knight since the hour of their first meeting. It ran looking on the ground, seeking and picking up things dropped and almost forgotten.

Knight had not been pleased when the Countess de Santiago talked to him of their being together on the *Monarchic*. The Countess had seemed wishful to annoy him in some way. She had taken that way. They had known each other well and for a long time. They knew a good deal about each other's affairs. Sometimes one would say that the Countess still liked to annoy Knight, and he resented that. He had been unwilling to have her asked to Valley House for Easter, though he knew she longed to come.

And Ruthven Smith! Knight had not wanted him. Could it possibly be on account of the blue diamond? Had Knight heard what *she* had heard there at the dinner-table, and was he anxious about what might happen next?

Hastily she flung a glance toward her husband. He was not looking at her, but it seemed—perhaps she imagined it—that his face had something of the same tense, strained expression she had caught on Charrington's.

How odd, if it were true, that both should have that look. One would almost fancy they shared a secret trouble. But Annesley shook the idea away, as she would have shaken a hornet trying to sting. How dare she let such a disloyal fancy even cross the threshold of her mind? A secret between her husband and his servant—a secret concerning the blue diamond, which stabbed them both with the same prick of anxiety at the mention of the jewel!

No sooner was the venomous thing dislodged than it crept back and settled close over her heart. For Knight's eyes turned to her, and in them was the look of a drowning man.

Just for the fraction of a second she saw it. Then the curtain was drawn over his real self that had come to the window and signalled for help. He smiled a friendly smile, and took up the conversation with his right-hand neighbour. But he had hidden his soul too late. The message could not be taken back, and Annesley was sure that he, too, had heard the story Ruthven Smith had told so loudly to Lady Cartwright.

The fact that he had lost his unruffled, nonchalant coolness even for a single instant warned Annesley that Knight must be desperately troubled.

"He bought the diamond for me, knowing what it was," she told herself, "and knowing that it must have been stolen. Of course that's why he made me wear it where nobody could see. But who else knew besides the man who sold it to Knight? *Somebody* must have known, and told Mr. Ruthven Smith. Perhaps the thief himself, hoping to be spared, and to get money from both sides. That is why Mr. Ruthven Smith accepted the invitation here, which I was so sure he would refuse. He has come because he thinks the Malindore diamond is in this house. That must be it! But how can he have found out that I am wearing it?"

As she thought these things, asking herself questions, sometimes answering them, sometimes unable to answer, she managed to keep up some desultory talk first with one of her neighbours, then with the other. It seemed to take all her strength to do this, and made her feel weak and broken, not excited and vital, as she had felt on the wonderful night at the Savoy when "Nelson Smith" had praised her pluck and presence of mind in saving him from a danger which had never been explained.

How she wished with all her anxious, troubled heart that she knew how to save him to-night!

It had been very wrong to buy a stolen diamond, but he had done it from no mercenary motives, for he had given it to her. She supposed that he had loved the beautiful thing, and felt when it was offered to him that he could not bear to let it go.... Perhaps the Countess de Santiago had stolen it on the *Monarchic*! That might be a cruel thought, but Annesley could not help having it, for it would explain many things.

Besides, it would help to exonerate Knight. He was very chivalrous where women were concerned, and he would have felt bound to protect his old friend. At all events, he could not have given her up to justice, and very likely she had been in debt and needed money. She had wonderful clothes, and must be extravagant.

Yes, the more Annesley dwelt on the idea the more convinced she became that Madalena de Santiago had stolen the blue diamond, and perhaps all the other things on the *Monarchic*, while pretending to have a vision in her crystal of the thief, and of the way the jewel had been smuggled off the ship. Then the Countess had been angry with Knight, and had tried to have him suspected, even of being mixed up in the theft—though that last idea seemed too far-fetched.

"How hateful, how mean of her!" Annesley thought, ashamed because it was so easy to believe bad things of the Countess, and to pile up one upon another. "Probably she put it into Constance's head to suggest having Mr. Ruthven Smith asked. And then she put it into his head to—to——"

The girl stopped short, appalled. *What* had been put into the jewel expert's head? What precisely had he come to Valley House to do?

"He has come to *find* the blue diamond!" the answer flashed into her brain.

Madalena de Santiago's eyes were as piercing as they were beautiful. She might have noticed the fine gold chain which her "pal's" wife wore always round her neck. She might have guessed that the ring with the blue diamond was hidden at the end of the chain; yet she could not *know for certain*, because Knight would never have told her that.

Therefore it followed that neither could Ruthven Smith know for certain. He meant to find out, and if he did find out, Knight would be punished far more severely than he deserved for buying a thing illegally come by.

"I will save him again," Annesley resolved.

But how? What might she expect to happen? And whatever it was, how could she prevent it happening?

CHAPTER XVIII.
THE STAR SAPPHIRE

Picture after picture grew and faded in her mind. She saw policemen coming to the house; she saw Ruthven Smith demanding that she and Knight be searched, and arrested if the diamond were found.

It might be difficult to prove that they had had nothing to do with the theft, especially as Knight had been on board the *Monarchic*. He must have travelled under his own name then, the name that he had not let her see when he wrote it in the register after the wedding. If Ruthven Smith knew about the *Monarchic* and the change of name, he might make things very unpleasant for Knight. And what must he himself be thinking at this moment as he peered through his eyeglasses?

Annesley had always told herself that Ruthven Smith looked like a schoolmaster. He looked more than ever like one to-night—a very severe schoolmaster, planning to punish a rebellious pupil.

"But he can't have accepted our invitation, and have come to this house to make a scene and a scandal before everybody," she tried to reassure her troubled heart. "Still, he wouldn't look like that if he didn't believe that I'm wearing the diamond, and if he did not mean to do something about it."

It was a terrifying prospect for Annesley, and suddenly, with a shock of certainty, she told herself that Ruthven Smith would not give her time, if he could help it, to get rid of the ring and conceal it somewhere else. "He'll think of an excuse after dinner to make me show what I have on my chain, or perhaps he has thought of the excuse already!"

It seemed to the girl that the room had become bitterly cold. She shivered slightly. "I must take off the ring and put something else on the chain when we go away and leave the men," she decided.

But no! Even then it might be too late. Ruthven Smith neither smoked nor drank. Very likely he would follow the ladies to the drawing room without giving her the chance of cheating him. If she were to save Knight from trouble she must do the thing she had to do at once.

That thing was to unfasten the clasp of the chain, slip off the ring with the blue diamond, substitute another ring, fasten the chain again and replace it inside her dress, all without letting Ruthven Smith across the table, or her neighbours, suspect what was being done.

Her plate was whisked away at that moment, and leaning back in her chair she seized the opportunity of looking at her hands. Brain and heart were throbbing so fast that she could not remember, without counting, what rings she had put on.

Knight had tried to console her for the loss she'd suffered through the burglary a fortnight before by making her a present of half a dozen new rings. Poor Knight! How anxious he always was to give her pleasure, no matter at what expense! He had such good taste in choosing jewellery, too, that one might almost fancy him as great an expert as Ruthven Smith.

But he had laughed when she said this to him, protesting that he was a "rank amateur."

The new rings were all beautiful, each unique in its way. The big white diamond of her engagement ring was the least original of her possessions. To-night, in addition to that and her wedding ring, she wore on her left hand a grayish star sapphire, of oval shape, curiously set with four small diamonds, white ones at top and bottom, pale pink and yellow at the sides. This ring was rather large for her, and as she wore it above the engagement ring, the stones easily slipped round toward the palm.

The dark blue scarab on her right hand Ruthven might have observed; but she was hopeful that the star sapphire had escaped his notice.

She took it off and laid it in her lap, ready.

Her dress of white charmeuse, embroidered with violets, was fastened in front under a folded and crossed fichu of "shadow" lace and a bunch of real violets held on by an old-fashioned brooch. Bending forward, she played at eating Punch à la Romaine, while with her left hand she contrived to undo three or four hooks from their delicately worked eyelets. Then, slipping two fingers into the aperture, she tore open her lace underbodice.

This accomplished, she felt the ring of the blue diamond; but she dared not break the chain, as she could easily have done. If Ruthven Smith were planning some trick by which to obtain a glimpse of ring and chain, the latter must be intact.

Pinching the chain between thumb and finger patiently, persistently, and very cautiously, she pulled it along until she touched the tiny clasp. As she did this she glanced down at the lace of her fichu now and then to make sure that she did not draw the thin line of gold so tightly across her neck that it became visible in moving.

At last she had the clasp in her hand. Pressed upon sharply, it opened, and the ring with the blue diamond fell into her palm. She pushed it inside her frock as far down as her fingers would reach and slid the star sapphire ring on to the chain before fastening the clasp again.

She was shivering still as if with cold, and her hands trembled so that she could hardly put the hooks of her dress into their eyelets. But somehow she did at last, and was sure that no one had seen.

More than one course had come and gone before her stealthy task was finished, and three or four minutes after the last hook had decided to bite, Constance looked at the Duchess of Peebles. Everyone rose, and, as Annesley had feared, Ruthven Smith followed the ladies out of the great dining hall.

Constance led them to the Chinese drawing room for coffee, and as the women grouped themselves to chat, or gaze at Buddhas and treasures of ancient dynasties, she suddenly recalled Madalena's latest vision in the crystal.

It seemed that it would interest rather than frighten her friends to hear of it. Besides, if it did frighten them a little, she didn't much mind. She bore the Duchess of Peebles and several others a grudge because they had come to Valley House not on her account, or Dick's, but because it was an open secret who were the real host and hostess on this occasion. Last year, if she had invited these people, they would have been "dreadfully sorry they were already promised for Easter."

It was Nelson Smith's money and popularity which had lured them. They knew they would have wonderful things to eat, and probably the women were counting on presents of Easter eggs in the morning with exciting surprises inside!

"Are you all very brave?" she asked aloud and gaily. "Because I've just remembered that the Countess de Santiago saw a picture of us in her crystal, grouped together as we are now, in this very room, and—something happening."

"Something nice, or horrid?" asked the Duchess, a tall, pretty woman, who looked as if Rossetti had created her, with finishing touches by Burne-Jones.

"Ah, she couldn't see. The vision faded," Constance replied. "But perhaps *we* shall see—if this is to be the night."

As she spoke the men came into the room. Ruthven Smith's example was contagious. They had been deserted by the ladies hardly ten minutes ago. Annesley felt sure that Knight had contrived to hurry the others. He, too, then, had guessed why Ruthven Smith had gone out of the dining hall with the women. Perhaps he also had a plan!

He came straight to his wife, who was standing with Lady Cartwright. Not far off was Ruthven Smith, still with his eyeglasses on. He was hovering with a nervous air in front of a cabinet full of beautiful things, at which he scarcely glanced.

Seeing Knight approach Annesley, he lifted his head, took a hesitating step in her direction, and stopped. He looked timid and miserable, yet obstinate.

"Anita, I've been telling the Duke about that star sapphire I picked up for you the other day," Knight began. "He says he never saw one with anything resembling a star in it. Will you fetch it for him to look at? I noticed as you got up from the table that you hadn't put it on to-night."

For an instant the girl could not answer. If only he had hit upon something else. If only it had occurred to her to hide her left hand after taking off the ring! But she could not have foreseen this.

For the first time she inclined to believe in the Countess de Santiago's supernatural power. Could it be that this scene had pictured itself in the crystal? Could it be that now in a moment something dreadful would happen?

She realized that Knight was trusting to the quickness of her wits; that not only had he overheard Ruthven Smith's talk about the Malindore diamond, but he credited her with having caught the drift of the words, and counted on her loyalty to help him. As he spoke he looked at her with the wistful, seeking look she had seen in his eyes when they were first married.

"He's afraid I'm angry with him for buying the diamond in spite of knowing what it was," she thought, "but he trusts me to stand by him now."

Her mind grew clear. After a pause no longer than the drawing of a breath she was ready to rise to the situation Knight had created. In fact, she saw safety for him and herself, as well as a realistic surprise for Ruthven Smith. But the latter, rendered brave to act through fear of loss, was too quick for her.

"I beg your pardon! Before you go, may I have the pleasure of a nearer look at that beautiful enamel brooch of yours?"

It was Annesley's impulse to step back as without waiting for permission the narrow head, sleekly brushed and slightly bald at the top, bent over her laces. But she remembered herself in time and stood still. She dared not glance at Knight, to send him a message of encouragement, but she knew that for once even his resourcefulness had failed, and that he must be steeling himself to the brutal discovery of his secret.

Yet even then she did not guess what Ruthven Smith's plan was until the thing had happened. He peered at the brooch, which represented a bunch of grapes in small cabochon amethysts and leaves of green enamel. Adjusting his eyeglasses, they slipped from his nose and fell on the lace of her fichu.

"Oh, how awkward of me! A thousand pardons!" he cried. Making a nervous grab for the glasses, which hung from a chain, he snatched up her chain as well, and with a quick jerk of seeming inadvertence wrenched from its warm hiding-place a ring with a flash of brilliants and a glint of blue.

Annesley's heart had given one great throb and then missed a beat, for there had been an awful instant as the "plan" developed when she feared that the ring with the blue diamond might, after all her pains, have become entangled with the chain. If it had, the violence of the jerk might have brought it to light.

But she had accomplished her task well. She could afford to smile, though her lips trembled, as she saw the bird-of-prey look fade from Ruthven Smith's face and turn into bewildered humiliation.

Right was on his side; yet he had the air of a culprit, and some wild strain in Annesley's nature which had been asleep till that instant sang a song of triumph in the victory of her "plan" over his. How delighted Knight would be, and how amazed and grateful—grateful as he had been when she "stood by him" with the watchers!

As Ruthven Smith stammered apologies her eyes flashed to Knight's; but there was none of the defiant laughter she had expected, and felt bound to reproach him for later.

He was pale, and though his immense power of self-control kept him in check, Annesley shrank almost with horror from the fury of rage against Ruthven Smith which she read in her husband's gaze and the beating of the veins in his temples.

Terrified lest his anger should break out in words, she hurried on to say what she would have said before the sudden move by the jewel expert.

"Here is the sapphire ring you asked about, Knight," she said. "I was just going to take off this chain and give it to you to show to the Duke when——"

"When Mr. Ruthven Smith took an unwarrantable liberty," Knight finished the sentence icily.

"I—I meant nothing. Really, I can't tell you how I regret——" the wretched man stuttered. But Knight was without mercy.

"Pray don't try any further," he cut in. "My wife is not a figurine in a shop window to have her ornaments stared at and pawed over. You are an old friend of hers, Mr. Ruthven Smith, and you are my guest—or rather my friend Annesley-Seton's guest—therefore I will say no more. But in some countries where I have lived such an incident would have ended differently."

"Oh, *please*, Knight!" exclaimed Annesley, thankful that at least he had spoken his harsh words in so low a voice that no one outside their own group of three could hear. But she was shocked out of her brief exultation by his white rage and the depths revealed by the lightning flash of anger. Also she was sorry for Ruthven Smith, even while she resented the plot which it was evident he had come to carry out.

With unsteady hands she lifted the delicate chain over her hair and gave it to her husband.

"The ring is rather large for my finger. Here it is for you to show to the Duke," she reminded him.

"Thank you, Anita," he said. And she knew that he thanked her for more than what she gave him.

"I am a thousand times sorry," Ruthven Smith persisted. "More sorry than I can ever explain, or you will ever know."

"Indeed it was nothing," the girl comforted him in her soft young voice. But she read in his words a hidden meaning, as she had read one into Knight's. She *did* know that which he believed she would never know: the meaning of his act, and the effort it had cost to screw his courage to the sticking place.

Also, as the star sapphire with its sparkle of diamonds had flashed into sight, she had seemed to read his mind. She guessed he must be telling himself that his informant—the Countess, or some other—had mistaken one blue stone for another.

"Let's go and join Constance and the Duchess," she went on, quietly. "They're looking at some lovely things you will like to see. And you must forget that Knight was cross. He has lived in wild places, and he has a hot temper."

"I deserved what I got, I'm afraid," murmured Ruthven Smith.

"After all, nothing exciting seems likely to happen to-night in this room, in spite of the Countess's prophecy," said Constance. "Perhaps it may be to-morrow or Monday."

"I hope nothing more exciting will happen then than to-night!" Annesley exclaimed, with a kindly glance at her companion. She pitied him, but she pitied herself more, for by and by she and Knight would have to talk this thing out together.

For the first time she dreaded the moment of being alone with her husband. There was a stain of clay on the feet of her idol, and though she had helped him to hide it from other eyes, nothing could be right between them again until she had told him what she thought—until he had promised to make restitution somehow of the thing he should never have possessed.

CHAPTER XIX.
THE SECRET

Knight and Annesley had a suite of rooms on the ground floor in what was known as "the new wing" at Valley House. On the floor above were the rooms occupied by Lord and Lady Annesley-Seton.

This wing was a dreadful anachronism, shocking to architects, for it had been tacked on to the house in the eighteenth century by some member of the family who had made the "grand tour" and fallen in love with Italy. Seeing no reason why a classic addition with a high-pillared loggia should be unsuitable to a house in England built in Elizabethan and Jacobean days, he had made it.

Fortunately it was so situated as not to be seen from the front of the building, or anywhere else except from the one side which it deformed; and there a more artistic grandson had hidden the abortion as much as possible by planting a grove of beautiful stone-pines.

As for the wing itself, the interior was the most "liveable" part of the house, and with the modern improvements put in to please the American bride before her fortune vanished, it had become charming within. Annesley's bedroom and her husband's adjoining had long windows opening out on the loggia and looking between tall, straight trunks of umbrella pines toward the distant sea.

It was late before she could slip away to her own quarters, for she had been wanted for bridge, an amusement which she secretly thought the last refuge for the mentally destitute. She had told her maid not to sit up; and she was thankful to close the door of the small corridor or vestibule which led into the suite, knowing that until Knight came she would be alone.

She wanted him to come, and meant to wait (it did not matter how long) until they could have that talk she wished for yet dreaded intensely. Meanwhile, however, it was good to have a few minutes in which to compose her mind, to decide whether she should begin, or expect Knight to do so; and how she could frankly let him see her state of mind without seeming too harsh, too relentless, to the man who had given her happiness with both hands—the only real happiness she had ever known.

She sat for a while in the boudoir, thinking that Knight might come soon, before she began to undress. There was a dying glow of coal and logs in the fireplace, but staring into the rosy mass brought no inspiration. She could not concentrate her thoughts on the scene which must presently be enacted; they would go straggling wearily to other scenes already acted, even as far back as that hour at the Savoy when a young man who looked to her like the hero of a novel begged to sit at her table.

He still seemed as much as ever like the hero of a novel in which he had splendidly made her the heroine; but it was not a pleasant chapter she had to read now. It reminded her too intensely of the mystery surrounding the hero, and forced her to realize that stories of real life have not always happy endings.

"But ours must!" she said to herself, springing up, unable to rest. "Nothing can break our love; and while we have that we have everything!"

She could no longer sit still, and going into her bedroom she peeped through the door into Knight's room beyond. It was dark, as she expected to find it; for she had been almost sure that she would have heard him if he had entered the vestibule.

Returning to her own rooms, she pulled back the sea-blue curtains which covered the large window looking on to the loggia. The sky was silver-white with moonlight between the black stems of the tall pines, and a flood of radiance poured into the room. It was so beautiful and bright, bringing with it so heavenly a sense of peace, that the girl could not bear to draw the curtains again. She began slowly to undress by moonlight and the faint red glow in the fireplace.

Her first act was to recover the blue diamond ring and to drop it with shrinking fingers into the jewel-case on her dressing table.

Taking off her dinner frock, she put on a white silk gown which turned her into a pale spirit flitting hither and thither in the silver dusk. Still Knight had not come. She pulled out the four great tortoise-shell pins which held up her hair, and let it tumble over her shoulders. As she began to twist it into one heavy plait, she walked to the window and stood looking out.

It seemed to her that the black trunks and outstretched branches of the trees were like prison bars across the moonlight. She wished she had not had that thought, but as it persisted, a figure moved behind the bars, the figure of a man.

At first she was startled, for it was very late, long after one o'clock; but as the man came nearer, she recognized him, although the light was at his back. It was Knight; and as though her thought called to him, he stopped suddenly, pausing on the lawn not far from the loggia. She could not see his face, but it seemed that he was staring straight up at her window.

"He has been walking in the moonlight, thinking things over just as I have in here!" the girl told herself. Surely he could see her! But no, he turned, and was striding away with his head down, when she knocked sharply and impulsively on the pane.

Hearing the sound, yet not knowing whence it came, he stopped again, and so gave Annesley time to open the window.

"Knight!" she called, softly.

Then he came straight to her across the strip of lawn and up the two steps that led to the loggia. She met him on the threshold and saw his face deadly pale in the moonlight. Perhaps it was only an effect of light, but she thought that he looked tired, even ill. Still he did not speak.

"Knight, you almost frightened me!" she said. "I was afraid for an instant you might be—might be——"

"A thief!" he finished for her.

"Or a ghost," she amended. "Weren't you coming in?"

"No," he said. "I hadn't thought of it. Do you want—shall I come in?"

"Yes, please do. I—I've been waiting for you."

"I'm sorry! I hoped you'd have gone to bed. But I might have known you wouldn't."

As she retreated from the window, he followed her, as if reluctantly, into the room.

"Shall I draw the curtains?" he asked. There was weariness in his voice, as in his face. Annesley's heart went out to her beloved sinner with even more tenderness than before.

"No, let's talk in the moonlight," she answered. "Oh, Knight, I *am* glad you've come! I began to think you never would!"

"Did you? That's not strange, for I was saying to myself that same thing."

"What same thing? I don't understand."

"That I—well, that I never ought to come to you again."

She sank down on a low sofa near the window, and looked up to him as he stood tall and straight, seeming to tower over her like one of the pine trees out there under the moon.

"Oh, Knight!" she faltered. "It's not—so bad as that!"

"Isn't it?" he caught her up sharply, eagerly. "Do you mean what you say? Isn't it, to you—as bad as that?"

"No—no," she soothed him. "You see, I love you. That's all the difference, isn't it? You've been everything to me. You've made my life—that used to be so gray—so bright, so sweet. Only the blackest thing—oh, an unimaginably blackest thing!—could come between us, or——"

Before she could finish, he was on his knees at her feet, holding her in his arms, crushing her against his breast, soft and yielding in her light dressing-gown, with her flowing hair.

"My God, Annesley, it's too good to be true!" he said, his breath hot on her face as he kissed her cheek, her hair, her eyes. "You can *forgive* me? I thought you'd go away. I thought you'd refuse to let me come near you. I was walking out there wondering how to make it easy for you—whether I could get rid of myself without scandal."

She had been sure that he must have repented long ago, and that it would hurt him dreadfully to have her find out the thing he had done, but she had not dreamed that his self-abasement would be so complete. She put her arms around him as he held her, and pressed his head against her neck—the dear, smooth black head which she loved better than ever in this rush of pardoning pity.

"Dearest!" she whispered. "Never, never think or speak of such a dreadful way out! Of course it was horribly wrong, and of course it was a great shock to me, but you might have known from my doing what I could to help that I didn't hate you. I said to myself there must be some excuse—some *big* excuse. And now, if only you wouldn't mind telling me about it from the beginning, I believe it would be the best way for us both. Then I might understand."

"You are God's own angel, Anita!" he said in a choked voice. "You don't know how I've learned to love you, better than anything in this world or the next—if there is a next. I knew you were a saint, but I didn't know that saints forgave men like me.... Shall I really tell you from the beginning? You'll listen—and bear it? It's a long story."

Annesley did not see why the story of his buying the historic stolen diamond and giving it to her should be so very long, even with its explanations; but she did not say this.

"I don't care how long it is," she told him. "But you will be tired—down on your knees——"

"I couldn't tell my story to you in any way except on my knees," he answered. And the new humility of the man she had loved half fearfully for his daring, his defiant way of facing life, almost hurt, as his sudden passion had startled the girl.

"I hardly know how to begin," he said. "Perhaps it had better be with my father and mother, because it was the tragedy of their lives that shaped mine." He was silent for a moment, as if thinking. Then he drew a long breath, as a man does when he is ready to take a plunge into deep water.

"My mother was a Russian. Her people were noble, but that didn't keep them from going to Siberia. She was brought to America by a man and woman who'd been servants in her family. She was very young, only fifteen. Her name was Michaela. I'm named after her—Michael. The three had only money enough to be allowed to land as immigrants, and to get out west—though her people had been rich." He paused a moment for a sigh.

"She and the servants—they passed as her father and mother—found work in Chicago. My father was a lawyer there. He was an Englishman, you know—I've told you that before—but he thought his profession was overstocked at home, so he tried his luck on the other side. The old Russian chap was hurt in the factory where he worked, and that's the way my father—whose name was Robert Donaldson—

got to know my mother. There was a question of compensation, and my father conducted the case. He won it.

"And he won a wife, too. She was nineteen when I was born. Father was getting on, but they were poor and had a hard time to make ends meet. They worshipped each other and worshipped me. You can think whether I adored them!

"Mother was the most beautiful creature you ever saw. Everyone looked at her. I used to notice that when I was a wee chap, walking with my hand in hers. When I was ten and going to school my father had a bad illness—rheumatic fever. We got hard up while he was sick; and then came a letter for mother from Russia. Some distant relations in Moscow had had her traced by detectives. It seemed there was quite a lot of money which ought to come to her, and if she would go to Russia and prove who she was she could get it.

"If father'd been well and making enough for us all he'd never have let her go, but he was weak and anxious about the future, so she took things into her own hands and went, without waiting for yes or no, or anything except to find a woman who'd look after father and me while she was gone. Well, she never came back. Can you guess what became of her?" he asked, huskily.

"She died?" Annesley asked, forgetting in her interest, which grew with the story, to wonder what the history of Knight's childhood and his parents' troubles had to do with the Malindore diamond.

"She died before my father could find her; but not for a long time. God—what a time of agony for her! Things happened I can't tell you about. We heard nothing, after a letter from the ship and a cable from Moscow with two words—'Well. Love.'

"For a while father waited and tried not to be too anxious; but after a time he telegraphed, and then again and again. No answer. He went nearly mad. Before he was well enough to travel he borrowed money and started for Russia to look for her. I stayed in Chicago—and kept on going to school. The friends who took care of me made me do that ... or thought so.

"But when I could, I played truant. I was in a restless state. I remember how I felt as if it were yesterday. Nothing seemed real, except my father and mother. I thought about them all the time. I couldn't sleep, and I couldn't study. I couldn't bear to sit at a desk. I picked up some queer pals in those months—or they picked me up. I suppose that was the beginning of the end.

"I think while he was away, finding out terrible, unspeakable things, my father forgot about me—or else he didn't realize I was big enough to mind. He never wrote. When he came back, after eleven months, he was an old man, with gray hair. I'll never forget the night he came, and how he told me about mother. It was a moonlight night, like this—with no light in the room. It was the last night of my childhood."

As the man talked, he had lifted his head from the soft pillow of the girl's white neck, and was looking into her eyes, his face close to hers. Annesley was not thinking about the diamond.

"For a long time," Knight went on, slowly, "father could not trace my mother. He expected to find the relations who had sent her word about the legacy, but they were gone—nobody could tell where. Nobody wanted to speak of them. They seemed afraid. Father went to the British and American Embassies; no use! But at last he got to know, in subterranean ways, that mother hadn't realized how dangerous it is to speak your mind in Russia. She'd left there before she was sixteen!

"She had said things about her father and mother, and what she thought of the ruling powers, and that same night—she'd been in Moscow two days—she and her relatives disappeared. It leaked out through a member of the secret police that she could have been saved by her beauty—someone high up offered to get her free. But she preferred another fate.

"She was sent to Siberia where her father and mother had gone, and had died years before. My father met a man who had seen her on the way as he was coming back. She was only just alive. The man was sure she couldn't have lived more than a few weeks.

"Yet father wouldn't give up. He went after her.... But what's the use of going on? He found the place where she had died.... Which ends that part of the story, as a story.

"Only it didn't end it for us. It filled our hearts with bitterness. We wanted revenge. Yet my father was too good a man to take it when his chance came. His conscience held him back. But he talked—talked like an anarchist, a man out to fight and smash all the hypocritical institutions of society. If it hadn't been for me he'd have killed himself in Siberia where his wife had died a martyr; and it would have been well for him if he had!

"Because of the wild way he talked when suspicion of fraud was thrown on him by a partner the fool public believed in his guilt. He died in prison when I was fifteen, and I swore to punish the beast of a world that had killed all I loved. I swore I'd make that my life's work, and I have. But—God!—I've punished myself, too, at last. I'm punished through you, because I've fallen in love with you, Anita, and for your sake I'd give the years that may be in front of me—all time but one day to be glad in, if I could blot out the past!"

"Maybe," the girl faltered, "maybe you're too hard on yourself. I can't believe that you, who have been so good to me, could have been very bad to others."

"If I could hope you wouldn't be too hard on me, that's all I care for now!" he cried, passionately. "You remember my saying that night in the taxi that the worst I'd ever done was to try and pay back a great wrong, and take revenge on society? If I could hope you meant what you said about understanding I'd tell you the story of that revenge."

"I *did* mean it, Knight. My love will help me to understand."

"You make me believe in a God, for surely only God could have sent such an angel as you into my life.... In a way, I haven't deceived you about myself, for I warned you I was a bad man. But when I think of the night we met and the trick I played on you, it makes me sick! I thought you'd loathe me if you ever found out. But I didn't intend to let you find out. It was to be a dead secret forever, like the rest. Yet if I tell you what my life has been you'll have to know that part, too. If I kept it back you might think it worse than it was."

"A trick?" echoed Annesley.

"Yes. A trick to interest you—to make you like and want to help me. Besides, it was to be a test of your courage and presence of mind. If you hadn't those qualities you'd have been a failure from my point of view. You see, I hadn't had time to fall in love with you then. And I wanted you for a 'help-mate' in the literal sense of the word. It seems a pretty sordid sense, looking back from where we've got to now. But that was my scheme. A mean, cowardly scheme! And it's thanks to you and your blessed dearness I see it in its true light.... Do you begin to understand, Anita—knowing something of what my life has been, or must I explain?"

"I—I'm afraid you must explain," she answered in a small voice, like a child's. She felt suddenly weak and sick, as if she might collapse in the man's arms. It was as if some terrible weapon wrapped round and half hidden in folds of velvet were lifted above her head to strike her down.

She shrank from the blow, yet asked for it. Already she guessed dimly that Knight's confession was to be very different from and far more terrible than anything she had expected.

"I was the man whose advertisement you answered—the man who wrote you the stiff letter in the handwriting you didn't like, signed N. Smith."

"Oh!" The word broke from her in a moan.

"Darling! Have I lost you if I go on?"

"You must go on!" she cried out, sharply. "For both our sakes you must go on!"

"I know how it looks to you. And it was vile. But I couldn't be sure when I advertised what an angel would answer to my call, and what a brute I should be to deceive her. I thought the sort of girl who'd reply to an 'ad' for a wife would be fair game; that I should be giving her an equivalent for what she'd give me.

"For my business that I had to carry out in England I needed a wife of another sort from any woman I knew, or could get to know, in an ordinary way; she had to be of good birth and education, nice-looking and pleasant-mannered—if possible with highly placed friends or relatives. Money didn't matter. I had enough—or would have. I got a lot of answers, but the only one that seemed good was yours. I felt nearly certain you were the woman I wanted, so I rigged up a plan. You know how it worked out."

"Maybe I'm stupid," Annesley said, dry-lipped. "I don't understand yet."

"Why, I thought the thing over, and it seemed to me that married life—if it came to that—would be easier for both if the man could make some sort of appeal to the love of romance in a girl. Well, she wouldn't think the man who had to get the right sort of wife by advertising much of a figure of romance. So the idea came to me of—of starting two personalities. I wrote you a stiff, precise sort of letter in a disguised business hand, making an appointment at the Savoy. When that was done, the writer went out of your life.

"He just ceased to exist, except that he sat behind a big screen of newspaper and watched for a girl in gray-and-purple, wearing a white rose, to pass through the foyer. That was his way of finding out if she'd suit. Jove, how beastly it does sound, put into words, and confessed to *you*! But you said I must go on."

"Yes—go on," Annesley breathed.

"You were about one hundred times better than my highest hopes. And seeing what you were, I was glad I'd thought out that plan. Even then, it was borne in on me that it wouldn't be long before I found myself falling in love, if I had the luck to secure you. And from that minute the business turned into an exciting play for me, just as I meant to make it for you. I let you wait for a while, but if you'd showed any signs of vanishing I'd have stepped up. I'd got a trick ready for that emergency.

"But I hoped you'd follow instructions and go to the restaurant. Once there, I was sure the head-waiter'd persuade you to sit down at a table; and the rest went exactly as I planned. The two men we called the 'watchers' used to be vaudeville actors—did a turn together, and their specialty was lightning changes. Their make-ups, even at short notice, could fool Sherlock Holmes. Even though you despise me for it, Anita, you must admit it was a smart way to make you take an interest, and prove your character.

"Lord, but you stood the test! I wouldn't have given you up at any price then, even if I hadn't begun falling in love. I saw how good you were; and in that taxi going to Torrington Square I felt mean as dirt for tricking you. But of course I had to go on as I'd begun.

"At first I thought it was luck, tumbling into the same house with Ruthven Smith; but now I see it was the devil's luck. If it hadn't been for Ruthven Smith I might have gone on living the part I played. You need never have known the truth. And I swear to you, Annesley, I'd made up my mind, after finishing off my work with the men who are with me, that I'd run straight for the rest of my days. The business was making me sick, for being close to your goodness threw a light into dark places.

"By heaven, Anita, it does seem hard, just as I was near to being the man you thought me, that that dried-up curmudgeon Ruthven Smith should call my hand and make me show you the man I was! But I can't help seeing there's a kind of—what they call poetical justice in it, the blow coming from him. I've always been like that: seeing both sides of a thing even when I wanted to see only one. But if *you* can see both sides, you will make the good grow, as the bright side of the moon grows, and turns the dark side to gold.

"Can you do that, do you think, Anita? Can you see any excuse for me in going against the world to pay it out for going against me and mine? If you've been piecing bits of evidence together since Ruthven Smith spoke, you'll have remembered that only heirlooms and things insured by, or belonging to, public companies, have been taken; no poor people have been robbed; and except in the case of Mrs. Ellsworth, where I wanted to see her paid out for her treatment of you——"

"'Robbed'!" Catching the word, Annesley heard none of those that followed. "*Robbed!* Oh, it's not possible you mean——"

Her voice broke. With both hands against his breast she pushed him off, and struggled to rise, to tear herself loose from him. But he would not let her go.

"What's the matter? How have I hurt you worse than you were hurt already by finding out?" he appealed to her, his arms like a band of steel round her shuddering body. "When you heard the truth about the diamond, it was the same as if you'd heard everything, wasn't it? You guessed Ruthven Smith suspected—someone must have told him—Madalena perhaps. You guessed he had some trick to play, and in the quietest, cleverest way you checkmated him, without hint or help from any one. You saved me from ruin, and not only me, but others. And on top of all that, when I hoped for nothing more from you, you promised me forgiveness. That's what I understood. Was I mistaken?"

"*I* was mistaken," she answered, almost coldly; then broke down with one agonized sob. "I thought—oh, what good is it now to tell you what I thought?"

"You must tell me!"

"I thought you had bought the blue diamond, knowing it had been stolen, but wanting it so much you didn't care how you got it. I didn't dream that you were a——"

"That I was—what?"

"A thief—and a cheat!"

"My God! And now you know I'm both, you hate me, Anita? You must, or you wouldn't throw those words at me like stones."

"Let me go," she panted, pushing him from her again with trembling, ice-cold hands.

He obeyed instantly. The band of steel that had held her fell apart. She stumbled up from the low sofa, and trying to pass him as he knelt, she would have fallen if he had not sprung to his feet and caught her.

But recovering herself she turned away quickly and almost ran to a chair in front of the dressing table not far off. There she flung herself down and buried her face on her bare arms.

Knight followed, to stand staring in stunned silence at the bowed head and shaking shoulders. He could hear the ticking of a small, nervous-sounding clock on the mantelpiece. It was like the beating of a heart that must soon break. At last, when the ticking had gone on unbearably long, he spoke.

"Anita, you called me a cheat," he said. "I suppose you mean that I cheated you by playing the hero that night at the Savoy, and stealing your sympathy and help under false pretenses; that I've been steadily cheating you and your friends every day since. That's true, in a way—or it was at first. But lately it's not been the same sort of cheating. It began to be the real thing with me. I mean I felt it in me to be the real thing. As for the other name you gave me—thief—I'm not exactly that—not a thief who steals with his own hands, though I dare say I'm as bad.

"If I haven't stolen, I've shown others the most artistic way to steal. I've shown men and women how to make stealing a fine art, and I've been in with them in the game. Indeed, it was my game. Madalena de Santiago, and the two men you knew first as the 'watchers,' then as Torrance and Morello, now as Charrington and Char, have been no more than the pawns I used, or rather they've been my cat's paws. There's only one other man at the head of the show besides me, and that is one whose name I can't give away even to you.

"But he's a great man, a kind of financial Napoleon—a great artist, too. He doesn't call himself a thief. He's honoured by society in Europe and America; yet what I've done in comparison to what he's done is like a brook to the size of the ocean. He has a picture gallery and a private museum which are famous; but there's another gallery of pictures and another museum which nobody except himself has ever seen. His real life, his real joy, are in them. Most of the masterpieces and treasures of this world which have disappeared are safe in that hidden place, which I've helped to fill.

"That man has no regrets. He revels in what he calls his 'secret orchard.' He thinks I ought to be proud of what I've done for him; and so I was once. I came here and brought the other people over to England to work for him.

"Not that that fact will whitewash me in your eyes; not that I wasn't working for myself, too, and not that I'm trying to make more excuses by explaining this. But I'd like you to understand, at least for the sake of your own pride, that you haven't been cheated into loving and living with a common thief. Does that make it hurt less?"

"No," she said in a strange tone which made her voice sound like that of an old woman. "That doesn't make it hurt less. It makes no difference. I think nothing can ever make any difference. My life is—over."

"Don't, for God's sake, say that! Don't force me to feel a murderer!" he cried out, sharply.

"There's nothing else to say. I wish I could die to-night."

"If one of us is to die," he said, "let it be me. If you hadn't happened to see me and call me in when I was under the trees bidding good-bye to your window, by this time I might have found a way out of the difficulty without any scandal or trouble to you whatever. No one would have known that it wasn't an accident——"

"I should have known."

"But if you had, it would have been a relief——"

"No. Because I—I hadn't heard the truth. I didn't understand at all. I thought you had done *one* unscrupulous thing. I didn't dream your whole life was—what it is. I loved you as much as ever. It would have broken my heart if you——"

"But now that you don't love me, it wouldn't break your heart."

"I don't seem to have any heart," Annesley sighed. "It feels as if it had crumbled to dust. But it would break my life if you ended yours. If anything could be worse than what is, it would be that."

"Very well, you can rid yourself of me in another way," the man answered. "You can denounce me—give me up to 'justice.' If you hand over the Malindore diamond to Ruthven Smith and tell him how you got it— —"

"You must know I wouldn't do that!"

"Why not?"

"Because I—couldn't."

"It needn't spoil your life. No one could blame you. I would tell the story of how I deceived you. You could free yourself—get a divorce— —"

"Don't!" the girl cut him short. "I'm not thinking of myself. I'm thinking of you. I can't love you again, and I wouldn't if I could, now that I—know. You're a different man. The one I loved doesn't exist and never did; yet you've told me your secret, and I'm bound to keep it. I don't need to stop and reflect about that. But as for what's to become of me, and how we're to manage not to let people guess that everything's changed, I don't know! I must think. I must think all to-night, until to-morrow. Perhaps by that time I can decide. Now—I beg of you to go and leave me—this moment. I can't bear any more and live."

He stood looking at her, but she turned her head away with a petulant gesture of repulsion; and lest her eyes might feel the call of his she covered them with her hands. Her hopelessness, her loathing of him enclosed her like a wall of ice.

"So! The dream's over!" he said. "'This woman to this man'! What a farce—what a tragedy!"

When she looked up again he had gone and the door between their rooms was shut.

The moon no longer lit the high window. With Knight's going darkness fell.

CHAPTER XX.
THE PLAN

Annesley sat as Knight had left her for a long time—minutes, perhaps, or hours. But at last she was very tired and very cold, so tired that she threw herself weakly on the bed, in her dressing-gown, because she couldn't sit up. All through the rest of the dark hours she lay shivering, and did not even trouble to roll herself in the warm down coverlet spread lightly over the bed.

It seemed right, somehow, that she should be cold and miserable physically. She did not care or wish to be comfortable.

Over and over again she asked herself: "What shall I do? What is to become of me—of both of us?" She tried to pray, but her heart was too hard toward the man who had trampled on her life and love for his own cruel purposes. It seemed to her that God would not hear a prayer sent up in such a mood; yet she did not want to soften her heart toward the sinner.

Because it had been so full of forgiveness before he poisoned the chalice with the bitter stream of confession, it was the more impossible to forgive now. It even seemed to Annesley that it would be monstrous to forgive, in the ordinary, human sense of the word, a man who was a living lie.

If there were room for thanksgiving in her wretchedness, it lay in the fact that her love had died a swift and sudden death. Had she gone on loving in spite of all, such love, she thought, must have brought death into her soul.

She did not know how to name her husband now. Even in thinking of him she would not call him "Knight."

What a mockery the name had been! How he must have laughed to know that she was fool enough to believe him a knight of chivalry, who had come like St. George to rescue her from the dragon!

She knew at last that the name he had not wished her to see in the parish register was Michael Donaldson. That meant, she supposed, that her name was Donaldson, too; a name he had dragged through the mire.

He pretended to love her. But such a man could not speak the truth. He had tried to excuse himself in every way. To talk of love and its purifying influence was only one of these ways. He would not even have confessed if he had not fallen into the mistake of thinking she understood that he was a thief, or head of a gang of thieves.

He seemed almost to boast of what he was.... Oh, how horrible life had become, and how she wished that it were over! She wondered if it would be wicked to pray that her heart might stop beating to-night.

Yet morning came and her heart beat on. She did not even feel very ill, only weak, with a wiry throbbing of each separate nerve in her head. She had meant to use the quiet hours to decide what must be done next, but always, when she had tried to pin her mind to the question, it had escaped like a fluttering moth, and turned to self-pity, or to calling up pictures of the past which brought tears to her eyes.

Now the time was upon her when realities must be faced. Before seven o'clock it was light, but neither she nor Knight were accustomed to early tea, and there was more than an hour to spare before they would be called by Parker.

The girl sat up shivering, though the room, heated by steam, had not grown bitterly cold when the grate fire died. She looked, heavy-eyed, toward her husband's closed door. They must talk things over, and make some plan.

She hated the very word "plan" since his story of the trick he had played at the Savoy. She hated the necessity to talk with him; but it *was* a necessity. They ought to arrange something for the future—the blank and hateful future—before Parker came, and daily life began. There would be many things to settle, questions to ask and answer; a sort of hideous campaign would have to be mapped out in details not one of which defined itself clearly in her tired brain.

"It's no use," she said to herself. "I can't think, after all, until I see him again. Perhaps he will make some suggestions, and I can accept or refuse. But I *can't* go to his door and call him."

As she hesitated, Knight—who was a knight no longer in her eyes—opened the door, very softly, not to disturb her if she slept. In the morning light which paled the uncurtained window their eyes met.

Annesley slipped off the bed and stood up, cloaking her bare white neck with her hair. Suddenly she felt that he was a strange man who had no right to be in her room. He was not the husband she had loved with a beautiful and sacred love.

"I won't come if you'd rather I didn't," he said. "I only looked in to see if you were awake. I thought if you were, and if you could stand it, it would be best to—talk about what's to be done." He spoke quietly, standing at the door. He was dressed for the day, as if nothing had happened; and Annesley felt dimly resentful because he looked bathed and well-groomed, his black hair smooth and carefully brushed; altogether his usual self, except that he was pale and grave.

"You had better come in, I suppose," the girl replied, grudgingly. "I was thinking, too, that we must talk. Let us—get it over."

"You haven't been to bed, I see," he said, his eyes lingering on her sadly. It flashed through Annesley's mind that it was as if he were looking for the last time at the sweetness and happiness of life. But her heart did not soften. It was his fault that there was no longer any happiness or sweetness left in their lives.

"No, I haven't been to bed," she returned. "But it doesn't matter. I am not ill. Please let us not waste time in discussing me. There are other things."

"Yes, there are other things," he agreed. "But we'll not begin to talk of them until you have got into bed and covered yourself up. You're as white as marble."

"I don't want——" she began; but he cut her short.

"What will Parker think if she finds your bed hasn't been slept in?"

"Oh, very well!" Annesley assented, impatiently. "I must get used to tricks!"

"Perhaps not," said Knight. "I've been thinking of ways and means. Have you? Because if there's anything you feel you would like to do, you've only to tell me."

"I haven't been able to think," she confessed.

"Well, then, I'll tell you what I've thought."

Annesley had now crept into bed; and before she could protest Knight had carefully covered her with the down quilt. Having done this, he drew a chair near, yet not too near, and sat down. It was as if he recognized her right to keep him at a distance.

"You said last night," he began, "that you didn't mean to denounce me. If you've changed your mind, I shan't blame you; I deserve it. All I ask is that you grant me time to warn certain persons who would go down if I went down, and give them time to make a bolt. Madalena de Santiago is one. I'm pretty sure that out of spite she put Ruthven Smith on to looking for the diamond, but I don't want to punish her. Evidently she—or whoever it was—didn't have much information to give, or the man wouldn't have backed down and apologized. I should like to find out exactly what he had to go upon. But if you've changed your mind, it's not worth while to bother about that——"

"I have not changed my mind," Annesley said.

"You are very good, a very noble woman. If I were the only one to suffer by being denounced, I don't think I'd care much, as things have turned out. But there are others. And above all, there's you. You could patch up your life, but you'd have to suffer more or less if I were dragged over the coals. And so, taking everything together, I'm thankful to accept your generosity.

"We'll call that settled. I don't think Ruthven Smith has any suspicion. We'll see about that later. Meanwhile, he doesn't count. And Madalena at her worst I can manage. There's nothing to be feared. But the question is, how are we two to go on?"

"You must—whatever else we decide—you must give up——" the girl stammered from her pillows, and could not bring herself to finish.

"That goes without saying, doesn't it? In any case, there was only to be one more *coup*. I'd warned everybody concerned of my decision as to that."

"*One more?* How terrible! Not—*here?*"

"Yes, if you must have that, too; it was to be here. It was to be a big thing. But there's time to stop it."

Annesley buried her head with a stifled moan.

"It wouldn't have hurt any of the people. Only family heirlooms again—everything insured. And as for the insurance companies, if you worry over them, it's part of the game. They're wallowing in money ... But I'll call the thing off. And that's the end for me. I'm not rich—not the millionaire I pose for; still, I've earned something. My 'Napoleon' has paid me well, and I've had a share now and then of some good things. There's enough to make you comfortable——"

"Do you think I'd take a penny of such money?" the girl cried, sick with indignation.

"I've worked for it," Knight said, with a kind of unhappy defiance, "and it was come by as honestly as a lot of fortunes made on the stock market. You must have money——"

"I can earn some, as I did before."

"No, *never* as you did before! Besides, I thought you'd decided on having no open break between us, no scandal. Or wasn't that what you meant?"

"It was. But—I don't see yet how it can be managed. Do you?"

"The way I had in my mind was, since I've lost your love—oh, I'm not complaining!—the way I had in my mind was to leave you over here with plenty of money, and be suddenly called to America on business. Then, if it would hurt your feelings to have me put myself out of the way, it needn't hurt them for something to *seem* to happen. Nelson Smith could be wiped off the map; and if you weren't free to marry somebody else, at least you'd be free of me.

"But if you won't take my money that plan will not work. You can hate me as much as you like, but I'm not going to leave you alone in the world without a penny. Neither you nor any one can force me to that.... I've thought of another thing, though, since we began to talk. Only I don't like to propose it, Anita. It isn't a good plan—from your point of view."

"I'd better hear it."

"Well, I might get a cable hurrying me across to the other side, and—you might go along."

"Oh!"

"I warned you you wouldn't think it a good plan. But since I've begun, let me finish. In Canada and the United States I'm known—in my least important character—as Michael Donaldson, and I've tried to keep the name clean because of my father and mother. When there's been anything shady doing I've taken a fancy name and made such changes as I could in myself. The reason I didn't want you to see the name in the register was because of what happened on the *Monarchic*. I'd given you that ring, you know. I couldn't resist doing that. I wanted you to have it, not because of its value, but because it's beautiful. I thought it was like you, somehow. I had to make up its loss in another way to the man who expected to have it—that 'Napoleon' I mentioned."

"I know, the old man—Paul Van Vreck," Annesley guessed with weary impatience.

"I'll not say yes or no to that. But it will be bad for me, and perhaps for you, too, if you ever mention Paul Van Vreck in such a connection. Not that you'd be believed."

"I sha'n't mention him again."

"Just as well not.... But it was my name and my plan I began to speak about. I was going to say, you needn't be afraid that if you took my name (which is yours now), you'd have to be ashamed of it. We could go to America, and in England Mr. and Mrs. Nelson Smith would soon be forgotten. I'd hand over the money you hate to charities—not the kind of charities I've been supporting here! They've all been part of what you call my fraud, and have only given me a chance to bring some rather queer-looking fish around me, who might have raised curiosity if I couldn't have accounted for them. But real charities.

"And if you'd stick by me—I don't mean love me; I know you can't do that; but live in the same house and not chuck me altogether, I'd turn over a new leaf. I'd begin again from the beginning.

"In Texas I've got some land—a ranch. It isn't worth much, I'm afraid, but I came by it honestly, for me. I won it at poker from a man named Jack Haslett. He was a devil for cards, but it didn't matter. He was rich; and he had a better ranch that he lived on. He's dead now—was near dead then, of consumption. He liked me. Said he was glad I'd won the ranch. It was only a bother to him.

"I was with Jack when he died, and did what I could to ease him at the end. He was grateful, and what money his bad luck at cards had left him he willed to me. It was only eight thousand dollars.

"If it had come to me any other way, I dare say I'd have chucked it away in a month. It wouldn't have seemed worth saving. But I was sort of sentimental about poor old Haslett and his feeling for me. I didn't care to lump his money in with what I got in my line of life. I made a separate fund of it.

"Some had to go toward improvements on the place before I could let the ranch to any one, but there's about six thousand dollars left, I guess. The fellow I let to wrote me a few weeks ago that he was tired of ranching and wanted to clear out. He hoped I could find someone to buy his cattle and the furniture he's put in the house. The letter was forwarded by a man I keep in touch with my business and whereabouts, so he can look after my interests. I've had no time to answer yet.

"I was going to write that I didn't know any one who cared to settle in Texas; but now what if I wrote that I'd take the place and everything on it off the fellow's hands myself?"

"I don't know what Texas is like," Annesley replied, coldly. "But anything would be better than the life you're leading now."

"I wasn't intending to go alone," Knight reminded her. "I said, if you'd stick by me, not throw me over altogether, I'd try and begin again. In that case, Texas would do as well as anywhere; and the place and the money are clean."

"How could I go with you, and live under the same roof, with everything so changed?" the girl exclaimed. "It would kill me!"

"As bad as that?... Well, then, I must rack my brains for something else. But I'm sorry this won't do. Would you care to live with Archdeacon Smith and his wife?"

"No. No! And they wouldn't want me."

"That seems queer to me: that any one should have the chance of keeping you with them, and not want you ... How would it be for you to go on the same ship with me, and find a little home somewhere on an allowance I could make you out of that fund? You see, you are my wife in the eyes of the law, so I'm bound to support you. And you're bound to let me do it, if I can do it honestly."

Annesley flung up her arms in a gesture of abandonment. "Let it go at that," she sighed, "until I can think of something better."

"Very well. We won't argue that part yet. The thing to make sure of at the moment is this: Do I get a cable, say on the day everyone's leaving Valley House, calling me back to America on urgent business, and do I take you with me?"

Annesley's thoughts raced through her head and would not stop. Knight did not speak. He was waiting with outward patience for her decision.

It seemed that she would never know what to say. She was about to tell him in despair that she must have the rest of the day to make up her mind, but before she could speak Parker knocked at the door.

"I'll go with you," the girl said, hastily. "On the ship. But after that— —"

Parker knocked again.

"Come in!" called Annesley.

"Thank you," Knight said, getting up from his chair near her bed.

"*Don't* thank me. I— —"

But Parker had opened the door. All that was conventional and agreeably commonplace in the lives of happy, well-to-do people seemed to enter the room with her.

CHAPTER XXI.
THE DEVIL'S ROSARY

Ruthven Smith summoned courage to ask for a few words alone with Knight that Easter morning, in order to explain as well as apologize for the "seeming liberty he had taken." By dint of stammering, and punctuating his sentences with short, dry coughs, he made "a clean breast," as he called it, of the "whole business."

He had come to Valley House, he confessed, because of an anonymous letter, written apparently by a person of education, to inform him that the Malindore diamond had come into the possession of the Nelson Smiths. Whether they were aware of its identity, the writer was not sure; but in any case their ownership of the jewel was kept secret.

Having got so far in his story, Ruthven Smith decided that the easiest way of finishing it would be to produce the letter. He did so (a typewritten sheet of plain creamy paper, in an envelope post-marked "West Hampstead"), and simplified things for himself by pointing to the last sentence.

> Mrs. Nelson Smith always wears a thin gold chain round her neck, which she lets drop to her shoulders for evening dress. What precious thing which has to be hidden hangs on that chain? Mr. Ruthven Smith is advised to find out.

"I see now," the unfortunate man excused himself, "that someone has been taking advantage of my anxiety about the losses of my firm to play a cruel practical joke on me. I can't help thinking, at the same time, that the person must have had a grudge against you and your wife also."

"Or else a desire to make mischief between you and us," was Knight's calm suggestion.

Ruthven Smith caught it up, eagerly. "Ah, that possibility hadn't occurred to me."

"I suppose we all have enemies." Knight pursued the subject without excitement. "The writer probably wished to put the idea in your head that I had deliberately bought an historic diamond which I knew to be stolen."

"But that would have been ridiculous!" exclaimed the jewel expert, and felt sincere in making his protest.

Nevertheless, he had glanced at Annesley's face while talking of the Malindore diamond to Lady Cartwright. It had been on the edge of his mind that, if she looked self-conscious, it would be a point against her and her husband. Also he had determined to make his daring attempt at discovery before she had time to get rid of the diamond if she were hiding it. Now, however, in the light of her shining innocence, he had almost forgotten that he had suspected an underhand design on her part.

He asked Nelson Smith if he could think of any one, man or woman, among his acquaintances capable of writing the anonymous letter. Nelson Smith replied that his brain was a blank, and that he hardly thought it worth while to follow the matter up, unless Ruthven Smith wished to do so. In that case they might put the affair in the hands of the police.

But the elder man was of the younger's opinion. He had made a fool of himself, and was ashamed that he had attached importance to an unsigned communication. All he desired was to let the unpleasant business drop.

This being settled, Knight, in whose hand was the typewritten letter, tossed the thing into the fireplace of the library, where the two had been talking. When he and Ruthven Smith had shaken hands and agreed to forget the whole incident the latter was glad to escape from the interview. He went to his room and lay down, to soothe his nerves and think of an excuse to return to London early on Monday morning.

As soon as his meagre back was turned Knight stooped and retrieved the letter in its envelope, unscorched, from the fireplace. There was nothing about it—not even a tell-tale perfume—to give any clue to the writer.

Nevertheless, Knight considered it of value. He intended to use it as a bluff to frighten the Countess de Santiago, for only through her own fear could he prove her treachery.

Most of the guests at Valley House went to church, to give thanks for the fairy-like Easter eggs they had received. Annesley had a headache, however, and no one was surprised that her husband should choose to stop at home to look after her.

His adoring devotion for the girl was no secret. People laughed at it, but admired it, too, and some women envied Annesley. They imagined him spending the morning with his wife, but as a matter of fact he did not go near her. He feared to speak lest she might change her decision and refuse to travel to America with him.

His one hope—a desperate hope—lay in her going. He decided not to see her alone again until Monday evening, after the arrival of the cable from America.

In order to insure the coming of this message, and to make it realistic, he motored into Torquay and sent a long telegram, partly in cipher. Returning, he had a conversation with Charrington, the butler, and Char, the chauffeur, a conversation which left the brothers grave and subdued. Later Char went off in the car again, though it poured with rain, and was gone until late at night.

Between twelve and one o'clock Knight, strolling toward the garage, heard the automobile return, and stopped in the blaze of the acetylene for the motor to slow down.

"Is it all right?" he inquired.

"It's all right," Char answered, somewhat sullenly, yet with a certain reluctant respect. "Nothing will happen here Monday night."

"Good!" his master answered, and smiled at the thought of Madalena's malicious prophecy which would not be fulfilled. It was not a pleasant smile, yet, as he had said to Annesley, he planned no revenge against the tigress—the woman whose claws had ripped his heart open.

Tigress or no, she was a woman, and he knew that, as far as she was capable of caring, she had cared for him.

Perhaps it had been partly his fault. She was handsome, and had been years younger when he had met her first. She was married then to an old man, jealous and suspicious, knowing that his money had won the beautiful wild creature for him. It was at Buenos Aires, and the husband had found Madalena out in an intrigue; partly political, partly mercenary, and partly passionate. He had turned her from his house without a penny, and Knight—not personally concerned in the intrigue, but interested—had been flush enough at the time to lend her a thousand dollars, enough to go away with. It had been called a loan, but he had not expected to get the money back, and never did get it.

In California she had set herself up as a palmist and had become successful, a success she duplicated in New York; and she had gladly made herself useful in many ways to "Don" and those with whom he "worked."

One way was to find out the number and worth of her rich clients' jewels, and where they were kept. Through her crystal gazing she was able to conjure women's secrets without their realizing that they, not she, gave them to the light. And aboard the *Monarchic* was not by any means the first time that Madalena had been invaluable in diverting suspicion by throwing it upon the wrong track.

Knight had consulted her, praised her, and flattered her from time to time. Now he told himself that he was paying for his thoughtlessness. He had taken Madalena for granted, regarding her as a machine rather than a woman; and though he owed to her the loss of his happiness, that happiness had been undeserved and, as he expressed it to himself, walking the wet paths at midnight, he had "stood to lose it anyhow."

He would frighten Madalena so that she would never dare to try her tricks again, and he would let her understand that because of what she had done their partnership had come to an end once and forever. Otherwise she should feel herself safe from him.

Bad he might be, and was, as he knew; but he didn't think it was in his make-up, somehow, to strike a woman.

He did not go back to the house, after his short talk with Char, until after he had heard the stable clock strike four. It was easier to think and see things clearly out of doors than in his room adjoining Annesley's—that closed room, forbidden to him now, where she was perhaps crying, and surely hating him. As for the long nightmare day he had lived through, it had been too full for much deliberate thinking; and he wanted to plan for the future: how to begin again, and how to keep the woman who had come to mean more for him than anything else had ever meant—more, he knew, than anything else could mean.

He was not sure whether the love in his heart was a punishment or a blessing, but there it was. It had come to stay.

"This woman to this man!"

He found himself repeating the words he remembered best in the marriage service, not bitterly as he had repeated them to Annesley, but yearningly, clingingly, groping after some promise of hope in them.

"She gave herself to me. I'm the same man she loved, after all, though she says I'm not," he told himself. "God! What's the good of being a man at all, if I can't get her back?"

As he wandered through one winter-saddened garden after another—the Italian garden, the Dutch garden, the rose garden—he searched his soul, asking it how much more he should have to tell the girl about his past. In a kind of desperate resignation he persuaded himself that there was nothing he would not be willing to tell her now, if it were for her good, and if she wished to hear.

But something within him said that she would wish to hear no more. She would deign to put no questions to him, even if she felt curiosity. She would doubtless refuse to listen if he volunteered a further confession. He was instinctively sure of his ground there; and in his bitterness of spirit there was a faint gleam of comfort; certain details of his degradation (she would think it that) might be kept decently hidden.

For instance, he would not have to tell her how, as a boy in Chicago, he had learned to make strange use of those clever, nervous hands of his, which she had lovingly praised as "sensitive and artistic." He could almost see the girl shudder and grow pale at hearing how proud he had been at sixteen of being admitted to friendship with a "swell mobsman" fascinating as any "Raffles" of fiction; how it had amused the fellow to teach him a deft and delicate touch, beginning his lessons with the game of jack-straws, in which he was given prizes if he could separate the whole stack, one straw from another, without disturbing the balance of the pile.

It would gain him no credit in Annesley's eyes if he should assure her that, though he knew how to pick pockets—none better—he had somehow never cared to put his skill in practice, but had always preferred, leaving that part of the industry to others. No excuse could help him with her, and he was glad she need not know all the ways in which he had served the eccentric friend and employer with whose interests he had been associated more or less since his twenty-fifth year.

How disgusting would seem to Anita the inside history of the *Monarchic* episode, upon which he had rather prided himself until love for her had begun making subtle changes in his view of life. He and old Paul Van Vreck had laughed together at the patent lock on which the agent depended—a lock invented by the retired member of the firm himself, and followed by a second invention, even more clever: a little instrument designed to open a door in spite of it.

There had been the drug, too, which leaving no odour behind, had the same effect as chloroform, and "took" even more quickly. Paul Van Vreck had read of certain experiments made by a professor of chemistry in Tours, had gone to France to see the man, had bought the formula, which had not yet proved itself entirely successful; had added an ingredient on his own account, and triumphed.

These parts of the complicated and well-fitting scheme had seemed deliciously amusing to Knight in those days; that Van Vreck should use his secret skill against his own brothers and nephews in the business he had made; that the great expert should add to his fortune by stealing from his own firm, or rather, from the great insurance company who would repay their losses; that in such ways, with such money, he could add treasures to his famous collection, practically at no expense to himself, and have besides the exquisite pleasure of laughing in his sleeve at the world.

It had all added zest to the work. And Knight had been pleased with some small inventions of his own, praised by Van Vreck: a smart hiding-place in the heel of a boot, almost impossible to detect, and another equally convenient and invisible in the jet standard of Madalena de Santiago's famous crystal. He had enjoyed the excitement when he and Madalena and their two assistants, among the other passengers on board ship, had consented to be searched for the missing jewels. And he had laughed sneeringly at the credulity of those who believed in Madalena's trumped-up vision "of the small fair man," the lighted life-preserver dropped into the sea at night, and the yacht which sent out a boat to pick it up.

For that other vision her crystal had supplied after the robbery in Portman Square he was not responsible; but it was he who had suggested the "pictures" for her to see on shipboard.

He hated the recollection now. Even Annesley could not think it more contemptible than he did.

Still worse was the remembrance of Mrs. Ellsworth's latchkey, the keeping of which had been accidental at first. Afterward he had gaily regarded its possession as a gift from Providence. The way to Ruthven Smith's house was made clear by it; and better still, through it the dragon could be punished for years of cruelty to the captive princess. "Char" had been the man to whom fell the honour of bestowing the punishment, and leaving a missive from the princess's rescuer.

Knight writhed in spirit as he wondered whether the princess guessed the fate of the key.

He wondered also if she asked herself what part he had had in the disappearance of the Valley House heirlooms. She would loathe him more intensely, if possible, could she know how her presence with him on that public "show day" had helped to cloak with respectability his secret mission. How mean he had been in distracting her attention from the two Fragonards and from the cabinets containing the miniatures and the carved Chinese gods of jade while he "marked" the prizes for the eyes of his two assistants. How unsuspicious and happy the girl had been, trusting him utterly, while behind her back he manipulated the diamond—the useful diamond—he always carried for such purposes!

Even then he had the grace to be ashamed of himself for disloyalty, though not for dishonesty, as deftly the diamond cut the glass faces of the cabinets directly opposite the miniatures and the Buddha meant to enrich Paul Van Vreck's secret collection. He had been glad to hurry his wife away, and let the eager pair of "tourists" crowding on his heels finish the work he had begun.

It seemed to Knight, as his thoughts travelled heavily along the past, that no other woman but Annesley Grayle, this fragile white rose that had freely given its sweetness, could have turned him from the vow of vengeance for his parents' fate which as a boy he had sworn against the world. Day by day, week by week, month by month, the fragrance of the white rose had so changed him that looking back at himself, he saw a stranger.

Had it not been for certain engagements made with Paul Van Vreck and others—engagements which had to be kept because there is honour among thieves—that "den" of his in Portman Square would long ago have been shut to his "at home" day visitors. No more "business" would have been done on those or any premises; this party of Easter guests would not have been invited to Valley House; and the Malindore diamond, sleeping away its secret on Annesley's breast, would still be guarding his secret, too.

While the others were at church she had sent him the diamond by Parker—the blue diamond, and the rose sapphire; her engagement ring also; the pearls he had given her the day before their marriage, and all his other gifts (except the wedding ring), which had not been stolen on the night when the Annesley-Setons' silver went.

It had been a blow to open the box brought to his room by the maid without a word of explanation—no lighter because it was deserved. It was only less severe than had the wedding ring been with the rest.

And perhaps, Knight reflected, it would have been there had Annesley known of another trick played upon her: those cleverly "reconstructed" pearls, gleaming ropes of them, and paste diamonds added to her collection only for the purpose of disappearing in the "burglary." A hateful trick, but he had believed it necessary at the time, while despising it.

Well, he was punished for everything at last—everything vile he had done and thought in his whole life; even those things the White Rose did not know!

He was young still, but he felt old—old in sin and old in hopelessness; for youth cannot exist in a heart deprived of hope. It seemed to Knight that his heart had been deprived of hope for years, yet suddenly he recalled the fact that a few moments before—up to the time when he had begun counting his sins one by one, like the devil's rosary—he had been thinking with something akin to hope of the future.

"What if, after all——" he began to ask himself.

But stumbling unseeingly from avenue to path, and path to lawn, he had wandered near the house.

By what seemed to him a strange coincidence he had come to a standstill almost on the spot where he had stood last night when Annesley, at her window, called him in.

She had loved him then! She had called him in to be forgiven. But her forgiveness, divine as it was, white and wide-winged as the flight of a dove—had not been wide enough to cover his guilt.

What a ghastly difference between last night and this! It was right that the face of the moon, so bright then, should be veiled with ragged black clouds. And yet, what if——

The man's eyes strained through the darkness of that dark hour before the dawn.

"If her window is uncurtained, I'll take it as a good omen," he said.

Noiselessly his feet trod the short, wet grass, going nearer to the shadowed loggia to make sure....

The curtains were drawn closely, and the window was shut.

CHAPTER XXII.
DESTINY AND THE WALDOS

After the cablegram came, calling them to America, it took the Nelson Smiths an incredibly short time to wind up their affairs and to break the ties—many and intricate as the clinging tendrils of a vine—which attached them to England.

Of course, as their friends pointed out, it wasn't as if they had had a home of their own. Luckily for them—unluckily for the Annesley-Setons—they had taken the Portman Square house only month by month. And in Devonshire they had been but paying—dearly paying!—guests, as the world surmised.

Everyone protested that they would be dreadfully missed, and begged to know their plans, and whether Mr. Nelson Smith's business on the other side (something to do with mines, wasn't it?) would not be finished, so that they might come back in time for Henley and Cowes?

But the American millionaire's answers were vague. He couldn't tell. He could only hope. And his manner, unflatteringly, was indifferent. It was Mrs. Nelson Smith who seemed depressed; "a changed girl," Constance said, "from the moment that cable message arrived at Valley House."

Connie thought, and mentioned her thought to others: very likely the truth was that Nelson Smith had lost money. In contradiction to this theory he was known to have given generously to charities just before starting; not those queer, new-fangled societies he had tried to bolster up while he was in London, but hospitals and orphan asylums, and organizations of that sort which opened their mouths wide.

Still, nobody could say for a certainty how much he gave, and it was argued that Lady Annesley-Seton was sure to know more than most people about Nelson Smith's private affairs. The story of possible money losses ran about and grew rapidly, healing regrets for his absence. Soon the pair dropped out of their late friends' conversation as a subject of living interest.

It was much the same with the Countess de Santiago. Whether her plans were affected by those of the Nelson Smiths, nobody knew; and she said that they were not. But about the time that their departure for America was decided upon, Madalena had a sharp illness. It was, she wrote Constance (who made inquiries, fearing something contagious), an unusual form of neuralgia, from which she had suffered before. The only doctor who had ever been able to relieve her pain lived in San Francisco, and in San Francisco she must seek him.

She had at first an idea of sailing on the same ship with the Nelson Smiths; but for a reason which she did not explain, she changed her mind the day after making it up, and engaged a cabin on a boat which started a week earlier.

She was missed, also, for a while. But then it was remembered that the crystal visions had been mysteriously more favourable for those who included the Countess in their nicest parties than for those who asked her to their second best. Little malicious digs which she had given were recalled, and those who had thought her wonderful when in their midst began to doubt her powers.

"Rather theatrical, don't you think?" said the Duchess of Peebles. "It's more satisfactory to go to a woman you can pay with money and not invitations."

So Madalena was not mourned for long; and the Annesley-Setons were fortunate enough to replace their lost American millionaire with one from Australia. He was old, and his wife was fat; but you can't have everything.

The Nelson Smiths took passage not on one of the great floating palaces patronized by millionaires, but on an obscure, cheap little ship, which bore out the gossip about the man's losses. As a matter of fact, however, they chose that way of going by Annesley's desire. It would have been Knight's way to vanish in a blaze of glory, as the setting sun plunges behind the horizon after a gorgeous day.

"I want to go on a ship," she said, "which none of the people we know have ever heard of. I couldn't bear to come across anyone I ever met before."

But, as it turned out, she was forced to bear what she had thought unbearable. At the top of the gangway as she went on board, a slightly shrill voice called out, "Why, how *do* you do! Who would ever have thought of meeting you two expensive creatures on board *this* tub?"

With a sinking heart Annesley recognized a Mrs. Waldo, an American woman (there was a husband in attendance) whom she and Knight had met during their honeymoon at the Knowle Hotel. The pair had been so friendly and kind that the Nelson Smiths had asked them to Portman Square more than once during the three gay months which followed.

But it was cruel, thought Annesley, that fate should bring them together again now, just when she and the man she had married were at the parting of the ways.

Little had the girl dreamed when she first conceived a mild fancy for the pretty, smiling woman and her silent, humorous husband, that the pair were destined to decide her future—decide it in a way precisely opposite to that in which she had decided it herself. But so it was to be.

Mr. and Mrs. Waldo were returning to New York in its waning season because the decorating of a house they had bought was just completed. They begged Annesley and Knight to be their first visitors, and the invitation was given so unexpectedly that Annesley, taken unawares, found herself at a loss.

"But I—I mean my husband—is going straight to Texas," she stammered.

"All the more reason, if he has to run off so far on business, and leaves you in New York, that you should stay with us, instead of in a hotel," argued Mrs. Waldo.

Annesley blushed, and for the first time since Easter eve looked for help to Knight. But he was silent, and she blundered on, not daring to pause lest the firm-willed little lady should seal her to a promise in spite of herself.

"You're very kind, and it would be delightful," she hurried along, "but I didn't mean that I was to stop in New York. I——"

"Oh, you are going together!" Mrs. Waldo caught her up. "I didn't understand. Well, I'm sorry for our sakes. But couldn't you spare us two or three days before you start?"

"I—am afraid we must wait for another time," said Annesley. "My husband has business. He can't waste a day——"

"Surely you won't turn your back on New York the day you arrive, the first time you've ever seen it!" cried the New York woman. "Why, it's sacrilege! You must stay with us one night. If you could see the *darling* new room we'll put you in: old rose and pearl gray, and Cupids holding up the bed curtains!"

In desperation the girl stuck to her point, no longer daring to look at Knight.

"Indeed we mustn't stay, even for one night. If there's a train the same afternoon——"

"There's a lovely train," Mrs. Waldo admitted, unable to resist praising the American railway system. "We call it the 'Limited.' You can have a beautiful stateroom, and run right through to Chicago without changing. If they must go, we'll see them off, won't we, Steve?" with a glance for the silent husband, "and bring them books and chocolates and flowers?"

What was left for Annesley to say? Short of informing the kindly couple that they were not wanted and had better mind their own business, and refusing to decide upon a train, she could do nothing except thank Mrs. Waldo.

"Perhaps," she thought, "they will forget, and things will settle themselves between now and then. Or else I shall patch up some excuse."

When the invitation was given, the *Minnewanda* was still four days distant from New York; but the four days, though seeming long, were not long enough to produce the prayed-for inspiration. Mrs. Waldo referred to the journey whenever she saw Annesley, so there was no hope of her scheme being forgotten; and the nearer loomed the new world, the more clearly the girl was forced to see the thing to which a few hasty words had committed her.

She and Knight had staterooms adjoining, with a door between. That was to save appearances, and it was no one's business that the door was never opened. In reality, they might as well have had the length of the ship between their cabins.

Annesley kept to her own quarters as constantly as her jangled nerves would allow; but the sea was provokingly smooth, and she proved to be a good sailor. She felt as if she might become hysterical, and perhaps do something foolish, if she tried the experiment of shutting herself up from morning to night. She paced the deck, therefore, and was dimly grateful to Knight because he seemed always to be in the smoking room when she took her walks.

At meals, however, unless she ate in her stateroom, they could not avoid each other; and again she felt cause for gratitude because Knight had accepted the Waldos' suggestion that they should take a table for four. In spite of the Waldos' unwelcome attentions, their society was preferable—infinitely preferable—to a duet with Knight.

They talked on such occasions; and the sharpest-eared scandal mongers could have guessed at nothing strange from their manner. But, save at these luncheons and these dinners, they scarcely spoke to each other.

Knight took his cue from Annesley. After the night when he had knelt at her feet and begged her forgiveness he had never forced himself upon his wife. He seemed to have a dread of being thought an intruder, and even withdrew his eyes guiltily if the girl caught him looking at her with the old wistful gaze to whose mystery she had now a tragic clue.

Annesley hoped that, before they landed, Knight might make some opportunity to discuss ways and means of getting out of the dilemma created by the Waldos. But he never attempted to begin a conversation with her, and she put off the evil moment from day to day, telling herself that there was time yet, and he had probably solved the problem—he, who was a specialist in solving problems.

Loving the man no longer, her heart seeming to die anew whenever she even thought of him, there remained still a ghost of her old trust; an almost resentful confidence that he who was so clever, so hideously clever, would be capable of overcoming any difficulty.

"I told him that I'd go with him on the ship, and that then we must part," she assured herself, lying awake at night, wondering feverishly what was to happen in New York. "He said we'd see about all that later, but he must know by the way I act that I haven't changed my mind. He will have to get me out of the trouble about the train."

The girl, in mapping the future, had thought of herself as being a governess for American children. She did not know many things which governesses ought to know, but if the children were small enough, she did not see why she mightn't do very well.

She could sing and play as nine girls out of ten could. She had been told that she had quite a Parisian accent in French; and as for arithmetic and geography and other alarming things which children ought to know and grown-up people forget, one could teach them with the proper books.

Besides, she had heard that Americans liked to have English governesses for their children; it was considered "smart."

She would go to an agent, and it ought to be easy to find a place in the country or suburbs. It must not be New York, for fear of some chance meeting with the Waldos. But if worst came to worst, and because of those everlasting Waldos she had to get into the train with Knight, she would get out again at the first good-sized place where it stopped. There must be agencies for governesses and companions in every large town. One would serve as well as another.

As for money, she knew that she must have some to go on with until she could begin to earn. So far she had been forced to let Knight pay her way, as he said, out of the "good" fund. Her coming with him had been for his sake, and to spare him from gossip. For herself, she was in no mood to care what people said.

But now, in sailing to America as his wife, she had done all that she had ever promised to do. He would have to arrange things as best he could.

Somehow the right time did not come to ask him what he intended to do; for at the table, or if occasionally they were on deck together, they were never alone.

The ship docked late in the morning, and Knight was busy with the custom-house men. It was noon when their luggage had been examined and could be sent away; and the Waldos, under letter "W," were released at the same moment that the Nelson Smiths, under "S," were able to escape.

"Let's have lunch at the dear old Waldorf, our pet place and almost namesake," proposed Mrs. Waldo. "You *owe* us that, after all the times you entertained us in London; and you really see New York in the restaurant. You've nothing to do till your train goes this afternoon, and your husband can get your reservations right there in the hotel."

Annesley's eyes went doubtfully to Knight's, and met a steady look which seemed to say that he had made up his mind to some course.

"Very well, we shall be delighted," she said, resignedly. "Shall we meet at the—Waldorf—is it?—at luncheon time?"

"Oh, *my*, no!" exclaimed the older woman, radiant in the joy of home coming. "It'll be lunch time in an hour. You *must* taxi up to Sixty-first Street with us, and just *glance* at the house, or we shall be *so* hurt. Then we'll spin you down to the hotel again in no time. I wish we could feed you at home, but nothing will be in shape there till tonight."

There was still no chance for Annesley to ask Knight the long-delayed question. They saw and duly admired the Waldos' house, and took another taxi to the hotel, the Nelson Smiths' luggage having been "expressed" to the Grand Central, to await them. Steve Waldo tried to engage his favourite table, and Mrs. Waldo suggested that it would be a good moment to get the reservations.

Again Annesley's startled glance turned to Knight. Again his eyes answered with decision. This time there was no longer any doubt in the girl's mind. The Waldos, persistent to the last, would compel her to leave New York with her husband.

But whatever happened she would part with him forever before darkness fell. "At the first big town," she told herself once more.

They were at the desired table, which Steve had secured, when Knight rejoined them, announcing that he had his tickets.

"I hope you were able to get a nice stateroom?" fussed Mrs. Waldo. "Such a *long* journey, and Mrs. Smith's first day in our country!"

"Yes. Everything satisfactory," said Knight, in the calm way which Annesley had once admired.

Mrs. Waldo would have asked more questions if at that moment her eyes had not lighted upon a couple at an adjacent table.

"*Well*, of all *things*!" she cried, jumping up to meet a pretty girl and a spruce young man, who had also jumped up. "George and Kitty Mason! What a coincidence!"

There were kissings and handshakings. Then Mr. and Mrs. Mason were introduced to Mr. and Mrs. Nelson Smith. They, it seemed, had been married in the early winter, just as Knight and Annesley had been. And to add to the strangeness of the coincidence, which drew birdlike exclamations from Jean Waldo, George and Kitty were starting for Kansas City that afternoon. They were going by the same train in which the Nelson Smiths would travel.

"Why, you'll be together for *two days*!" shrieked Jean. "For goodness' sake, look at your reservations, and see if you're in the same car!"

George Mason pulled out his tickets. "We're in a boudoir car all the way," he said. "We start in one called 'Elena.' After Chicago we're in 'Alvarado.'" Knight followed suit, not ungraciously, though without enthusiasm. Annesley's heart was tapping like a hammer in her breast. She felt giddy. There was a mist before her eyes; yet she saw clearly enough to see that there were two railway tickets, alike in every way, even to what seemed their extraordinary length. A flashing glance gave her the name of the last station, at the end. It was in Texas.

And their two staterooms were also in "Elena" and "Alvarado."

CHAPTER XXIII.
THE THIN WALL

"How *dared* he buy a ticket for me all the way to Texas!" Annesley asked herself. "But I might have known how it would be," she thought. "Why expect a man like him to keep a promise?"

Yet she *had* expected it. She constantly found herself expecting to find truth and greatness in the man who was a thief—who had been a thief for half his life. It was strange. But everything about him was strange; and stranger than the rest was his silent power over all who came near him, even over herself, who knew now what he was. It would have seemed that after his confession there would be no further room for disappointment concerning his character; yet she was disappointed that his "plan," on which she had been counting, had been nothing more original than to break his word and "see what she would do."

After luncheon, when the Waldos and Masons became absorbed for a few minutes in talk, she turned a look on her husband. "I saw the tickets," she said.

"Did you?" he returned, pretending—as she thought—not to understand.

"You bought one for me to Texas."

"Of course. Did you think I wouldn't? That would have been poor economy in the game we've been playing."

It was her turn to show that she was puzzled. "What do you mean?"

"You never cared to talk things over. I saw you didn't want to, so I didn't press. And when this complication about the Waldos came up, I thought—perhaps I was mistaken—that you—trusted me to do the best I could."

"Yes. That's why I expected you not to get me a ticket to Texas."

"How far *did* you expect me to get it?"

"I—don't know."

"That's just it. Neither did I know. I got the whole ticket, so you might choose your stopping-place."

"Oh!" Annesley was ashamed, though she was sure she had no need to be. "That was why!"

"That was why. Things being as they are, it was well I had your ticket to show with mine, wasn't it?"

"I—suppose so. But—what am I to do?"

"We'll talk of that in the train. There won't be time before, because of these people, and because I must leave you for two hours before the train goes."

"Leave me!" Annesley echoed the words blankly, then hoped that he had not noticed the dismay in her tone.

"You will be all right with the Waldos and their friends. I'll explain to them. There's no time to lose. I must go off at once."

Annesley was pricked with curiosity to know why and where he must go. She would not ask. But while he was away and she was being whirled through the park and along Riverside Drive at lightning speed, "to see New York in a hurry," her thoughts were with her husband, imagining fantastic things.

"My mind is like a ghost," she thought, bitterly, "haunting what once it loved. It seems doomed to follow wherever he goes, whatever he does. But it will be different when we're parted. I shall escape in soul and body. I shall have my own life to live."

"That wonderful Italian house," Mrs. Waldo was saying, as the taxi slowed down for one of her lectures, "is Paul Van Vreck's New York home. They say it's a museum from garret to cellar (not that there *is* a garret!), and I believe it's a copy of some palazzo in Venice. It's shut up now; perhaps he's in Florida, or Egypt, where he—but look, somebody's coming out—why, Mrs. Nelson Smith, it's your *husband*! Shall we stop——"

"No, let's drive on," Annesley begged, anxiously. "My husband knows Mr. Van Vreck. They have business together. He won't want us."

The taxi was allowed to go on to the next place of interest. Annesley had flung herself back in the seat, but she was not sure that Knight hadn't seen her. She knew what powers of observation his quiet almost lazy manner could hide.

This chance meeting took place on the way to the Grand Central Station, where they met the Masons, and were joined almost at the last moment by Knight, just as Annesley had begun to wonder if, after all, he were not coming.

He was as calm as though there were no haste, and said he had been delayed in collecting the luggage from the ship. He had a good deal to say about that luggage; and what with thanks to the Waldos for books and flowers and chocolates, and their kindness to Annesley, Mrs. Waldo (with the best intentions) found no chance to mention Paul Van Vreck.

Annesley had not meant to refer to him, though seeing Knight come out of his shut-up house had given her a shivering sense of mystery; but when the train had started, Knight came to the door of her stateroom.

"There are one or two things I should like to speak to you about, if you don't mind," he said, in the kind yet distant manner which had replaced the old lover-like way when they were alone together.

"Come in," she replied, and added, lowering her voice: "Mr. and Mrs. Mason are next door."

"They are too much in love to be thinking about us, or listening," he answered; and Annesley imagined a ring of bitterness in his tone. "I've come to talk over plans, but before we begin I want to explain something. Once you made a guess in connection with Paul Van Vreck. Probably you think that what you saw confirms it. Of course, the Waldos were telling you whose house it was; and as luck would have it, I came out at that instant.

"Whether there was anything in your guess or not doesn't matter. You're too sensible to mention it to any one except me. But I can't have you torturing yourself with the idea that such dealings as you imagine with Van Vreck are still going on, if they ever did go on. Because I have faith in your discretion, and because I owe it to you, I'm going to explain why I went to Van Vreck's house this afternoon — why I was obliged to go. I knew he would have got back from Florida.

I hear from him sometimes, and I had to tell him that any business I'd ever done for him was done for the last time, because—I was going to settle down to ranch life in Texas.

"Also I handed to him the Malindore diamond. His firm lost it. His firm has by this time been paid the insurance. It's up to him how to dispose of the property.

"That's all I have to say about Van Vreck. I thought in fairness you ought to know that I didn't keep the diamond. And I thought I might tell you that my call at Van Vreck's didn't mean entering any new deal."

"Thank you," Annesley said, stiffly. "I am glad."

She *was* glad, yet she wished the man to understand how impersonal was her gladness; how impossible it was that any atonement could bring them together again in spirit; how dead was the past which he had slain. And he did understand as clearly from her few words as if she had preached him an hour's sermon.

"Now, for what you are to do," he went on, crisply. "Although you and I never discussed the situation on board ship, I realized what the Waldos were letting you in for. I supposed you'd feel that your staying in New York was out of the question. I bought our tickets to Texas. At the same time I got a map and a guide-book which gives information about places on the way and beyond.

"The Masons being on the train to Kansas City was a new complication. But it wasn't my fault. And it only means that the game of keeping up appearances must be played a little farther.

"Would you like to go to California? If you want to take back your maiden name and be Miss Grayle—or if you care to have a new name to begin a new life with, a quite respectable fellow called Michael Donaldson could introduce you to a few influential people in Los Angeles. No danger of meeting Madalena de Santiago there, though it's only a day's journey from San Francisco, where she's very likely arrived by this time. She has reasons for not liking Los Angeles. In her early days she had some—er-financial troubles there, and she wouldn't enjoy being reminded of them."

"Is Los Angeles farther than El Paso?" Annesley inquired, keeping her voice steady, though there was a sickly chill in her heart.

"A good way farther," Knight went on, in the same businesslike tone which separated him thousands of miles from the Knight she used to know. "Here, I'll show you how the land lies."

Opening a map of a western railroad, he drew a little closer to her on the seat, and pointed out place after place along the black line; told her when they would arrive at Kansas City, and how they would go on without change to Albuquerque.

There, he said, he must take another train for El Paso, and from El Paso he must go a distance of twenty miles to the ranch, which lay close to the border of Mexico, on the Rio Grande.

"But you," he said, quietly, "you can keep straight along in the train we'll get into at Chicago till you come to Los Angeles. There'll be time in Chicago to buy your ticket to California, and I can write letters of introduction. They'll be to good people. You needn't be afraid."

Yet Annesley *was* afraid, deathly afraid. Not that Knight's friends would not be "good people," but of going on alone to an unknown place in an unknown country. It would not have been so terrible, she thought, to have stayed in New York—if only the Waldos hadn't interfered. But to have this man—who, after all, was her one link with the old world—get out of the train which was hurling them through space and leave her to go on alone!

That was a fearful thing. She could not face the thought—at least not yet. Perhaps she would feel more courageous to-morrow. On the ship she had slept little. Her nerves felt like violin strings stretched too tight—stretched to the point of breaking.

"Does that plan suit you—as well as any other?" Knight was asking.

"I—can't decide yet," the girl answered; and to keep tears back seemed the most important thing just then. "It doesn't matter, does it, as I *must* go on past Kansas City?"

"No, it doesn't matter," Knight agreed. "You've plenty of time. I suppose you'd like me to leave you now, to rest till dinner time? Here's the guide-book. You might care to look it over."

But when he had gone Annesley let the book lie unopened on the seat. She was very tired. She could not think far ahead. Her mind would occupy itself with the features of the journey, not with her own affairs.

Everything was strange and new. Even the train was wonderful. She had thought, in the immense station, that the cars looked like a procession of splendidly built bungalows each painted a different colour and having brightly polished metal balconies at the end. And inside, the car was still like a bungalow, or perhaps a houseboat, with neat little panelled rooms opening all the way down a long aisle.

The coffee-coloured porter and maid were delightful. They smiled at her kindly, and when they smiled it seemed sadder than ever not to be happy.

The Masons' talk at dinner was disconcerting. They took it for granted that she and Knight were an adoring newly married couple, like themselves. Annesley was thankful to escape, and to go to bed in her little panelled room.

"To-morrow, when I'm rested, things will be easier," she told herself.

But to-morrow came and she was not rested; for again she had not slept.

In Chicago there were hours to wait before train time. The Masons proposed taking a motor-car to see the sights, and lunching together at a famous Chinese restaurant.

At a sign from her, Knight consented. It was better to be with the Masons than with him alone. After luncheon, however, Knight drew her aside.

"What about Los Angeles?" he inquired. "Have you decided?"

Annesley felt incapable of deciding anything, and her unhappy face betrayed her state of mind.

"If you'd rather think it over longer," he said, "I can buy your ticket at Albuquerque."

"Very well," Annesley replied. She did not remember where Albuquerque was, though Knight had pointed it out on the map; and she did not care to remember. All she wanted was not to decide then.

Knight turned away without speaking. But there was a look almost of hope in his eyes. Things could not be what they had been; yet they were better than they might be.

At Kansas City the Masons bade the Nelson Smiths good-bye. And from that moment the Nelson Smiths ceased to exist. There were no initials on their luggage.

The man kept to his own stateroom. Annesley, alone next door, had plenty of books to read, parting gifts from the Waldos; but the most engrossing novel ever written could not have held her attention. The landscape changed kaleidoscopically. She wondered when they would arrive at Albuquerque, wondered, yet did not want to know.

"Would you rather go to the dining car alone, or have me take you?" Knight came to ask.

"It's better to go together, or people may think it strange," she said. Even as she spoke she wondered at herself. The Masons having gone, the other travellers—strangers whom they would not meet again—were not of much importance. Yet she let her words pass. And at dinner that evening she forced herself to ask, "Do we get to Albuquerque to-night?"

"Not till to-morrow forenoon," Knight informed her casually. He feared for a moment that she might say she could not wait so long before making up her mind; but she only looked startled, opened her lips as if to speak, and closed them again.

Next day there were no more apple orchards and flat or rolling meadow lands. The train had brought them into another world, a world unlike anything that Annesley had seen before. At the stations were flat-faced, half-breed Indians and Mexicans; some poorly clad, others gaily dressed, with big straw hats painted with flowers, and green leggings laced with faded gold. In the distance were hills and mountains, and the train ran through stretches of red desert sprinkled with rough grass, or cleft with river-beds, where golden sands played over by winds were ruffled into little waves.

Toward noon Knight showed himself at the open door of the stateroom.

"We'll be in Albuquerque before long now," he announced. "That's where I change, you know, for Texas. The train stops for a while, and I can get your ticket for Los Angeles. Those letters of introduction I told you about are ready. I've left a blank for your name. I suppose you've made up your mind what you want to do?"

Some people with handbags pushed past, and Knight had to step into the room to avoid them. The moment, long delayed, was upon her!

Annesley remembered how she had put off deciding whether or not to sail for America with Knight. Now a still more formidable decision was before her and had to be faced. She glanced up at the tall, standing figure. Knight was not looking at her. His eyes were on the desert landscape flying past the windows.

"What I *want* to do!" she echoed. "There's nothing in this world that I want to do."

"Then"—and Knight did not take his eyes from the window—"why not drift?"

"Drift?"

"Yes. To Texas. Oh, I know! I asked you that before, and you said you wouldn't. But hasn't destiny decided? Would it have sent you these thousands of miles with me unless it meant you to fight it out on those lines? You've travelled far enough, side by side with me, to learn that a man and a woman with only a thin wall between them can be as far apart as if they were separated by a continent.

"Now, this minute, you've got to decide. It isn't *I* who tell you so. It's fate. Will you go on alone from the place we're coming to, or—will you try the thin wall?"

CHAPTER XXIV.
THE ANNIVERSARY

The girl felt as if some great flood were sweeping her off her feet. She clutched mechanically at anything to save herself. Knight was there. He stood between her and desolation; but if he had spoken then—if he had said he wanted her, and begged her to stay, she would have chosen desolation.

Instead, he was silent, his eyes not on her, but on the desert.

"You—swear you will let me live my own life?" she faltered.

"I swear I will let you live your own life."

He repeated her words, as he had repeated the words of the clergyman who had, according to the law of God, given "this woman to this man."

The train was stopping.

Annesley knew that she could not go on alone.

"I will try—Texas," she said in final decision.

Las Cruces Ranch was named, not after the New Mexico town thirty or forty miles away, but in honour of the Holy Crosses which had rested there one night, centuries ago, while on a sacred pilgrimage.

It was a lonely ranch, as far from El Paso in Texas as it was from the namesake town in New Mexico. Even the nearest village, a huddled collection of low adobe houses and wooden shacks on the Rio Grande ("Furious River," as the Indians called it), was ten miles distant. Only the river was near, as the word "near" is used in that land of vast spaces. At night, if a great wind blew, Annesley fancied she could hear the voice of the rushing water.

When she first saw the place where she had bound herself to live, her heart sank. It seemed that she would not be able to support the loneliness; for it would be desperately lonely to live there, lacking the companionship of someone dearly loved. But afterward—afterward she could no more analyze her feeling for the country than for the man who had brought her to it.

Lonely as she was, she was never homesick. Indeed, she had no home to long for, no one whose love called her back to the old world. And she was glad that there were no neighbours to come, to call her "Mrs. Donaldson" and ask questions about England.

She had nobody except the Mexican servant woman and the cowboys who stayed with the new rancher when the old one went away.

Knight had suggested that she should wait in El Paso until he had seen whether the house was habitable for her, and had made it so, if it were not already. But Annesley had chosen to begin her new life without delay, for she was in a mood where hardships seemed of no importance. It was only when she had to face them in their sordid nakedness that she shrank.

Yet, after all, what did it matter? If she had stepped into the most luxurious surroundings she would have been no less unhappy.

The low house was of adobe, plastered white, but stained and battered where the walls were not hidden by rank-growing creepers, convolvulus, and Madeira vines. If the girl had read its description in some book—the veranda, formed by the steep-sloping roof of the one-story building; the patio, walled mysteriously in with a high, flower-draped barrier; the long windows with green shutters—she would have imagined it to be picturesque.

But it was not picturesque. It was only shabby and uninviting; at least that was her impression when she arrived, toward evening, after a long, jolting drive in a hired motor-car.

The paintless wooden balustrade and flooring of the veranda were broken. So also were the faded green shutters. The patio was but a little square of dust and stringy grass. A few dilapidated chairs stood about, homemade looking chairs with concave seats of worn cowskin.

Inside the house there was little furniture, and what there was struck Annesley as hideous. Nothing was whole. Everything was falling to pieces. Illustrations cut out of newspapers were pasted on the dirty, whitewashed walls.

The slatternly servant, who could speak only "Mex," had got no supper ready. Knight would let Annesley do nothing, but he deftly helped the woman to fry some eggs and make coffee. He tried to find dishes which were not cracked or broken, and could not.

If he and Annesley had loved each other, or had even been friends, they would have laughed and enjoyed the adventure. But Annesley had no heart for laughter. She could only smile a frozen, polite little smile, and say that it "did not matter. Everything would do very well." She would soon get used to the place, and learn how to get on.

When she had to speak to Knight she called him "you." There was no other name which she could bear to use. He had had too many names in the past!

As time went on, however, the girl surprised herself by not being able to hate her home. She found mysteriously lovely colours in the yellow-gray desert; shadows blue as lupines and purple as Russian violets; high lights of shimmering, pale gold.

Spanish bayonets, straight and sharp as enchanted swords which had magically flowered, lilied the desert stretches, and there were strange red blossoms like drops of blood clinging to the points of long daggers. Bird of Paradise plants were there, too, well named for their plumy splendour of crimson, white, and yellow; and as the spring advanced the China trees brought memories of English lilacs.

The air was sweet with the scent of locust blossoms, and along the clear horizon fantastically formed mountains seemed to float like changing cloud-shapes.

The cattle, which Knight had bought from the departing rancher, had their corrals and scanty pastures far from the house, but the cowboys' quarters were near, and Annesley never tired of seeing the laughing young men mount and ride their slim, nervous horses.

This fact they got to know, and performed incredible antics to excite her admiration. They thought her beautiful, and wondered if she had lost someone whom she loved, that she should look so cold and sad.

These men, though she seldom spoke to any, were a comfort to Annesley. Without their shouts and rough jokes and laughter the place would have been gloomy as a grave.

There was a colony of prairie dogs which she could visit by taking a long walk, and they, too, were comforting. It was Knight who told her of the creatures and where to seek them; but he did not show her the way.

If things had been well between them, the man's anxiety to please her would have been adorable to Annesley. As soon as he saw the deficiencies of the house, he went himself to El Paso to choose furniture and pretty simple chintzes, old-fashioned china and delicate glass, bedroom and table damask. He ordered books also, and subscribed for magazines and papers.

Returning, he said nothing of what he had done, for he hoped that the surprise might prick the girl to interest, rousing her from the lethargy which had settled over her like a fog. But her gratitude was perfunctory. She was always polite, but the pretty things seemed to give her no real pleasure.

Knight had to realize that she was one of those people who, when inwardly unhappy, are almost incapable of feeling small joys. Such as she had were found in getting away from him as far as possible.

She practically lived out of doors in the summertime, taking pains to go where he would not pass on his rounds of the ranch; and even after the sitting room had been made "liveable" with the new carpet laid by Knight and the chintz curtains he put up with his own hands, she fled to her room for sanctuary.

Knight's search for capable servants was vain until he picked up a Chinaman from over the Mexican border, illegal but valuable as a household asset. Under the new régime there was good food, and Annesley had no work save the hopeless task of finding happiness.

It was easy to see from the white, set look of her face as the monotonous months dragged on that she was no nearer to accomplishing that task than on the day of her arrival. Nothing that Knight could do made any difference. When an upright cottage piano appeared one day, the girl seemed distressed rather than pleased.

"You shouldn't spend money on me," she said in the gentle, weary way that was becoming habitual.

"It's the 'good fund' money," Knight explained, hastily and almost humbly. "It's growing, you know. I've struck some fine investments.

And I'm going to do well with this ranch. We don't need to economize. I thought you'd enjoy a piano."

"Thank you. You're very kind," she answered, as if he had been a stranger. "But I'm out of practice. I hardly feel energy to take it up again."

His hopes of what Texas might do for her faded slowly; and even when their fire had died under cooling ashes, his silent, unobtrusive care never relaxed.

Only the deepest love—such love as can remake a man's whole nature—could have been strong enough to bear the strain.

But Annesley, blinded by the anguish which never ceased to ache, did not see that it was possible for such a nature to change. She who had believed passionately in her hero of romance was stripped of all belief in him now, as a young tree in blossom is stripped of its delicate bloom by an icy wind. Not believing in him, neither did she believe in his love.

She thought that he was sorry for her, that he was grateful for what she had done to help him; that perhaps for the time being he intended to "turn over a new leaf," not really for her sake, but because he had been in danger of being found out.

Scornfully she told herself that this pretence at ranching was one of the many adventures dotted along his career; one act in the melodrama of which he delighted to be the leading actor. His own love of luxury and charming surroundings was enough to account for the improvements he hastened to make at the ranchhouse.

Anxiously she put away the thought that all he did was for her. She did not wish to accept it. She did not want the obligation of gratitude. It even seemed puerile that he should attempt to make up for spoiling her life by supplying a few easy chairs and pictures and a Chinese cook.

"He likes the things himself and can't live without them," she insisted. And it was to show him that he could not atone in such childish ways that she lived out of doors or hid in her own room.

At first she locked the door of that room when she entered, thinking of it defiantly as her fortress which must be defended. But when weeks grew into months and the enemy never attacked the fortress her vigilance relaxed. She forgot to lock the door.

Summer passed. Autumn and then winter came. Knight was a good deal away, for he had bought an interest in a newly opened copper mine in the Organ Mountains, and was interested in the development which might mean fortune. At night, however, he came back in the second-hand motor-car which he had got at a bargain price in El Paso, and drove himself.

Annesley never failed to hear him return, though she gave no sign. And sometimes she would peep through the slats of her green shutters on one side of the patio at the windows of his bedroom and "office," which were opposite. It was seldom that his light did not burn late, and Annesley went to bed thinking hard thoughts, asking herself what schemes of new adventure he might be plotting for the day when he should tire of the ranch.

Often she wondered that her life was not more hateful than it was; for somehow it was not hateful. Texas, with its vast spaces and blowing gusts of ozone, had begun to mean more for her than her cold reserve let Knight guess, more than she herself could understand.

On Christmas morning, when she opened her bedroom door, she almost stumbled over a covered Mexican basket of woven coloured straws. Something inside it moved and sighed.

She stooped, lifted the cover, and saw, curled up on a bit of red blanketing, a miniature Chihuahua dog. It had a body as slight and shivering as a tendril of grapevine; a tiny pointed face, with a high forehead and immense, almost human eyes.

At sight of her a thread of tail wagged, and Annesley felt a warm impulse of affection toward the little creature. Of course it was a present from Knight, though there was no word to tell her so; and if the dog had not looked at her with an offer of all its love and self she would perhaps have refused to accept it rather than encourage the giving of gifts.

But after that look she could not let the animal go. Its possession made life warmer; and it was good to see it lying in front of her open fire of mesquite roots.

She had no Christmas gift for Knight.

He had made, soon after their coming to the ranch, a cactus fence round the house enclosure; and seeing the dry ugliness of the long, straight sticks placed close together, Annesley disliked and wondered at it. At last she questioned Knight, and complained that the bristly barrier was an eyesore. She wished it might be taken down.

"Wait till spring," he answered. "It isn't a barrier; it's an allegory. Maybe when you see what happens you'll understand. Maybe you won't. It depends on your own feelings."

Annesley said no more, but she did not forget. She thought, if her understanding of the allegory meant any change of feeling which the man might be looking for in her, she would never understand. She hated to look at the line of stark, naked sticks, but they, and the "allegory" they represented, constantly recurred to her mind.

One day in spring she noticed that the sticks looked less dry. Knob-like buds had broken out upon them, the first sign that they were living things. It happened to be Easter eve, and she was restless, full of strange thoughts as the yellow-flowering grease-wood bushes were full of rushing sap.

A year ago that night her love for her husband had died its sudden, tragic death. In the very act of forgiveness, forgiveness had been killed.

Knight had gone off early that morning in his motor-car, the poor car which was a pathetic contrast to the glories of last year in England. He had gone before she was up, and had mentioned to the Chinese cook that he might not be back until late.

"That means after midnight," she told herself; and since she was free as air, she decided to take a long walk in the afternoon, as far as the river. It seemed that if she stayed in the house the thought of life as it might have been and life as it was would kill her on this day of all other days.

"I wish I could die!" she said. "But not here. Somewhere a long way off from everyone—and from *him*."

As she passed the cactus fence the buds were big.

Across the river, where the water flowed high and wide just then, lay Mexico. Annesley had never been there, though she could easily have gone, had she wished, from the ranch to El Paso, and from El Paso to the queer old historic town of Juarez. But she could not have gone without Knight, and there was no pleasure in travelling with him.

Besides, there was trouble across the border, and fierce fighting now and then. There had been some thievish raids made by Mexicans upon ranches along the river not many miles away, and that reminded her how Knight had remarked some weeks ago that she had better not go alone as far as the river bank.

"It isn't likely that anything would happen by day," he said, "but you might be shot at from the other side." Annesley was not afraid, and there was a faint stirring of pleasure in the thought that she was doing something against his wish on this anniversary. Deliberately, she sat alone by the river, waiting for the pageant of sunset to pass; and when she reached home the moon was up, a great white moon that turned the waving waste of pale, sparse grasses to a silver sea.

She had taken sandwiches and fruit with her, telling the cook that she would want no dinner when she came back. Away in the cow-punchers' quarters there was music, and she flung herself into a hammock on the veranda, to rest and listen.

There was a soft yet cool wind from the south, bringing the fragrance of creosote blossoms, and it seemed to the girl that never had she seen such white floods of moonlight, not even that night a year ago at Valley House.

Even the sky was milk-white. There were no black shadows anywhere, only dove-gray ones, except under the veranda roof. Her hammock was screened from the light by one dark shadow, like a straight-hung curtain. Save for the music of a fiddle and men's voices, the silver-white world lay silent in enchanted sleep.

Then suddenly something moved. A tall, dark figure was coming to the veranda. It paused at the cactus fence.

Could it be Knight, home already and on foot? No, it was a woman.

She walked straight and fast and unhesitating to the veranda, where she sat down on the steps.

Annesley raised herself on her elbow, and peered out of the concealing shadow. Who could the woman be? It was on the tip of her tongue to call, "Who are you?" when a sudden lifting of the bent face under a drooping hat brought it beneath the searchlight of the moon.

The woman was the Countess de Santiago, and the moon's radiance so lit her dark eyes that she seemed to look straight at Annesley in her hammock. The girl's heart gave a leap of some emotion like fear, yet not fear. She did not stop to analyze it, but she knew that she wished to escape from the woman; and an instant's reflection told her that she could not be seen if she kept still.

She began to think quickly, and her thoughts, confused at first, straightened themselves out like threads disentangled from a knot.

The woman had marched up to the veranda with such unfaltering certainty that it seemed she must have been there before. Perhaps she had arrived while the mistress of the house was out, and had been walking about the place, to pass away the time.

"But she hasn't come to see me," the girl in the hammock thought. "She has come to see Knight. It's for him she is waiting."

Anger stirred in Annesley's heart, anger against Knight as well as against Madalena.

"Has *he* written and told her to come?" she asked herself. "Does she think she can stay in this house? No, she shall not! I won't have her here!"

She was half-minded to rise abruptly and surprise the Countess, as the Countess had surprised her; to ask why she had come, and to show that she was not welcome. But if Madalena were here at Knight's invitation she would stay. There would be a scene perhaps. The thought was revolting. Annesley lay still; and in the distance she heard the throbbing of a motor.

CHAPTER XXV.
THE ALLEGORY

Annesley knew that Knight was in the habit of coming home that way, in order not to disturb her with the noise of the car if she had gone to bed. If he were bringing parcels from the little mining town, he drove to the house, left the packets, and ran the auto to a shanty he had rigged up for a garage.

A few seconds later the small open car came into sight, and Madalena sprang up, waving a dark veil she had snatched off her hat. She feared, no doubt, that the man might take another direction and perhaps get into the house by some door she did not know before she could intercept him. From a little distance the tall figure standing on the veranda steps must have been silhouetted black against the white wall of the house, clearly to be seen from the advancing motor.

Quick as a bird in flight the car sped along the road, wheeled on to the stiff grass, and drew up close to the veranda steps.

"Good heavens, Madalena!" Annesley heard her husband exclaim. "I thought it was my wife, and that something had gone wrong."

The surprise sharpening his tone did away with the doubt in the mind of the hidden listener. She had said to herself that the woman was here by appointment, and that this hour had been chosen because the meeting was to be secret.

"I wanted you to think so, and to come straight to this place," returned the once familiar voice. "Don, I've travelled from San Francisco to see you. Do say you are glad!"

"I can't," the man answered. "I'm not glad. You tried to ruin me. You tried in a coward's way. You struck me in the back. I hoped never to see you again. How did you find me?"

"I've known for a long time that you were in Texas," said Madalena. "Lady Annesley-Seton and I kept up a correspondence for months after you—sent me away so cruelly, in such a hurry, believing hateful things, though you had no proof. She wrote that 'Mr. and Mrs. Nelson Smith' would probably never come back to England to settle, as she'd heard from a Mrs. Waldo that they'd gone to live in Texas. She asked if I knew whether 'Nelson Smith' had lost his money. I forgot to answer that question when I answered the letter. But when she said 'Texas' I felt sure you must be somewhere in this part. I remembered your telling me about the ranch that consumptive gambler left to you on the Mexican frontier."

"What a fool I was to tell you!" Knight exclaimed, roughly.

The words and his way of flinging them at her were like a box on the ear; and Annesley, lying in her hammock, heard with a thrill of pleasure. She was ashamed of the thrill, and ashamed (because suddenly awakened to the realization) that she was eavesdropping.

But it seemed impossible that she should break in upon this talk and reveal her presence. She felt that she could not do it; though, searching her conscience, she was not sure whether she clung to silence because it was the lesser of two evils or because she longed with a terrible longing to know whether these two would patch up their old partnership.

"If you knew why I have come all these miles, maybe you would not be so hard," Madalena pleaded.

"That I can't tell until I do hear," said Knight, dryly.

"I am going to explain," she tried to soothe him. "A great thing has happened. I can be rich and live easily all the rest of my years if I choose. But—I wanted to see you before deciding.

"I arrived in El Paso yesterday, and went to the Paso del Norte Hotel, to inquire about you. I was almost certain you would have taken back your own name, because I knew you used to be known by it when you stayed in Texas. I soon found out that I'd guessed right. I heard you'd stopped at that hotel last year on the way to your ranch. I hired a motor-car and came here to-day; but I didn't let the man bring me to the house. I didn't want to dash up and advertise myself.

"I questioned some of your cowmen. They said you'd gone off, and would be getting back at night in your automobile, not earlier than ten and maybe a good deal later. So I waited. The car I hired is a covered one, and I sat in it, a long way from the house out of sight behind a little rising of the land. Perhaps you call it a hill."

"We do," said Knight.

"I brought some food and wine. The chauffeur's there with the car now. He has cigarettes, and doesn't mind if we stay all night."

"I mind," Knight cut her short. "You can't stay all night. The road's good enough with such a moon for you to get back to El Paso. You'd better start so as to reach there before she sets."

"Wait till you hear why I've come before you advise me to hurry!" the Countess protested. "There's no danger of our being disturbed, is there? Where is your wife?"

"In bed and asleep, I trust."

"I'm glad. Then will you sit on the top of these steps in this heavenly moonlight and let me tell you things that are important to me? Perhaps you may think they are important to you as well. Who knows?"

"I know. Nothing you can have to say will be important to me. I won't sit down, thank you. I've been sitting in my car for hours. I prefer to stand."

"Very well. But—how hard you are! Even now, you won't believe I was innocent of that thing you accused me of doing?"

"I think now what I thought then. You were not innocent, but guilty. You were just a plain, ordinary sneak, Madalena, because you were jealous and spiteful."

"It is not true! Spiteful against *you*! It was never in my heart to lie. Jealous, perhaps. But that is not to say I wrote the letter you believe I wrote. You didn't give me time to try and prove I did not write the letter. You accused me brutally. You ordered me out of England, with threats. I obeyed because I was heartbroken, not because I was afraid."

"Why trouble to excuse yourself?" he asked. "It's not worth the time it takes. If you've come to tell me anything in particular, tell it, and let's make an end."

"I have an offer of marriage from a millionaire," the Countess announced in a clear, triumphant tone.

"Which no doubt you accepted, not to say snapped at."

"Not yet. I put him off, because I wanted to see you before I answered."

"You flatter me!" Knight laughed, not pleasantly. "If you've come from San Francisco to get my advice on that subject, I can give it while you count three. Make sure of the unfortunate wretch before he changes his mind."

"Ah, if I could think that your harshness comes from just a little—*ever* so little, jealousy!" Madalena sighed. "He won't change his mind. There is no danger. He is old, and I seem a young girl to him. He adores me. He is on his knees!"

"Bad for rheumatism!"

"He thinks I am the most wonderful creature who ever lived. I met him through my work. He came from a friend of his who told him about my crystal, and about me, too."

"You are still working the crystal?"

"But, of course! It has always given me the path to success. If I marry this man I shall be able to rest."

"On your laurels—such as they are!"

"On his money. He can't live many years."

"You are an affectionate fiancée!"

"I am not a fiancée yet. Not till I give my answer. And that depends on you.... Oh, Don, surely you must be sick of this—this existence, for it is not life! I know you are angry with me, but you can't hate me really. It is not possible for a man with blood in his body to hate a woman who loves him as I love you.

"I have tried to get over it. At first I thought I was succeeding. But no, when the reaction came, I found that I cared more than ever. We were born for each other. It must be so, for without you I am only half alive. I haven't come for your advice, Don, but to make you an offer. Oh, not an offer of myself. I should not dare, as you feel now. And it is not an offer from me only; it is from a great person who has something to give which is worth your accepting, even if my love is not!"

"You've got in touch with *him*, have you?" Knight broke into the rushing torrent of her words as a man might take a plunge into a cataract.

"Why not?" she answered. "I didn't seek him out. It was he who sought me."

"You don't know how to speak the truth, Madalena! You said you found me through Lady Annesley-Seton hearing from Mrs. Waldo, whereas you wrote to Paul Van Vreck."

"You do me injustice—always! I *did* hear from Constance. Then I—merely ventured to write and ask Mr. Van Vreck if he kept up communication with you, and——"

"You said in your letter to him that you knew where I was, and gave him to understand that we were in touch with each other, or he would have let out nothing."

"He has written and told you this!" She spoke breathlessly, as if in fear.

"Ah, you give yourself away! No, I haven't heard from Van Vreck since I saw him in New York, and thought I convinced him that my working days for him were over. I simply guessed—knowing you—what you would do."

"I may have mentioned Texas," Madalena admitted. "I supposed he knew where you were. I couldn't have told him, because I didn't know. But he wrote and suggested I should use my influence with you to reconsider your decision. Those were his words."

"How much has he paid you for coming here?"

"Nothing. As if I would take money for coming to *you*!"

"You have taken it for some queer things, and will again if you don't settle down to private life with your millionaire.... It's no use, Madalena. Go back to San Francisco. Send in your bill to Van Vreck. Tell him there's nothing doing. And make up your mind to marriage."

"But, Don, you haven't heard what he offers."

"It can't be more than he offered me himself when I saw him in New York——"

"It is more. He says that particularly. He raises the offer from last time. It is *three times* higher! Think what that means. Oh, Don, it means life, real life, not stagnation! I would give up safety and a million to be with you—as your partner again, your humble partner.

"Here, on this bleak ranch, it is like death—a death of dullness. I know what you must be suffering because you are obstinate, because you have taken a resolve, and are determined not to break it. You are afraid it will be weakness to break it. There can be no other reason.

"I have asked questions about your life here. I have learned things. I know *she* is cold as ice. If you stay you will degenerate. You will become a clod.

"Leave this hideous gray place. Leave that woman who treats you like a dog. Let the ranch be hers. Send her money. You will have it to spare. She can divorce you, and you will be freed forever from the one great mistake you ever made. As for me— —"

"As for you—be silent!" The command struck like a whiplash. "You are not worthy to speak of 'that woman,' as you call her. If I did what you deserve, I'd send you off without another word—turn my back on you and let you go. But—" he drew in his breath sharply, then went on as if he had taken some tonic decision—"I want you to understand why, if Paul Van Vreck offered me *all* his money, and you offered me the love of all the women on earth with your own, I shouldn't be tempted to accept.

"It's because of 'that woman'—who is my wife. It may be true that she treats me like a dog, for she wouldn't be cruel to the meanest cur. But I'd rather be her dog than any other woman's master.

"So you see now. It's come to that with me. I won her love and married her for my own advantage. I lost her love because she found me out—through you. Mild justice that, perhaps! But all the same, getting her for mine *has* been for my advantage. In a different way from what I planned, but ten thousand times greater. Though she's taken her love from me, she's given me back my soul. Nothing can rob me of that so long as I run straight.

"And I tell you, Madalena, this ranch, where I'm working out some kind of expiation and maybe redemption, *is* God's earth for me. *Now* do you understand?"

For an instant the woman was silent. Then she broke into loud sobbing, which she did not try to check.

"You are a fool, Don!" she wept. "A fool!"

"Maybe. But I'm not the devil's fool as I used to be. Don't cry. You might be heard. Come. It's time to go. We've said all we have to say to each other except good-bye—if that's not mockery."

Madalena dried her tears, still sobbing under her breath.

"At least take me to the automobile," she said. "Don't send me off alone in the night. I am afraid."

"There's nothing to be afraid of," Knight answered, the flame of his fierceness burnt down. "But I'll go with you, and put you on the way back to El Paso. Come along!"

As he spoke, he started, and Madalena was forced to go with him, forced to keep up with his long strides if she would not be left behind.

When they had gone Annesley lay motionless, as though she were under a spell. The man's words to the other woman wove the spell which bound her, listening as they repeated themselves in her mind. Again and again she heard them, as they had fallen from his lips.

His expiation—perhaps his redemption—here on his bit of "God's earth" ... "It may be true that she treats me like a dog.... But I'd rather be her dog than any other woman's master...." And this was Easter eve, a year to the night since his martyrdom began!

Something seemed to seize Annesley by the hand and break the bonds that had held her, something strong although invisible. She sat up with a faint cry, as of one awakened from a dream, and slipped out of the hammock. There was a dim idea in her mind that she must go along the road where they had gone, so as to meet Knight on his way back. She did not know what she should say to him, or whether she could say anything at all; but the something which had taken her hand and snatched her out of the hammock dragged her on and on.

At first she obeyed the force blindly.

"I must see him! I must see him!" The words spoke themselves in her head. But when she had hurried out of the enclosure walled in by the cactus hedge, the brilliant moonlight seemed to pierce her brain, and make a cold, calm appeal to her reason.

"You can't tell him what you have heard," it said. "He would be humiliated. Or"—the thought was sharp as a gimlet—"what if he *saw* you, and knew you were listening? What if he talked just for effect? He is so clever! He is subtle enough for that. And wouldn't it be more *like* the man, than to say what he said *sincerely*?"

She stopped, and was thankful not to see her husband returning. There was time to go back if she hurried. And she must hurry! If he had seen her in her hammock, and made that theatrical attempt to play upon her feelings, he would laugh at his own success if she followed him. And if he had not seen her, and were in earnest, it would be best—indeed the only right way—not to let him guess that the scene on the veranda steps had had a witness.

Annesley turned to fly back faster than she had come. But passing the cactus hedge her dress caught. It was as if the hedge sentiently took hold of her.

She bent down to free the thin white material; and suddenly colour blazed up to her eyes in the rain of silver moonlight. The buds had opened since she noticed them last.

No longer was the hedge a grim barricade of stiff, dark sticks. Each stalk had turned into a tall, straight flame of lambent rose. From a dead thing of dreary ugliness it had become a thing of living beauty.

Knight's allegory!

He had said, perhaps she might understand when the time came; and perhaps not.

She *did* understand. But she had not faith to believe that the miracle could repeat itself in life—her life and Knight's. She shut her eyes to the thought, and when she had freed her dress ran very fast to the house.

CHAPTER XXVI.
THE THREE WORDS

Knight was generally far away long before Annesley was up in the morning, and often he did not come in till evening. She thought that on Easter Day, however, he would perhaps not go far. She half expected that he would linger about the house or sit reading on the veranda; and she could not resist the temptation to put on one of the dresses he had liked in England.

It was a little *passé* and old-fashioned, but he would not know this. What he might remember was that she had worn it at Valley House.

And the wish to say something, as if accidentally, about the flaming miracle of the cactus hedge was as persistent in her heart as the desire of a crocus to push through the earth to the sunshine on a spring morning. She did not know whether the wish would survive the meeting with her husband. She thought that would depend as much upon him as upon her mood.

But luncheon time came and Knight did not appear.

Annesley lunched alone, in her gray frock. Even on days when Knight was with her, and they sat through their meals formally, it was the same as if she were alone, for they spoke little, and each was in the habit of bringing a book to the table.

But she had not meant it to be so on this Easter Day. Even if she did not speak of the blossoming of the cactus, she had planned to show Knight that she was willing to begin a conversation. To talk at meals would be a way out of "treating him like a dog."

The pretty frock and the good intention were wasted. Late in the afternoon she heard from one of the line riders whom she happened to see that something had gone wrong with a windmill which gave water to the pumps for the cattle, and that her husband was attending to it.

"He's a natural born engineer," said the man, whose business as "line rider" was to keep up the wire fencing from one end of the ranch to the other. "I don't know how much he *knows*, but I know what he can *do*. Queer thing, ma'am! There don't seem to be much that Mike Donaldson *can't* do!"

Annesley smiled to hear Knight called "Mike" by one of his employees. She knew that he was popular, but never before had she felt personal pleasure in the men's tributes of affection.

To-day she felt a thrill. Her heart was warm with the spring and the miracle of the cactus hedge, and memories of impetuous—*seemingly* impetuous—words of last night.

If she could have seen Knight she would have spoken of his allegory; and that small opening might have let sunlight into their darkness. But he did not come even to dinner; and tired of waiting, and weary from a sleepless night, she went to bed.

Next morning a man arrived who wished to buy a bunch of Donaldson's cattle, which were beginning to be famous. He stayed several days; and when he left Knight had business at the copper mine—business that concerned the sinking of a new shaft, which took him back and forth nearly every day for a week. By and by the cactus flowers began to fade, and Annesley had never found an opportunity of mentioning them, or what they might signify.

When she met Knight his manner was as usual: kind, unobtrusive, slightly stiff, as though he were embarrassed—though he never showed signs of embarrassment with any one else. She could hardly believe that she had not dreamed those words overheard in the moonlight.

Week after week slipped away. The one excitement at Las Cruces Ranch was the fighting across the border; the great "scare" at El Paso, and the stories of small yet sometimes tragic raids made by bands of cattle stealers upon American ranches which touched the Rio Grande. The water was low. This made private marauding expeditions easier, and the men of Las Cruces Ranch were prepared for anything.

One night in May there was a sandstorm, which as usual played strange tricks with Annesley's nerves. She could never grow used to these storms, and the moaning of the hot wind seemed to her a voice that wailed for coming trouble. Knight had been away on one of his motoring expeditions to the Organ Mountains, and though he had told the Chinese boy that he would be back for dinner, he did not come. Doors and windows were closed against the blowing sand, but they could not shut out the voice of the wind.

After dinner Annesley tried to read a new book from the library at El Paso, but between her eyes and the printed page would float the picture of a small, open automobile and its driver lost in clouds of yellow sand.

Why should she care? The man was used to roughing it. He liked adventures. He was afraid of nothing, and nothing ever hurt him. But she did care. She seemed to feel the sting of the sharp grains of sand on cheeks and eyes.

She was sitting in her own room, as she was accustomed to do in the evening if she were not out on the veranda—the pretty room which Knight had extravagantly made possible for her, with chintzes and furnishings from the best shops in El Paso. On this evening, however, she set both doors wide open, one which led into the living room, another leading into a corridor or hall. She could not fail to hear her husband when he came, even if he left his noisy car at the garage and walked to the house.

A travelling clock on the mantelpiece—Constance Annesley-Seton's gift—struck nine. The girl looked up at the first stroke, wondering if serious accidents were likely to happen in sandstorms; and before the last note had ended she heard steps in the patio.

"He has come!" she thought, with a throb of relief which shamed her. But the step was not like Knight's. It was hurried and nervous; and as she told herself this there sounded a loud knock at the door.

There was an electric bell, which Knight had fitted up with his own hands, but it was not visible at night. No one except herself could hear this knocking, for the servants' quarters were at the far end of the bungalow. A little frightened, recalling stories of cattle thieves and things they had done, Annesley went into the hall.

"Who is there?" she cried, her face near the closed door, which locked itself in shutting. If a man's voice—the voice of a stranger—should reply in "Mex," or with a foreign accent, the girl did not intend to let him in. A man's voice did reply, but neither in "Mex" nor with a foreign accent. It said: "My name is Paul Van Vreck. Open quickly, please. I may be followed."

Annesley's heart jumped; but without hesitation she pulled back the latch, and as she opened the door a rush of sand-laden wind wrenched it from her hand. She staggered away as the door swung free, and there was just time to see a tall, thin figure slip in like a shadow before the light of the hanging-lamp blew out. The girl and the newcomer were in the dark save for a yellow ray that filtered into the hall from her room, but she saw him stoop to place a bag or bundle on the floor, and then, pulling the door to against the wind, slammed it shut with a click.

Having done this, the tall shadow bent to pick up what it had laid down.

"Thank you, Mrs. Donaldson, for letting me in," said the most charming voice Annesley had ever heard—more charming even than Knight's. "Evidently you've heard your husband mention me, or you might have kept me out there parleying, if you're alone, for these are stirring times."

"Yes, I—I've heard you mentioned by—many people," the girl answered, stammering like a nervous child. "Won't you come in—into the living room? Not the room with the open door. That's mine. It's another, farther along the hall. I'm sorry my husband's out."

As she talked she wondered at herself. She knew Van Vreck for a super thief. He did not steal with his own hands, but he commanded other hands to steal, and that was even worse. Or she had thought it worse in her husband's case, and for more than a year she had punished him for his sins. Yet here she was almost welcoming this man.

She did not understand why she felt—even without seeing him except as a shadow—that she would find herself wishing to do whatever he might ask. It must be, she thought, the influence of his voice. She had heard Paul Van Vreck spoken of as an old man, but the voice was the voice of magnetic youth.

He opened the door of the living room, and, carrying his bundle, followed her as she entered. There was only one lamp in this room, a tall reading-lamp with a green silk shade, which stood on a table, its heavy base surrounded by books and magazines. A good light for reading was thrown from under the green shade on to the table, but the rest of the room was of a cool, green dimness; and, looking up with irresistible curiosity at the face of her night visitor, it floated pale on a vague background, like a portrait by Whistler.

It was unnaturally white, the girl thought, and—yes, it *was* old! But it was a wonderful face, and the eyes illumined it; immense eyes, though deepset and looking out of shadowed hollows under level brows black as ink. Annesley had never seen eyes so like strange jewels, lit from behind.

That simile came to her, and she smiled, for it was appropriate that this jewel expert should have jewels for eyes. They were dark topazes, and from them gazed the spirit of the man with a compelling charm.

Under a rolled-back wave of iron-gray hair he had a broad forehead, high cheekbones, a pointed prominent chin, a mouth both sweet and humorous, like that of some enchanting woman; but its sweetness was contradicted by a hawk nose. Had it not been for that nose he would have been handsome.

"I guessed by the startled tone of your voice, when you asked, 'Who is there?' that your husband was out," explained the shadow, now transformed by the light into an extremely tall, extremely thin man in gray travelling clothes. "I had a moment of repentance at troubling a lady alone; but, you see, the case was urgent."

He had carelessly tossed his Panama hat on to the table, but kept the black bag, which he now held out with a smile.

"Not a big bag, is it? And so common, it wouldn't be likely to tempt a thief. But it holds what is worth—if it has a price—about half a million dollars."

"Oh!" exclaimed Annesley. She looked horrified; and through the green gloom the old man read her face.

"I see!" he said, with a laugh in his young voice. "You have heard the great secret! That makes another who knows. But I'm not afraid you'll throw me to the dogs. You wouldn't do that even if you weren't Donaldson's wife. Being his wife, you could not."

"My husband has told me no secret about you, none at all," the girl protested, defending Knight involuntarily. "I beg you to believe that, Mr. Van Vreck."

"I do believe it. If there's one thing I pride myself on, it's being a judge of character. That's why I've made a success of life. You wouldn't lie, perhaps not even to save the one you love best. I believe that he did not tell you the secret. Yet I'm certain you know it. I suppose other discoveries you must have made gave you supernatural intuition. You guessed."

Annesley did not answer. Yet she could not take her eyes from his.

"You needn't mind confessing. But I won't catechize you. I'll take it for granted that what Donaldson knows you know — not in detail, in the rough.... In this bag are six gold images set with precious stones. They are of the time of the Incas, and they've been up till now the most precious things in Mexico. From now on they will be among the most precious things in Paul Van Vreck's secret collection.

"Some weeks ago I hoped that Donaldson would get them for me. He refused, so I had to go myself. I couldn't trust any one else, though the only difficulty was getting to Central Mexico with Constitutionals raging on one side and Federals on the other. A man promised to deliver the goods to my messenger. I've been bargaining over these things for years. But, as I said, Don wouldn't go, so I had to do the job myself. You see, Mrs. Donaldson, your husband is the only honest man I ever came across."

"Honest!" The exclamation burst from Annesley's lips.

"Yes. Honest is the word. I might add two others: 'true' and 'loyal.'" Paul Van Vreck held her with his strange, straight look, commanding, yet amused. "That is the opinion," he added after a pause, "of a very old friend. It's worth its weight in — gold images."

The girl gave him no answer. But the effort of keeping her face under control made lips and eyelids quiver.

"May I sit down, Mrs. Donaldson?" Van Vreck asked in a tone which changed to commonplaceness — if his voice could ever be commonplace. "I'm a fugitive, and have had a run for my money, so to speak. I'm seeking sanctuary. Also I came in the hope of trying my eloquence on Donaldson. But now I've seen you, I will not do that. In future he's safe from me, I promise you."

"Oh!" Annesley faltered. And then: "Thank you!" came out, grudgingly. How astonishing that *she* should thank Paul Van Vreck, the monster of wickedness and secrecy she had pictured, for "sparing" her husband—her husband whom *he* called loyal, true, and honest; whom she had called in her heart a thief!

"Do sit down," she hurried on, hypnotized. "Forgive my not asking you. I——"

"I understand," he soothed her. "I've taken advantage of you—sprung a surprise, as Don would say, and then turned on the tortures of the Inquisition. Aren't *you* going to sit? I can't, you know, if you don't."

"I thought you might like something to eat," the girl stammered. "I could call our cook——"

"No, thank you," replied Van Vreck. "I'm peculiar in more ways than one. I never eat at night. I live mostly on milk, water, fruit, and nuts. That's why I feel forty at seventy-two. I give out that I'm frail—an invalid—that I spend much time in nursing homes. This is my joke on a public which has no business to be curious about my habits. While it thinks I'm recuperating in a nursing home I—but no matter! That won't interest you."

When she had obediently sat down, her knees trembling a little, Van Vreck drew up a chair for himself, and, resting his arms on the table, leaned across it gazing at the girl with a queer, humorous benevolence.

"How soon do you think your husband will come?" he asked, abruptly.

"I don't know," Annesley replied. "He told our Chinese boy he'd be early. I suppose the sandstorm has delayed him."

"No doubt.... And you're worried?"

"No-o," she answered, looking sidewise at Van Vreck, her face half turned from him. "I don't think that I'm worried."

"May I talk to you frankly till Don does come?" the old man asked.

"Certainly."

"I'll take you at your word!... Mrs. Donaldson, when your husband called on me a year ago last spring, in New York, he said nothing about you. I knew he'd married an English girl of good connections (isn't that what you say on your side?), and why he thought it would be wise to marry. But when he informed me that our association was to be ended, that nothing would induce him to continue it, I read between the lines. I'm sharp at that! I knew as well as if he'd told me that he'd fallen in love with the girl, that she'd unexpectedly become the important factor in his life, and that—she'd found out a secret she'd never been meant to find out: *his* secret, and maybe mine.

"I realized by his face—the look in the eyes, the tone of the voice, or rather, the tonelessness of the voice—what her finding out meant for Don. I read by all signs that she was making him suffer atrociously and I owed that girl a grudge. She'd taken him from me. For the first time a power stronger than mine was at work; and yet, things being as they were, my hope of getting him back lay in her."

"What do you mean?" The question spoke itself. Annesley's lips felt cold and stiff. Her hands, nervously clasped in her lap, were cold, too, though the shut-up room had but lately seemed hot as a furnace.

"I mean, if the girl behaved as I thought she would behave—as I think you have behaved—he might grow tired of her and the cast-iron coat of virtue he'd put on to please her. He might grow tired of life on a ranch if his wife made him eat ashes and wear sack-cloth. That was my hope. Well, I sent a messenger to find out how the land lay a few weeks ago."

"The Countess de Santiago!" Annesley exclaimed.

"He told you?"

"No, I saw her. I—by accident—(it really was by accident!) I heard things. He doesn't know—I believe he doesn't know—I was there."

"Perhaps that's just as well. Perhaps not. But if I were you I'd tell him when the right time comes. The Countess wrote me she'd had her journey in vain, and why. She said—spitefully it struck me—that Don was bewitched by his wife, a cold, cruel creature with ice in her veins, who treated him like a dog."

"She said that to you, too?"

"Yes, she said that. She seemed to gather the impression. But the dog stuck to his kennel. Nothing *she* could do would tempt him to budge. So I decided to call here myself, on the way back from Mexico. I couldn't delay the trip. A man was waiting for me. And waiting quietly is difficult in Mexico just now. I got what I wanted, and crammed the lot into this bag, which cost me at the outside, if I remember, five dollars. A good idea of mine for putting thieves off the track. They expect sane men to carry nightgowns and newspapers in such bags. I thought I'd managed so well that I'd put the gang who follow me about, generally on 'spec,' off the track.

"I speak Spanish well. I've been passing for a Mexican lawyer from Chihuahua. But to-day I caught a look from a pair of eyes in a train. I fancied I'd seen those eyes before—and the rest of the features. Perhaps I imagined it. But I don't think so. I trust my instinct. I advise you to! It's a tip.

"At El Paso I bought a ticket for Albuquerque. The eyes were behind me. I got into the train. So did Eyes, and a friend with a long nose. Not into my car, however, so I was able to skip out again as the train was starting. Not a bad feat for a man of my age! I hope Eyes and Nose, and any other features that may have been with them, travelled on unsuspectingly. But I can't be sure. Instinct says they saw my trick and trumped it.

"I oughtn't to have come here, bringing danger to your house, Mrs. Donaldson. But I want to see Don, and I know he is afraid neither of man nor devil—afraid of nothing in the world except one woman.

"As for her—well, what I'd heard hadn't prepossessed me in her favour. I sacrificed her for the safety of my golden images and my talk with Don. But the sound of your voice behind the shut door broke the picture I'd made of that young woman. And when I saw you—well, Mrs. Donaldson, I've already told you I don't intend to exert my influence over your husband, though to do so was my principal object in coming. Even if I did, I believe yours would prove stronger. But if I could count on all my old power over him, I wouldn't use it now I have seen you.

"I adore myself, and—my specialties. But there must be an unselfish streak in me which shows in moments like this. I respect and admire it. You may treat Don like a dog, but he'd never be happy away from you. And I am fool enough to want him to be happy. This kicked dog of yours, madame, happens to be the finest fellow I ever knew or expect to know."

"You say I treat him like a dog!" cried Annesley, roused to anger. "But how ought I to treat him? He came into my life in a way I thought romantic as a fairy tale. It was a trick—a play got up to deceive me! I knew nothing of his life; but because of the faith he inspired, I believed in him. No one except himself could have broken that belief. I would not have listened to a word against him. But when he thought I'd discovered something, the whole story came out. If I hadn't loved him so much to begin with, and put him on such a high pedestal, the fall wouldn't have been so great—wouldn't have broken my heart in pieces."

"But Don gave up everything pleasant in his life, and came down here to this God-forsaken ranch—a man like Michael Donaldson, with a few hundred dollars where he'd had thousands—all for you," said Van Vreck, "and he's had no thought except for you and the ranch for more than a year. Yet apparently you haven't changed your opinion. By Jove, madame, you must somehow, through your personality and God knows what besides, have got a mighty hold on his heart, in the days when you loved him, or he wouldn't have stood this dog's life, this punishment too harsh for human nature to bear. Good Lord, how were you brought up? Evidently not as a Christian."

"My father was a clergyman," said Annesley.

"There are many clergymen who have got as far from the light as the moon from the earth. I know more about Christianity myself than some of those narrow men with their 'cold Christs and tangled Trinities'! That is, I know all this on principle. I don't practise what I know, but that's my affair. Did Don ever excuse himself by mentioning the influence I brought to bear on him when he was almost a boy?"

"No," breathed Annesley. "He didn't excuse himself at all except to tell me about his father and mother, and a vow he'd made to revenge them on society."

"It was like him not to whine for your forgiveness."

"He would never whine," the girl agreed. But she remembered that night of confession when on his knees he had begged her to forgive, to grant him another chance, and she had refused. He had never asked again. And he had struggled alone for redemption.

"I haven't forgotten some early teachings which impressed me," said Paul Van Vreck. "Christ made a remark about forgiving till seventy times seven. Did you forgive Donaldson four hundred and eighty-nine times, and draw the line at the four hundred and ninetieth?"

"No, I never had anything to forgive him—till that one thing came out. But it was a very big thing. Too big!"

"*Too* big, eh? There was another saying of Christ's about those without sin throwing the first stone. Of course I'm sure *you* were without sin. But you look as if you might have had a heart—once."

"Oh, I had, I had!" Tears streamed down Annesley's pale face, and she did not wipe them away. "It's dead now I think."

"Think again. Think of what the man is—what he's proved himself to be. He's twice as good now as one of your best saints of the Church. He's purified by fire. You've got the face of an angel, Mrs. Donaldson, but in my opinion you're a wicked woman unworthy of the love you've inspired."

"You speak to me cruelly," the girl said through her tears. "I've been very unhappy!"

"Not as unhappy as you've made Don by *your* cruelty. Good heavens, these tender girls can be more cruel when they set about punishing us, than the hardest man! And to punish a fellow like that by making him live in an ice-house, when you could have done anything with him by a little kindness! Don't *I* know that?

"I'm the sponsor for such sins as Don's committed. He was meant to be straight. But I got hold of him through an agent, and caught his imagination when that wild vow was freshly branded on his heart or brain. I have the gift of fascination, Mrs. Donaldson. I know that better than I know most things. *You* feel it to-night, or you wouldn't sit there letting me tear your heart to pieces—what's left of your heart. And I have an idea there's a good deal more than you think, if you have the sense to patch the bits together.

"I have fascination, and I've cultivated it. Napoleon himself didn't study more ardently than I the art of winning men. I won Don. I appealed to the romance in him. I became his hero and—slowly—I was able to make him my servant. Not much of my money or anything else has ever stuck to his hands. He's too generous—too impulsive; though I taught him it was necessary to control his impulses.

"What he did, he did for love of me, till you came along and lit another sort of fire in his blood. I saw in one minute, when he called on me, what had happened to his soul. It's taken you more than a year to see, though he's lived for you and would have died for you.

Great Heaven, young woman, you ought to be on your knees before a miracle of God! Instead, you've mounted a marble pedestal and worshipped your own purity!"

Annesley bowed her head under a wave of shame. *This* man, of all others, had shown her a vision of herself as she was. It seemed that she could never lift her eyes. But suddenly, into the crying of the wind, a shot broke sharply; then another and another, till the sobbing wail was lost in a crackling fusillade.

The girl leaped to her feet.

"Raiders!" she gasped. "Or else— —"

Paul Van Vreck sprang up also, his face paler, his eyes brighter than before.

"They've come after me," he said. "Clever trick—if they've bribed ruffians from over the border to cover their ends. The real errand's here, inside this house."

Annesley's heart faltered.

"You must hide," she breathed. "I must save you—somehow."

"Why should you save *me*?" Van Vreck asked, sharply. "Why not think about saving yourself?"

"Because I know Knight would wish to save you," she answered. "I want to do what he would do.... God help us, they're coming nearer! Take your bag, and I'll hide you in the cellar. There's a corner there, behind some barrels. If they break in, I'll say— —"

"Brave girl! But they won't break in."

"How do you know?"

"Your husband won't let them. Trust him, as I do."

"He's not here. Do you think I told you a lie? Thank Heaven he *isn't* here, or they'd kill him, and I could never beg him to forgive— —" She covered her face with her hands.

The old man looked at her gravely.

"You don't understand what's happening," he said, with a new gentleness. "Don's out there now, defending you and his home. That's what the shooting means. Do you think those brutes would advertise themselves with their guns if they hadn't been attacked?"

With a cry the girl rushed to the long window, and began to unfasten it, but Van Vreck caught her hands.

"Stop!" he commanded. "Don't play the robbers' own game for them! *How do you know which is nearer the house, Don and his men, or the others?*"

She stared at him, panting, "Don and his men?" she echoed.

"Yes. Even if he were alone to begin with, I'll bet all I've got he roused every cowpuncher on the ranch with his first shot; and they'd be out with their guns like a streak of greased lightning. If you open that window with a light in the room, the wrong lot may get in and barricade themselves against Don and his bunch—to say nothing of what would happen to us. But——"

Annesley waited for no more. She ran to the table and blew out the flame of the green-shaded lamp. Black darkness shut down like the lid of a box. But she knew the room as she knew her own features. Straight and unerring, she found her way back to the window.

This time Van Vreck stood still while she opened it and began noiselessly to undo the outside wooden shutters. As she pushed them apart, against the wind, a spray of sand dashed into her face and Van Vreck's, stinging their eyelids. But disregarding the pain, the two passed out into the night.

Clouds of blowing sand hid the stars, yet there was a faint glimmer of light which showed moving figures on horseback. Men were shouting, and with the bark of their guns fire spouted.

Annesley rushed on to the veranda, but Van Vreck caught her dress.

"Stay where you are!" he ordered. "Our side is winning. Don't you see—don't you hear—the fight's going farther away? That means the raid's failed—the skunks have got the worst of it. They're trying to get back to the river and across to their own country. There'll be some, I bet, who'll never see Mexico again!"

"But Knight——" the girl faltered. "He may be shot——"

"He may. We've got to take the chances and hope for the best. He wouldn't leave the chase now if every door and window were open and lit for him. Wait. Watch. That's the only thing to do."

She yielded to the detaining hand. All strength had gone out of her. She staggered a little, and fell back against Van Vreck's shoulder. He held her up strongly, as though he had been a young man.

"How can I live through it?" she moaned.

"You care for him after all, then?" she heard the calm voice asking in her ear. And she heard her own voice answer: "I love him more than ever." She knew that it was true, true in spite of everything, and that she had never ceased to love him. It would be joy to give her life to save Knight's, with just one moment of breath to tell him that his atonement had not been vain.

Away out of sight the chase went, but the watching eyes had time to see that not all the figures were on horseback. Some ran on foot; and some horses were riderless. As Van Vreck had said, there was nothing for him and for Annesley to do except to wait. They stood silent in the rain of sand, listening when there was nothing more to see. The shots were scattered and blurred by distance. Annesley realized how a heart may stop beating in the anguish of suspense.

But at last when the fierce wind, purring like a tiger, was the only sound in the night, there came a sudden padding of feet. A form stumbled up the veranda steps, and before she could cry out in her surprise, the girl recognized their Chinese servant.

She had fancied him in bed. But she might have known he would be out!

He had been running so fast that his breath came chokingly.

"What is it?" Annesley implored.

The boy pointed, trying to speak, "Bling Mist' Donal back," he gulped. "Me come tell."

Annesley pushed past him, and springing down the steps ran blindly through the sand cloud, taking the way by which the Chinese boy must have come home. Her mind pictured a procession carrying a dead man, or one grievously wounded; but at the cactus hedge she came upon three men—one in the centre, who limped, two who supported him on either side.

"Why, Anita!" exclaimed her husband's voice.

"Knight!" she sobbed. It was the first time since Easter a year ago that she had given him the old name.

"Thank God you're alive!"

"If you thank Him, so do I," he answered, whether lightly or gravely she could not tell. His tone was controlled, as if to hide pain.

"It's all right. You mustn't worry any more. Wish I could have sent you news sooner. I hoped you'd guess we were getting the upper hand when the shots died away. Coming home I spotted the sneaks fording the river. I turned the car, and stirred up the boys. Then we had a shindy, and scared the dogs cold—bagged a few, but I guess nobody croaked—anyhow, none of our crowd. Half a dozen are after the curs.

"As for me, I feel as if I'd got a dum-dum in my ankle, but I'll be fit as a fiddle in a week or two. I'm afraid you had a fright."

How strange it was to hear him speak so coolly after what she had endured! But his calmness quieted her.

"Mr. Van Vreck was with me," she said.

"Van Vreck! Great Scott, then the raid was a frameup! I see. Boys, let's get along to the house quick."

"Wait an instant!" the girl intervened. "Knight, I never had a chance to tell you—about the cactus blossoms. I understood. I understand even better now. Mr. Van Vreck has made me understand. That is all I can tell you. Let them help you to the house. I'll follow. Some other time I'll explain."

"No—now!" he said. "Let go a minute, boys. I can stand by myself. Three words with my wife."

As the two men moved off hastily, Annesley sprang forward, giving her shoulder for her husband's support.

"Lean on me," she said. "Oh, Knight, you don't need an explanation, for the three words are, love—love and forgiveness. Forgiveness from *you* to *me*."

He held out his arms, and caught her to him fiercely. Neither could speak. The past was forgotten. Only the present and future counted. Both the man and woman had atoned.

THE END